T4-AKF-450

INFORMATION PROFICIENCY

Your Key
to the
Information
Age

THOMAS J. BUCKHOLTZ

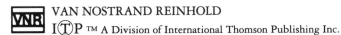
VAN NOSTRAND REINHOLD
I(T)P ™ A Division of International Thomson Publishing Inc.

New York • Albany • Bonn • Boston • Detroit • London • Madrid • Melbourne
Mexico City • Paris • San Francisco • Singapore • Tokyo • Toronto

I(T)P™ A division of International Thomson Publishing, Inc.
The ITP logo is a trademark under license

Printed in the United States of America

For more information, contact:

Van Nostrand Reinhold
115 Fifth Avenue
New York, NY 10003

International Thomson Publishing GmbH
Königswinterer Strasse 418
53227 Bonn
Germany

International Thomson Publishing Europe
Berkshire House 168–173
High Holborn
London WCIV 7AA
England

International Thomson Publishing Asia
221 Henderson Road #05-10
Henderson Building
Singapore 0315

Thomas Nelson Australia
102 Dodds Street
South Melbourne, 3205
Victoria, Australia

International Thomson Publishing Japan
Hirakawacho Kyowa Building, 3F
2-2-1 Hirakawacho
Chiyoda-ku, 102 Tokyo
Japan

Nelson Canada
1120 Birchmount Road
Scarborough, Ontario
Canada M1K 5G4

International Thomson Editores
Campos Eliseos 385, Piso 7
Col. Polanco
11560 Mexico D.F. Mexico

1   2   3   4   5   6   7   8   9   10   QEBFF   01   00   99   98   97   96   95

Library of Congress Cataloging-in-Publication Data

Buckholtz,Thomas J.
    Information proficiency : your key to the information age / Thomas
J. Buckholtz.
        p.   cm.
    Includes bibliographical references and index.
    ISBN 0-442-01954-8
    1. Information technology—Management. 2. Information resources
management. 3. Employees—Training of. 4. Information society.
HD30.2.B83   1995
    658.4′038—dc20   94–49396
                                                            CIP

CONTENTS

FOREWORD

The publication of *Information Proficiency* marks a turning point in the Information Age. Finally, there is a comprehensive basis for understanding, anticipating, mastering, and even shaping the dramatic changes we are all experiencing.

Tom Buckholtz presents a thorough guide to the Information Age. For everyone—executives, empowered employees, technologists, academics, and people in all walks of life—*Information Proficiency* provides an easy-to-use roadmap to success in these most challenging times.

Organizations and individuals will gain immensely from perspective and practical suggestions throughout a gamut of opportunities: setting goals and achieving results, enhancing proficiency at making and implementing decisions, building teamwork, enhancing people's capabilities, and maximizing the benefits derived from information, information technologists, and information systems.

For example, the information proficiency paradigm focuses the central concepts of total quality management on people's key Information Age opportunity: setting goals through quality decisions and accomplishing goals by implementing decisions well.

As well as supplying a useful basis for applying total quality management and business process reengineering to today's work, Tom Buckholtz provides practical insight into the next steps in our Information Age journey. We learn the keys to building knowledge bases and enhancing overall information proficiency.

This book also provides significant, easily implemented techniques for success in building teamwork within and between organizations, working with information, developing information systems, and acquiring information technology. A highlight is the practical program to bring information technologists into the mainstream of the organizations they support.

The publication of Tom Buckholtz's *Information Proficiency* provides all of us with a vital, penetrating, and stimulating look at the past, present, and future of the Information Age. This superb book is packed with advice on how to find and make the best of our opportunities.

KOJI YAMAZAKI
Deputy Chairman of the Board of Counselors
The Japan Research Institute, Limited
Tokyo, Japan
January 1995

PREFACE

The Information Age pervades our lives, extending our abilities to think, compressing time scales, and changing the way we work, shop, and use our leisure time.

You sense progress. The world is at your fingertips. Instantaneous communications are yours to enjoy when talking by telephone, sending a facsimile message, or transmitting data between computers. Up-to-the-moment world news and securities prices are yours for the asking.

You sense uncertainty. Society struggles with organizational right-sizing and changes in the job market; we need perspective to adapt to the swift pace of change. Relations between information technologists and their clients drift while the two communities grope for a common understanding and agenda.

Everyone faces Information Age challenges. Sometimes the challenge is to reengineer a company's processes. Sometimes the challenge is to learn to use a new software package.

Everyone needs perspective . . . Where is the Information Age headed? To what should you pay attention? How can you keep pace with the changes? Ultimately, how can you lead change?

Having been blessed with opportunities to help individuals and organizations succeed in this age, I have used insights gained to write this book *to help you understand the Information Age and to give you vital techniques—techniques that you, your colleagues, and your organizations can use to succeed in these challenging times.* The following are some of the questions I will help you answer:

- What is an appropriate framework to guide your comprehension and action in the Information Age?
- How can an organization, individual, or all society raise its proficiency? How can you measure and enhance proficiency, whether for making strategic decisions or employing new technology?
- Will mastering technology and reengineering business processes suffice to ensure organizational competitiveness?
- How can you maximize the value of your information resources?
- How can information technologists and their clients develop and achieve optimal common goals?
- What should you know about fundamental changes in the evolution of information systems?
- How can you and your colleagues deal most effectively in the information technology marketplace?

Through this book, you will gain a context and incisive techniques for success in the Information Age. Apply them personally . . . as a member of organizations . . . and as a constituent of information systems and technology. In addition, if you are an information technology developer, vendor, academic, or student, you can apply this book's perspective to your special interests.

Use this book to gain a context for evaluating and acting on the Information Age transformation of business and society. Obtain valuable methods for excelling. Learn how information proficiency provides a paradigm for measuring and enhancing all your organizations' endeavors and accomplishments.

Learn how to engage an organization's information systems community for maximal impact. Gain practical insight into changes affecting the design, deployment, and use of information systems.

If you invest in companies, use this book to gain perspective to help you determine how well your companies are generating competitive advantage.

If you work for an organization that creates or markets information technology or educational services, use this book to gain vital ideas for your organization's strategy, products, and business practices.

I want to give you your key to the Information Age—concepts, a program, and techniques so that you thrive in this challenging era. Your key will be easy to use and will open many doors. These doors lead to opportunities for you, the groups with which you work, and society as a whole.

Your key is improving information proficiency, the making and implementing of decisions.

TOM BUCKHOLTZ
Portola Valley, CA
September 1994

To Helen and Catheryne

and

In memory of Joe and Sylvia

ACKNOWLEDGMENTS

As a first-time author, I would like to acknowledge individuals who formed the direct chain leading to the publishing of this book. Bob Metcalfe wrote a column in the June 21, 1993 *Infoworld* discussing ideas from the first draft of this book. Larry Press read the article, asked for my book proposal, and forwarded it to the New York office of Van Nostrand Reinhold. There, Dianne Littwin asked for the draft and made suggestions for improving the book. Jeanne Glasser took over this project and has seen it through to publication.

Having seen the need for this book for several years, I was fortunate that George Flynn and Jerry Brilliant of the U.S. General Services Administration suggested that I talk to George Washington University about teaching. George Washington's Ed Cherian recommended me to Jerry Learmonth, who asked me to teach information resources and security management for the Executive Master in Information Systems program. As there was no book covering the topic thoroughly, I wrote the first draft of this book for my students.

Several people made useful suggestions based on preliminary versions of this book. These individuals include Russell Acree, Jr., Adrain Brown, Barbara Cerny, Don Driscoll, Stefano Ghielmetti, Marilyn Hartwell, Marian Holton, Cathy Kreyche, Diana Mixon, Fred Morris, Wilson Parran, Lee Swent, Ben Wu, and Van Nostrand Reinhold reviewers whose names I do not know. Jerry Learmonth made several key suggestions about the content.

I am especially grateful to Marilyn Hartwell for the extensive time and editing contributed toward the final manuscript. Cathy Kreyche edited early drafts and my proposal.

I want to acknowledge all the people who contributed to the successes I have described in this book. While I am acquainted with only some of you, I want to thank all of you. Learning about your work has allowed me to formulate and articulate methods through which other successes will be achieved.

Numerous people provided me advice on publishing. They include Steve Alter, Bruce Armbruster, Pat Baker, Ed Bersoff, Katie Boyd, C. Stewart Brewster, Ed Cherian, John Cogan, Mike Crisp, Barbara Culliton, Bill Davidow, Omar El Sawy, George Ferguson, Roger Freeman, Sheryl Fullerton, John Gardner, Kevin Gilmore, Sam Hamod, Stan Holditch, John Kilcullen, Fred Kily, Don Knuth, Jim March, Bob Metcalfe, Roby Shotwell Metcalfe, Becky Morgan, Mike Morgan, Fred Murphy, Pauline Naftzger, Tim O'Reilly, Jim Patell, Claire Pyle, Bill Raduchel, Jack Roberts, Michael Rothschild, Joan Shih, Mike Spence, Paul Strassmann, David Taylor, and Koji Yamazaki.

Finally, I would like to acknowledge the contributions of Helen, my wife, who encouraged me to write this book and provided support that I needed in order to devote a substantial period of my life to this endeavor.

To each and every one of you: Thank you!

P A R T *1*

Introduction

CHAPTER 1

Discovering a Problem and Everyone's Opportunities

The Information Age has broad, dramatic, ever-changing impact. It is hard to keep up. Information proficiency provides each person and each organization with the power to succeed in these challenging times.

KEEPING UP IS DIFFICULT

You want to keep up with the Information Age. Yet you know you cannot stay abreast of the myriad of new technological products, let alone the proposed technologies. You wonder what else you are missing. Just how difficult is it to keep up?

Here is an Information Age awareness test: How well did people anticipate the fall of the Soviet Union?

That collapse was an Information Age transformation, from top to bottom. Soviet leaders could no longer escape the evidence that traditional policies and processes were not sustainable. The Soviet populace had learned about non-Soviet concepts and prosperity through foreign broadcasts, foreign contacts, and underground information. Individuals used facsimile machines, printing presses, photocopiers, videotapes, and other technology to hasten the debate over ideas for new political and economic systems.

The Information Age set the pace for the collapse of the old order. Knowledge and technology played pivotal roles. Progress depended on people formulating, debating, and working toward a future differing markedly from the past.

Even better than keeping abreast of the Information Age and its impact on our world, you can get ahead of the changes. You can stay ahead. It is time to articulate, and take advantage of, a framework for the Information Age and the many practical suggestions that spring from that framework.

LITTLE DID I KNOW . . .

In 1982, I joined a large company to lead its office automation program. It was a fresh start for the company and for me. The company had no personal computers. I had not previously worked with the company or in its field. My hands-on experience with personal computers totaled, at most, two hours.

Little did I know that I would take my employer from 0 to 10,000 personal computers in less than five years, that I would initiate a change in corporate culture, that I would establish a new business practice in the software marketplace, or that the company would achieve $100 million in recurring annual benefits as a result of this office automation program.

Little did I know that I would go on to lead deployment of computing and telecommunications throughout the executive branch of the United States federal government or that I would catalyze federal government achievements far beyond those anticipated from information technologists.

And little did I know that a single observation at the beginning of the office automation project would guide me through that project and beyond and that it would alert me to the need for this book. That observation is one you can still make today: *Most Information Age conversations start and end with technology.*

People like to talk about technology. They debate which hardware, software, and services to buy. They compare the "power" of various computers. They contrast the features of similar software packages. They debate the merits of various telecommunications services. In leading my employer's office automation program, was I to limit my thoughts and conversations to this sort of technological concern? Was I to limit my activities to putting technology on people's desks? Even if I did more than that, was I to be perceived simply as a supplier of technology? If office automation was equated to technology, would my employer be well served? The answers, of course, are no, no, no, and no.

Indeed, there are better questions. Perhaps you have already thought of some, such as these:

- What is a context for understanding the Information Age?
- Beyond technology, what are the foci of this age?
- What should you spend your valuable time on?
- What thoughts and actions will make you most effective in conducting your activities and in contributing to the success of organizations with which you work?
- How can you survive and thrive in the Information Age?

This book will help you answer these questions. Based on a decade of experience and analysis, I have written this book to provide a useful context for understanding the Information Age and a variety of new or underutilized suggestions for how to succeed in these challenging times.

CHALLENGES AND OPPORTUNITIES

Most Information Age conversations start and end with technology. This observation contains good news and bad news.

First, some good news. The technology is proving to be immensely useful. Indeed, we find it difficult to imagine conducting business without modern telecommunications, facsimile machines, and computers. We find it difficult to imagine society not having these and other information technologies such as television. Technological improvement continues at a vigorous pace.

Now, some bad news. Overattention to technology distracts us. We spend precious time debating which technology to use. Additional time goes to buying, installing, and maintaining technology. Still more time goes into learning to use new technology and trying to cope with differences between systems.

Where is the attention to *information*? After all, this is supposed to be the Information Age. Where is the attention to *how we use information*? Where is the attention to our *goals*, for which information and technology are but means to ends? Where is attention to *people*? Without people, the goals cannot be pursued.

These questions present opportunities for you. You can succeed in the Information Age by focusing on your goals and then considering the more specific issues, such as working with people, understanding and using information, and using information technology.

Organizations face the same challenges. Your employer, a community group you support with time or money, a business supplying you goods or services, a government agency—each faces similar opportunities to pursue its goals through appropriate attention to people, information, and technology.

Context: Goals and results
Focus: Achievement
Definition 1: The effective use of information to define and achieve
        goals

Context: Process
Focus: Quality
Definition 2: Quality in making and implementing decisions, including

Proficiency *with* information to make decisions and thereby set
goals
              and
Proficiency *through* information to implement decisions and
thereby achieve results specified by goals

FIGURE 1–1   Two Definitions of Information Proficiency.

INFORMATION PROFICIENCY— THE CONSUMMATE OPPORTUNITY

Information proficiency is the effective use of information to define and achieve goals. Operationally, information proficiency denotes quality in making and implementing decisions (Fig. 1–1).

Information proficiency provides the power to accomplish your objectives. The components of this power are quality decision making and incisive implementation.

Information-proficient decision making leads to optimal goals. Information-proficient implementation achieves the results specified by those goals. The vital link between your goals and people, information, and technology is information proficiency.

CHAPTER 2

Developing a Framework for the Information Age

A framework for the Information Age and the paradigm of information proficiency facilitate the understanding and capture of Information Age opportunities.

THE ELEMENTS OF AN INFORMATION-PROFICIENT WORLD

Some elements of a framework (Fig. 2–1) for the Information Age are common to this and all eras of civilization. The focus is on goals, results, and how people achieve them. Information proficiency is a concept denoting quality—how well people define goals and achieve results (Fig. 1–1). People's use of information plays a major role in determining the objectives they set and the results they accomplish. These elements are timeless.

Today, we recognize that information constitutes a resource to be managed. Information resources and information resources management belong in the framework for the Information Age. Because of the role of computing, telecommunications, and other information technologies in our world, information systems and technology are also included in the framework.

*   *   *

Goals express the aspirations of people and organizations for future results. For a business, an example of *results* can be a successful product, such as a new airplane or a new service that enhances competitiveness. For a government agency, a result may be an improvement in service to the public, such as a new way for people to obtain or renew permits without appearing at a government office, or a reduction in cost, such as a saving achieved by substituting automation for

---

- Goals and Results
- People and Information Proficiency
- Information and Information Resources Management
- Information Systems
- Technology

FIGURE 2–1   The Framework for the Information Age.

clerical work. For you, results may include enhancements to your professional or personal life derived by applying what you learn from this book.

Results are neither elementary nor final. Every result is found in the midst of others: A scientific discovery, a decision to explore a potential improvement in work processes, or an assignment of people to work on a project contributes to other results. A medical discovery leads to improved health. A governmental cost reduction frees moneys for other uses by taxpayers or government. A project team invents a new product.

The concept denoted by *people* includes individuals, groups, and patterns of behavior. People determine goals, whether through explicit decisions or implicitly by default. People create and pursue activities, seemingly goal-directed or not. People interpret and act on, or ignore, information. People judge and talk about the results of efforts—human, natural, or automated; intended or unintended; seemingly complete or not.

Information proficiency denotes the effectiveness of an organization or individual in producing two types of results: decisions and implementations (Fig. 1–1). A decision is a result that sets direction and helps people work toward goals. Implementing a decision is necessary—why make a decision if you don't intend to implement it? Enhancing one's information proficiency is crucial to success and is, therefore, a goal for every organization and individual.

Information is a diverse concept that encompasses human sensory perceptions, articles in newspapers, a televised movie, data in a corporation's financial records, pictures returned from the camera of a spacecraft orbiting another planet, computer-manipulated images of the surface of that planet, and results from a computerized simulation of airflow around an aircraft that has yet to be built. Additionally, information includes processes, such as those used to make decisions, the procedures through which a company maintains financial records, and the steps, expressed in software, that a computer follows to maintain such records.

Information also constitutes a resource that individuals and organizations generate, acquire, and accumulate. Every person and organization manages *information resources.* Many organizations employ specialists, such as computer professionals and librarians, to build information resources and provide information services.

In 1980, the U.S. federal government defined the term *information resources management* to merge, and provide a basis for extending the combination of, three disciplines: records management, computing, and telecommunications. The term is now used extensively outside the federal government.

Managing information resources in today's world depends heavily on *information systems,* both automated and manual. Such systems are essential for collecting, storing, analyzing, transmitting, and presenting information.

Traditionally, *information technology* includes technology and services in at least two areas: computing and telecommunications. Other information-delivering technologies, such as motion pictures, radio, and television, have had pervasive impact and are destined to join computers and telecommunications equipment in future "multimedia" combinations that will include at least these five technologies.

Putting these concepts together produces the framework for the Information Age and the outline for this book. The framework invites a results-oriented view of this challenging era.

APPLICABILITY OF THE FRAMEWORK

This framework for the Information Age applies throughout human endeavors (Fig. 2–2). It pertains to:

- Society as a whole.
- Macroentities, such as nations.
- Informal groups, such as the residents of a neighborhood.
- Formal organizations, such as corporations.
- Individuals acting alone.

Each entity has foci that include goals and results, effectiveness in defining goals and achieving results, and information resources.

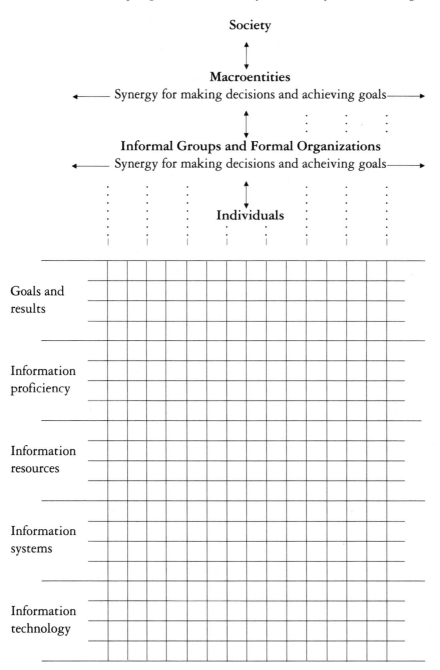

FIGURE 2–2   The Modular Society: Entities and Foci.

Today, essentially all entities rely on information systems and technologies—at the very least, telephones and television. Thus, most entities have points of interest throughout the five layers of the framework.

Individuals having common interests form groups that share and pursue those interests. For example, six people share a common goal: to persuade their city government to plant shrubs in their neighborhood's unused rights-of-way. These people also have a mutual interest in information technology: They use the local telephone system to talk with each other. They want to create an informal group that develops enough information proficiency to gather public support for getting the shrubs planted and persuade the government to plant the shrubs.

Members of the informal neighborhood beautification coalition have disparate views on goals other than those of their group. Generally, any two entities will have some interests that fall at different points within the same level of the framework.

Similarly, informal groups, formal organizations, and individuals having common interests band together into a macroentity. The macroentity succeeds to the extent that it develops sufficient information proficiency to serve the common interest of its perhaps constantly changing membership. The macroentity also depends on information, systems, and technology.

As well as constituents forming and affecting coalitions, groups impact their own components in the hierarchy and network of entities. For example, a decision by a corporation to offer employees flexible benefits influences those individuals' goals and decisions about health insurance coverage.

Many such connections associate individuals, informal groups, formal organizations, and macroentities with points in the framework. Each connection contributes to the fabric and course of society.

PART *2*

Goals and Results

3

Setting Goals and Striving for Results

As information overload and the wealth of "good ideas" threaten to swamp us, concentrating on making and implementing decisions well becomes crucial. Finding appropriate goals, pursuing them tenaciously, and focusing on appropriate issues enhances decision making.

THE WORLD OF "WHY NOT?"

Life is getting more complicated. Every day, we face too many choices. There are a multitude of goals to pursue, instantaneous demands to meet, and many good ideas to explore.

We live in an age of *why not?* Why not add one more goal to the agenda? Why not activate one more project? Why not explore yet another alternative?

Organizations and individuals face similar challenges. Customers, suppliers, friends, and other constituents often dream up new why-not's. Perhaps you are a demanding dreamer, one who develops many good ideas for yourself and other people.

Why not be able to design and order a highly customized automobile for yourself? Today, you can choose an affordable car with a combination of options. Tomorrow, perhaps you can design the body and other components with personally customized features.

Why not be able to access any government service easily? Today, financial service corporations offer one-stop shopping covering all their services. Tomorrow's government, if it wants to meet your demands, will have to offer convenient ways for you to learn anything you need to know about your government accounts, as well as governmental policies and proceedings. Furthermore, you will want that service anytime and anywhere—at home or in a hotel room, car, or office.

Why not have this level of information-delivery service for most catalogued information? You want the world's information at your fingertips.

As a consumer, you wonder what is holding us back. Not the laws of nature. Not a lack of natural resources. Not even laws propagated by man. Yet an organization's taking steps to provide you such service is becoming harder . . .

*   *   *

On the one hand, individuals and organizations need to think globally. There are no isolated peoples or geographic regions. Commerce is global. Businesses that once marketed their products only domestically now compete internationally. Companies form alliances with firms previously viewed as competitors and encounter new, unexpected rivals.

Even governments form macroentity partnerships (Fig. 2–2). National governments cooperate on security or commerce. Local governments join to solve regional problems. National programs, such as food stamps in the United States, are administered by state and local governments. Private-sector banks administer government lending programs. Within national governments, separations between domestic and foreign policies are diminishing.

The world is becoming smaller. We now find overlaps among formerly disparate topics and issues. More than ever, opportunities are tackled through cooperative efforts.

*   *   *

On the other hand, new complexities arise in old issues. A scientific breakthrough generates new areas of specialized research. A new environmental law spawns a new legal specialty. Evolving "sophistication" leads to growing complexity in areas such as rules governing evidence admissible in court proceedings, schedules of airline fares, and regulations pertaining to constructing or modifying buildings.

Yesterday's understanding of a topic or issue becomes tomorrow's starting point for a whole new field and a new specialized vocabulary. Disciplines continue to subdivide into smaller, more highly differentiated units, forcing us to cope with finer and finer levels of detail.

Today's world is filled with detail. Consider, for instance, the detail required for the programming of software. Many software programs consist of millions of digits and letters. If you have experience with spreadsheets, you probably know that, while there are many "right" ways to code a program, a single mistake can lead to a very wrong program and unacceptable results.

Attention to detail is important and often provides early warning of a growing problem or an attractive opportunity. People who piece together snippets of evidence may be the first to spot a business headed for financial difficulties. An unusually large number of late-night pizza deliveries to a business or governmental headquarters

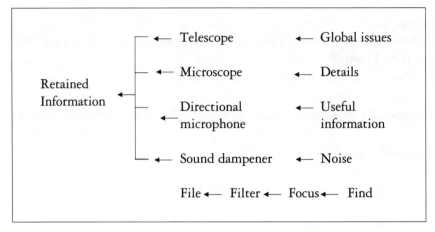

FIGURE 3–1   Sensing the World of "Why Not?"

may indicate a growing crisis somewhere in the world. Futurists comb the news, hoping to find the first signs of a new trend.

*   *   *

Individuals and organizations are challenged to think, on the one hand, more broadly across issues and, on the other, more deeply about, single issues. It seems difficult to gain perspective with, in effect, one eye looking through a telescope, the other eye looking through a microscope and, with our ears picking up both useful information and distracting noise (Fig. 3–1). We try to focus on potentially relevant data and to filter even that to find the most useful in-

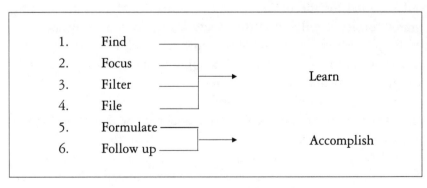

FIGURE 3–2   Functioning in the World of "Why Not?"

formation. Learning is not enough (Fig. 3–2). We need to be information-proficient (Fig. 1–1): We need to formulate plans and follow up to accomplish them.

And yet, as complex as life may be today, we anticipate continued diversification in society's pursuits.

THINKING GLOBALLY AND IN DETAIL

Today's business decisions take into account global considerations such as markets for products, sources of financing, currency fluctuations, trade tariffs, export and import restrictions, costs of labor and other means of production, and political climates.

Business decisions are based on interactions with, and perceptions about, many constituencies: current customers, potential customers, shareholders, individual employees, unions, business partners, lenders, suppliers, government regulators, government policymakers, public advocacy groups, competitors, trade associations, political candidates whose campaigns seek contributions, the general public, and the news media.

Business decisions depend on attention to detail, such as local laws, cultural nuances, customs, regulations, tax policies, and the competitive advantage of dealing appropriately, transaction by transaction, with each constituent. Attention to detail increases as businesses encourage employees to consider that one instance of poor service can result in loss of current and future business from a customer. If the customer tells other potential customers, the loss is magnified.

Individuals face the same challenges. You can find much in your life that mirrors business decision making. For example, if you own or work with a business or other organization, you contribute to business decisions.

Your personal life is filled with needs for attention to both broadening and deepening issues. If you pay income taxes in the United States, you experience the increasing complexities of the tax codes. The laws and regulations have become so encompassing and complex that many people seek expert tax advice when deciding on an investment, planning an individual retirement account, or doing estate planning. Filing income tax returns is likely to require software to tabulate data and the advice of experts.

If you buy shares of stock in a business, you bet on other people's skills to make business decisions on your behalf. When you review your investment portfolio, you have the challenge of guessing the relative merits of current and alternative investments. You want to estimate the future success of various management teams in making and implementing business decisions and you want to outguess other people's estimates of the marketplace.

SIMPLIFYING DECISIONS

Information proficiency emphasizes the processes used to arrive at decisions. Consider the following example in which a decision that could have been protracted and could have generated considerable emotion was made quickly and well.

In this example, an entirely new generation of computers was emerging. A manager was in charge of selecting the type of computer to be used throughout a large organization.

Some organizations have made such decisions several times, perhaps for mainframe computers for administrative applications in the 1950s and again in the 1960s, for possibly different mainframe computers for engineering use during the same two decades, for minicomputers in the 1970s, for microcomputers and "engineering workstations" in the 1980s, and for "parallel-processing" computers in the 1990s. These decisions have traditionally focused on system capabilities, such as speed in doing arithmetic and capacity for storing information, and on costs. Traditionally, many people in an organization take an interest in such a decision and want to be heard before it is made. The decision maker potentially faces considerable controversy before the decision is made, just after it is announced, and if the decision proves poor, for a long time into the future.

In this instance, the manager made the decision easily. He discovered that a preponderance of software developers were working on new products primarily for one type of the newly available class of computers. A single principle was used to make the decision: The organization would be best served by using computers that ran the widest variety of software.

The traditional topics of computing capabilities and cost were not researched. The manager believed that the software creators knew enough to invest their efforts wisely. The software developers would focus on a computer product line with a bright future, and they would help create the market for that product family. From the point of view of the decision maker, market forces would ensure that the chosen line of computers would remain competitive in terms of capability and cost.

The decision was successful. The software and the family of computers provided good service to the organization. Constituents appreciated the choice.

*   *   *

In an era of growing complexity, there is a tendency to assume that decisions must be made by striving for consensus and eventually making a "tough call" only in areas of continuing disagreement. It is possible, however, to simplify decision making.

The first step in information-proficient decision making is to think globally and determine the most important goals and principles on which to focus. If, as in the example just cited, you can identify one overriding principle, use it. If there are several paramount principles, all pointing in one direction, follow them. If there are several important principles and applying them leads to conflict, assign priorities to them.

If you and your colleagues cannot reach a decision, you are on to a second step in your process. As you are drawn into details, try from time to time to go back to first principles. Perhaps you have discovered a new principle or have had an insight about the principles you already considered. Perhaps you have learned enough at this point to extricate yourselves from the quagmire of details.

You may be noticing that the principle-based decision is a key tool, enabling you to thrive in the demanding world of why-not. It is a powerful tool for avoiding unnecessary complexity and wasted time.

A decision is a result, but a more important result lies in implementing the decision well. Keep in mind the principles that led to a decision and use them again in implementing the decision.

When you make a decision, you need to explain it to other people. Describing the principles that led to a decision provides important .information that helps other people implement your decision. Announcing the principles may capture the support of people who otherwise would oppose the decision. In any event, you maximize the possibility of earning respect for you and the decision while minimizing the chance that any disagreement will turn disagreeable.

Letting other people know the principles behind your decision increases the possibility that their decisions will parallel and reinforce yours.

Thus, you want to make a good decision, with minimum effort and maximum ability to explain it to other people. In short, you want to make a decision based on principles.

STICKING TO PRINCIPLES

Sometimes, sticking to principles requires steadfast resolve over a period of decades.

A few decades ago, a group of citizens found themselves struggling to block a series of proposals to develop their city's shoreline and parklands. The proposals included boat harbors, tennis clubs, parking lots, a city hall, and a city maintenance yard. The citizens fought the proposals one by one, winning narrow majority votes from a divided city council.

During the third battle, one member of this citizens' coalition spotted the trend and recognized that why-not ideas would continue to arise. This person proposed a new strategy and a new goal: Preempt future development proposals by establishing a wildlife preserve.

Establishing the preserve took decades of sticking to that one goal. First, preservationists received appointments, one by one, to the city planning commission. A majority was achieved, thereby slowing down the stream of proposals. Preservationists were elected to the city council, virtually shutting off the development proposals and finally setting up the opportunity to act on the goal.

The city council secured a bill from the state legislature granting the city title to the shoreline if the city adopted and implemented a plan for the land. After decades of sticking to the preservation principle, the citizens' group got its wish. Today, four "shoreline preserve" signs stand on the cliffs overlooking four miles of undeveloped shoreline.

*   *   *

Perhaps no decision can be more far-reaching than a government's choosing to go to war. The United States' yes or no decision to declare war in the Persian Gulf had wide-ranging and varied consequences for individuals, families, businesses, and nations: deaths, absences from families and from jobs, and other consequences. In areas near military bases, businesses suffered—soldiers sent overseas could not buy goods at home, and family members became cautious. Some businesses got a boost. For example, the United States government made massive purchases of food rations for soldiers.

Presumably, many such consequences could have been foreseen and widely debated for a long time before the decision was made.

Declaring war was, however, a rapidly made, principle-based decision that featured one clearly delineated goal. The more than two-dozen countries constituting the "coalition" decided to drive Iraqi forces out of Kuwait. The objective was, of course, later realized.

*   *   *

Electorates can also make decisions with clear purposes. The following example features a state's populace voting to keep property taxes within the means of homeowners. It also illustrates that, as with other decisions, principle-based decisions require maintenance when subtle issues are subsequently found.

In the 1970s, the California electorate voted in favor of Proposition 13, a constitutional amendment limiting the two factors used to compute property taxes, namely, the value assessed to a parcel and the tax rate applied to that value.

The main principle is straightforward, even quantitative. Yet, over the years, various issues and a series of further ballot measures have arisen. For example, what should the assessed value be if a new home is built after an existing one was destroyed in a fire? Or suppose someone sells a house and buys a less expensive one having a purchase price greater than the assessed value of the house being sold; is it fair for that person to face an increased property tax bill?

The Proposition 13 change in tax policy occurred in relative isolation from other issues, such as the consequences of reductions in property tax revenues. Adjustments to Proposition 13 have been considered based on their fairness to property owners within the principles of the original proposition.

With all the simplicity of this situation, it has taken far more than a decade to discover subtleties and to fine-tune Proposition 13.

*   *   *

Sticking to principles sometimes produces a breakthrough in thinking. The following example gives the history of the creation of the information-proficiency paradigm.

In late 1989, the United States General Services Administration (GSA) developed a mission statement befitting its role of providing services to other federal agencies: "To provide quality services required by our clients in a timely manner and ensure the best value to the government and the public, thereby enhancing our clients' ability to accomplish their mission" (Austin, 1990).

Each major GSA unit also developed a mission statement. One unit, the Information Resources Management Service (IRMS), could have developed a statement emphasizing computing and telecommunications products and services. Such a statement would, however, have been incomplete for two reasons: (1) About a decade had passed since federal law established the concept of information resources management, which emphasizes information as well as technology; and (2) a "products and services" mission statement would be interpreted as overlooking IRMS's role of overseeing information resources management practices throughout the federal executive branch.

Information Resources Management Service employees considered "an information-rich environment" as the key theme for a mission statement. An information-rich environment helps federal agencies be effective. Fostering such an environment seemed the most important contribution the information resources community could make. The Information Resources Management service is a leader for that community.

The draft mission statement had weaknesses. People might not understand "information-rich environment." The concept might connote "information overload." "Information-rich" hardly encompasses the main principles behind the use of information and information technology in the federal government.

Further thought raised the issue of how closely people associate information resources management with the missions of federal agencies. Perhaps National Archives and Records Administration employees think of themselves as managing information as a resource, but most federal employees and other people might not perceive such a direct connection between information resources management and the missions of agencies.

It was time to change the question. It was time to find a new paradigm and a new principle.

Finding a satisfactory mission statement depended on answering the question, "What is the relationship between information resources management and governmental mission?" Providing information, or fostering an information-rich environment, falls short.

The missing link is the effective use of information to accomplish goals. The Information Resources Management Service developed its mission statement around the theme of helping clients make effective use of information to accomplish their work and their agencies' missions. The wording is a statement followed by a definition: "To help clients achieve information proficiency. Information proficiency is the effective use of information to accomplish a person's job or an organization's mission" (Information Resources Management Service, 1990).

Thus, people discovered a principle with which to make decisions about managing information resources and deploying information technology. Society gained a paradigm and goal for people's use of Information Age techniques (Fig. 1–1).

CLIMBING APPROPRIATE MOUNTAINS

As the previous examples illustrate, sticking to principles need not imply staying with one principle. People should always be looking for a broader, better perspective.

Visualize a mountain range, with each mountain symbolizing a key principle or opportunity. Climbing one mountain represents maximizing the use of that principle or opportunity. To gain more perspective and possibly capture a better opportunity, you need to explore more than one mountain.

The creation of the information-proficiency paradigm demonstrates the benefits of looking for new mountains to climb. Trying to formulate a mission statement featuring the principle of an information-rich environment can be thought of as exploring one mountain. The view from the top of this mountain represents the best possible mission statement featuring the information-rich theme.

The Information Resources Management Service found it necessary to explore mountains other than the "information-rich" mountain. One of the other mountains, producing a "products and services" mission statement, would have been easier to climb—such a mission statement could have been adapted from the General Services Administration's overall mission statement. However, the peak would not have been as high—the mission statement would be seen as excluding important goals—and the view would not have been as good—the vision implicit in the mission would be too narrow.

The "information-proficiency" mountain took longer to find, proved easy to climb, and provided the best view.

Similarly, the story of the shoreline preservationists demonstrates the value of finding the most appropriate mountain. While the coalition could not abandon climbing the mountains representing countering the development proposals, it was necessary to find an additional mountain. The "shoreline preserve" mountain provided the opportunity for a long-term strategy and permanent solution. This mountain's view, the shoreline preserve, exists today for all people to see and enjoy.

RECOGNIZING YOUR OPPORTUNITIES

Your life doubtless contains opportunities to find better mountains to climb. You can find such opportunities if you take the time and effort to review current goals and methods and to look out into the world around you. The paradigm of information proficiency provides a new perspective for improving the effectiveness of organizations of which you are a part. Refocusing your Information Age attention on results and people provides another opportunity.

Your decisions, both personal and on behalf of organizations, reflect complex global issues and challenges to pay attention to necessary detail. You need to focus on important matters and avoid clutter.

The real question lies in choosing goals: Which opportunities should you pursue? The answer lies in making and implementing the decisions implicit in those opportunities (Fig. 1–1).

DECIDING AND ACHIEVING

When you consider what organizations and individuals produce, you are likely to think of tangible products and services. Automobile manufacturers produce cars for dealers to sell, financing plans for car buyers to use, and profits for shareholders. Governments produce services, information, and financial grants. People create the processes that make these products. Also, our processes and products generate by-products, intended and unintended,

What do all these products have in common? We can extract a powerful, simple conclusion: *Society's products are decisions and their implementations.*

Your world depends on the processes and products of the past: issues people addressed, choices made, and the results that followed. Your activities consist of selecting issues on which to act, making decisions, and taking action. Even inaction is a decision.

Decisions are results, but not final results. In focusing on an issue, you give importance to some concerns and downplay others. By making a decision, you produce a concept for the future, but that is all. For example, engineering plans and production schedules are decisions. They are tangible products, but they are not cars. The cars must get built. Turning a decision into a complete result requires further action: The decision must be implemented.

As you work to produce results—decisions and implementations—you doubtless notice that your world continues to suggest more why-not options, to demand broader global thinking, and to force attention to fine details. You need to become more proficient at making and implementing decisions. You need to improve your information proficiency (Fig. 1–1).

REFERENCES

Austin, Richard G., 1990. *Strategic Plan of the U.S. General Services Administration.* U.S. General Services Administration, Washington, DC.

Information Resources Management Service, 1990. *Strategic Plan of the Information Resources Management Service.* U.S. General Services Administration, Washington, DC.

PART *3*

*People and
Information
Proficiency*

CHAPTER 4

Understanding Information Age Changes to Organizations

Information Age change pervades society, affecting work, jobs, the workplace, and the economy. Decision making is supplanting analytic and clerical endeavors as the focus of work. The Peer Paradigm for organizational behavior provides one context for understanding the Information Age transformation. Levels of increasing information proficiency provide a second context. History provides a third.

WORK AND JOBS IN
THE INFORMATION AGE

The Information Age has not changed the objectives of work, but it has changed how work is done and has dramatically decreased employment in some types of jobs.

*   *   *

Clerical work involves recording, matching, combining, synthesizing, storing, and retrieving information. Although combining and synthesizing are less routine than the other functions, much clerical work falls into patterns. In the Information Age, patterned work is subject to automation.

In the past, many organizations hired people to work in data-entry pools. The primary skill was the ability to type information rapidly and accurately, day after day. This work is being supplanted as other employees, close to the sources of data, use handheld computers or barcode readers to record inventory in stores and warehouses, time-card data at work sites, and utility meter readings at customers' homes.

Computerizing data at its source eliminates extra steps. Errors are significantly reduced because data is captured either automatically or by people familiar with the information. The new procedures are more accurate, faster, and less expensive than the ones they replaced. Such procedures can be fully automated if the data sources contain information technology.

Many data-entry clerks have talents that can be used elsewhere. One employee had worked for several years in a data-entry pool. Her job was being eliminated by automation. She had skills that were not being used in that job and that had not been recognized by her employer. For eight hours a day, she was simultaneously doing good data-entry work and thinking about other aspects of her life—she was planning the development of her family and the management of a business in which she was a part owner. She and her employer created a new job that used more than her typing skills.

Beyond data entry, other clerical work is being eliminated or automated. Sometimes, a reduction in jobs exceeds the reduction in, and automation of, the work; the remaining work is left to people not paid to be clerks.

*   *   *

Secretarial work traditionally involves meeting callers, whether in person or over the phone, drafting and producing correspondence and other documents, arranging schedules, and doing clerical work for an individual or a work group. Automated answering systems and other technology are taking up telephone-related work. Scheduling and clerical work are being automated. Some of the steps in producing documents have moved from central typing pools to secretaries, and on to the individuals and groups supported by secretaries.

Secretarial work is being reshaped to incorporate more personal interactions with people from other groups, budget and administrative work, operational support for the group's automation tools, and types of work specific to the mission of the group.

While secretarial work takes on new aspects, the fraction of workers considered secretaries and the fraction of the workday spent on traditional secretarial activity continue to decline.

Again, change summons previously unused personal potential and provides a win-win scenario for companies and their workers. Another employee changed jobs from secretary to administrative assistant and then to budget analyst. Later, this employee received another promotion, this time to join a controller's department.

*   *   *

Middle-management jobs are also disappearing. Middle managers used to be essential for reporting information to more senior management. Today, information technology is taking over some of this work.

Middle managers served as repositories of knowledge about work processes; work groups are now redefining how work is done, however, and information systems are becoming the repositories of that information.

Current trends to empower all workers to make and implement decisions are redefining company culture, thereby reducing the role middle managers had in teaching traditional culture.

Once, middle managers served as coaches on how to find information elsewhere within the organization or beyond it and on how to secure cooperation from people in other groups. Now, information systems and work group colleagues are becoming directories of choice for locating information. Whether as a first choice or last resort, electronic mail provides a means to ask widely and quickly how to locate information. Similarly, E-mail can be used to initiate dialogue leading to teamwork with other components of the organization.

For example, one consulting firm uses E-mail as a primary means for employees to obtain answers to questions. An employee sends a question to a "topic." Automation converts the topic into a list of employees expert in that topic. The addressees want to help—answering a question may be the first step toward working on a new project and advancing one's career.

As with clerical and secretarial positions, the need for middle-management positions will continue to decline based in large part on use of information technology. None of these three types of jobs is headed for extinction, but each is being automated into narrower niches.

The evolutions of these three job groups have much in common. Routine work is subject to automation. Work unique to the goals of the organization remains.

*   *   *

For a sales force, information technology facilitates closing business and contacting more customers. It allows the salesperson to present to a customer a complete, up-to-date product catalog, including detailed product specifications, still pictures, and even movies. The customer easily explores choices. Orders are closed and recorded electronically at the time of contact. Through information technology, the sales call becomes more effective, and a larger fraction of a salesperson's time is devoted to selling.

Sometimes, customers do not require much personal help and the sales function is performed without a salesperson. For example, for some buying and selling of securities, a computer takes the order. In some such cases, a customer's computer makes buy and sell decisions and places orders.

*   *   *

For engineers designing products, information technology provides opportunities to perform larger portions of a piece of work with greater effectiveness than before. It is now possible to design an airliner without much use of paper. Computer-based modeling leads to an aerodynamic exterior design, with reduced reliance on building models and testing them in wind tunnels. Computerization supports producing, recording, and checking designs of parts, assemblies, and the whole product.

Workers and work groups are truly benefiting from a new standard of empowerment. They have the freedom to concentrate on the work, as opposed to procedures supporting work. Sophisticated tools perform complex parts of the work.

* * *

Common to all these types of work—clerical, secretarial, middle-managerial, sales, and engineering—is improvement in information proficiency. Haphazard approaches yield to patterned behavior. Patterned behavior is replaced by organized, procedural behavior. Procedural behavior is being automated. While taking advantage of the automation, workers also guide and optimize further automation. Most important, people have the information proficiency, means, and time to do work that is valued more highly and is less routine.

The balance of "knowledge-based" work is shifting from clerical to analytic. The change will not stop at analysis but will continue on to the making and implementing of decisions (Fig. 1–1).

Concurrent with these changes comes another demand for enhanced information proficiency—a shift from management to leadership.

* * *

Much executive work is ad hoc. Traditionally, information systems are applied to repetitive work. Executives want some information that today's systems can supply, but they need far more than routine information. Only today can we begin to conceive of a worldwide, broad-based amalgam of information sources that meets some of this need. Only today can we begin to conceive of techniques to filter such a vast resource to make it useful.

The information-proficiency paradigm invites executives to improve the processes by which they make decisions. While issues may change, decision-making patterns exist. As competition and other factors drive executives to improve their processes for making and implementing decisions, new opportunities for useful automation tools will arise.

Common to all jobs are four alternatives:

- Automate the work.
- Hire new employees or contractors to do the work well.
- Improve the information proficiency of the incumbent workforce quickly.
- Cease the activity.

For an executive, the standard for adding value continues to rise, and the choice is between the last two: improve or leave.

QUANTIFYING TODAY'S WORK

A recent study of the United States federal workforce (Personnel Research and Development Center, 1994) provides useful insight into today's work, as well as a baseline for future studies of this and other segments of the world's workforce.

> A survey . . . of the Federal workforce was undertaken to determine how employees identify, use and manage the information they need for their jobs and to support their agency missions. The results provide the General Services Administration the data that it needs for its governmentwide information resources management role to help agencies become more information proficient.

More than 5000 employees responded to this survey. With regard to the entire population of federal civilian employees, the percentage figures reported are "accurate within +/− 1.3 percent, at the 95 percent level of confidence."

The study addresses how far along the workforce is in the transition from clerical work to decision making. The survey indicates that federal employees emphasize decision making over analysis. Furthermore, communicating information, an activity crucial to making and implementing decisions, has virtually the same emphasis as decision making.

The survey probed the types of information-related tasks employees perform. The tasks, with the percentage of employees that perform each on a typical day, are:

- Make decisions, 75%.
- Communicate information, policies, or decisions to others, 74%.
- Analyze information, 69%.
- Enter or compile information into an existing form, format, or program, 61%.
- Retain, preserve, or store information, 53%.
- Create documents, databases, or spreadsheets, 48%.
- Perform general administration tasks, 44%.

In an era of growing complexity, you probably suspect that employees' gaining knowledge of processes and procedures is important. The survey backs that conclusion.

The survey studied the information employees need for performing work for their agencies. The types of information, and the percentage of employees needing each type, are:

- Internal agency policies and procedures, 81%.
- Federal regulations and laws, 78%.
- Federal agency activities, 37%.
- Reportings or filings from vendors, companies, or individuals required to report specific information to the agency, 35%.
- Requests from the public, 33%.
- Information from vendors for purchases or contracts, 32%.
- Personnel data, 32%.
- Financial or accounting statements, 30%.
- Scientific data, 27%.
- State and local government activities, 25%.
- Congressional activities, 22%.
- Results of surveys and questionnaires, 21%.

Having adequate information of appropriate quality is essential to performing one's job. The survey provides data about information and its quality.

Federal employees reported on whether they have the right amount of information to do their jobs. About 1 in 10 has more than is needed. About 3 in 5 have about the right amount. About 1 in 4 reported having somewhat less information than is needed.

The survey asked about the quality of information. Eighty-seven percent of the employees surveyed believe the information they receive is accurate and complete. The following sources of quality assurance are used by the indicated percentage of employees:

- Personal knowledge and skills, 92%.
- Supervisors, 57%.
- Co-workers, 52%.
- Using computer programs or applications, 31%.
- Feedback from other agencies, 22%.

THE CHANGING WORKPLACE

The definition of *workplace* is changing, and this change, in turn, causes ripples throughout the economy.

One change in the way people work involves the expectation that people be present at a central workplace. In a traditional manufacturing plant, being away from the assembly line meant being nonproductive. Although traditions of being present and looking busy linger and many people are reluctant even to take time for training or vacations, changes in the places and circumstances in which people work proceed apace.

As products shift from tangible goods to intangibles such as software and decisions, the need to be present in a traditional workplace decreases. A software programmer needs to use a computer, but neither the computer nor the display terminal needs to be at the employer's office. Much of the information needed to make a decision need not be in such an office either. Research and discussion can be conducted using telephone calls, electronic mail messages, documents sent via facsimile, video conferences, and other means that do not involve showing up at a central workplace.

A term has been invented for this new style of work. *Telecommuting* denotes working *with* the office but not *at* the office. Telecommuters can devote more time to work or personal matters than regular commuters. They save gasoline and tires but generate increased telecommunications costs.

The focus of sales work is the customer, not the office. Unless one is part of business in which customers visit stores, a salesperson need not "come to work." Sales calls can be made in person or electronically.

Companies are reducing the office space provided to sales staffs. For example, many salespeople can share an office with a few desks. Each person has a locker that can be moved to any desk. When a person leaves the office, the desk must be cleared and the locker returned to its usual spot. In some cases, a secretary is present to support the sales force and keep the office supplied. In some cases, there is a nearby conference room that can be rented for a staff meeting.

Recognizing that some people want work facilities away from their employers' locations, some suburban communities are providing office space so that residents can "come to work" while avoiding the commute to their organizations' traditional offices.

With the shift in the locations at which work is performed, at least two challenges arise.

One challenge is to corporate culture. Organizations must foster ways for people to feel comfortable working with seldom-seen colleagues. New techniques will be needed to help groups form, work together, and produce beneficial results. Appropriate measures of, and rewards for, success are needed.

Another challenge is evident in the real estate marketplace as the Information Age changes people's needs. In the U.S. commercial real estate marketplace, various factors have led to vacancies. Overbuilding has been followed by declines in needs for space that are driven by information technology. Organizations continue to "right-size" their in-house workforces and find that employees need not go to an office as often or, in some cases, at all. The new style of work affects the residential real estate marketplace; for example, telecommuting increases the demand for storage and work space in houses and apartments. There are ramifications for the hotel industry: videoconferencing and other means of communications decrease individual's needs for business travel but, when people travel on business, they want more technology-based facilities and services.

Shopping from home has occurred for decades, based on catalogs, telephones, and delivery services. Recently, some catalogs have been brought into homes via television. The advent of two-way video and computer services will result in more opportunities to shop from home. There is no reason why the electronic sales brochure of the future cannot offer a customer essentially all desired details about a specific product. Customers will be able to synthesize charts comparing competing products. Orders will be placed electronically. Although people do like to touch products before buying them and many like to get out of the house to shop, one may well wonder how many retail shops will survive.

A further pressure on both retail businesses and commercial and retail real estate will occur to the extent that clothing manufacture adopts a customized, just-in-time approach. For example, an individual customer orders a jacket based on choices of style and fabric from a catalog, and a computer-driven laser fabric cutter cuts the material to fit the customer. The costs could be competitive, based on the elimination of warehouses, retail display space, transportation costs, and much of the labor and risk associated with today's method of doing business.

Such analyses of impacts are relative, not absolute. For real estate, they do not predict overall demand or prices, but they do indicate Information Age effects.

You might want to think about how the Information Age affects other segments of the economy, including transportation, energy, and telecommunications. If you invest in stocks or will be seeking employment or are planning to go into business, such contemplation can be beneficial to you. Consider transportation, for example.

Telecommuting and electronic conferencing will increase demand for more sophisticated automobiles that accommodate electronic equipment but will soften demand for commercial and corporate airplanes.

The Peer Paradigm for Organizational Behavior

Organizations use a vertical chain of command. The organization chart resembles the roots of a tree, with each manager's responsibility branching to several subordinates.

Traditionally, attention focused vertically, especially upward. Information flowed upward before it flowed across (Fig. 4–1). Organizational units sought to be self-sufficient. If work could not be handled within one unit, it was handled sequentially by various units, each functioning in isolation.

One metaphor sums this up: Organizations erected Berlin Walls that kept individuals and groups from mingling, sharing information, and working together. Computer systems reinforced those walls with barriers of their own—walls that kept people from getting information from more than one system at a time and walls that prohibited information flow between systems.

You doubtless have experienced some of the consequences. Perhaps you felt obligated to chase a permit application or other matter from desk to desk through a bureaucracy, acquainting each employee with particulars of your case.

While organizations still have vertical chains of command, other aspects of the traditional vertical paradigm are in decline. The depth of the organization chart has decreased. Clerical units have disappeared from the bottom. Layers of managers have disappeared from the middle. Further flattening occurred as spans of control increased throughout.

The walls are falling. Today's organization tackles challenges by building teams composed of employees from many units. For example, an automobile manufacturer's 1992 advertisement featured the

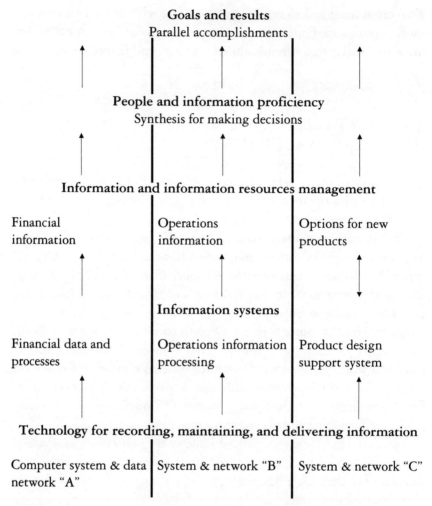

Goals and results
Parallel accomplishments

People and information proficiency
Synthesis for making decisions

Information and information resources management

| Financial information | Operations information | Options for new products |

Information systems

| Financial data and processes | Operations information processing | Product design support system |

Technology for recording, maintaining, and delivering information

| Computer system & data network "A" | System & network "B" | System & network "C" |

FIGURE 4–1   The Traditional Paradigm for Organizations, Information, and Accomplishments.

team concept; designers, engineers, and production workers worked together to design a new model and get it ready for manufacturing in less time than it took for previous models. Curiously, the ad did not mention any role of customers. One of the first principles of "quality" is to involve customers in product design, and mentioning that customers have contributed to the design makes a strong selling point.

Along with the shift from vertical information flow to horizontally constituted teams comes an emphasis on empowering teams and individuals to make and implement decisions. You may have read of a government assigning one person to decide on, or marshal the resources needed to handle, permit applications or other classes of cases. You have doubtless read of automobile companies in which assembly workers halt production until they figure out how to avoid further occurrences of a defect.

Implicit in the new paradigm is a concept of *modularity*. For a specific opportunity, a team forms, works together in person or via communications, completes or abandons its task, and dissolves.

Organizations strive for modularity. The term *virtual corporation* has been coined to denote a business that is proficient in hiring, or otherwise allying with, groups outside the company to accomplish needed tasks. Unless one can be competitive at a type of work that one will do continuously, why devote employees to it? At the extreme, a corporation brings a product to market without using its own employees to perform design, testing, manufacturing, marketing, or distribution work. The business contracts for each of these services, though it needs to foster teamwork among contractors supplying different services.

Information Age techniques and technology are facilitating these changes, especially as computer and telecommunications systems transcend the walls implicit in past systems. Interpersonal communications are facilitated. Routine work is automated. Organizations focus on the important aspects of their work. They meet their goals through increased information proficiency.

People have referred to this new organizational behavior as the "horizontal paradigm," thereby emphasizing horizontally constituted teams and reduced layers of management. Although this is an era of growing horizontal operational cooperation, vertical chains of command will continue to exist. The change to horizontal teams is but one hallmark of this new era.

The term Peer Paradigm captures this broader change (Fig. 4–2). This is an era of peer cooperation involving:

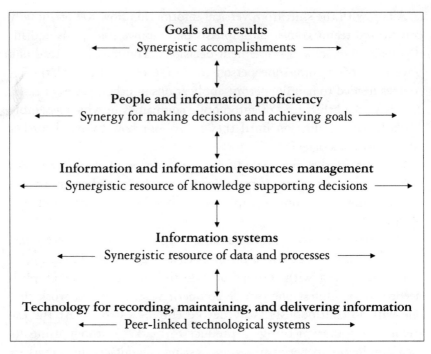

FIGURE 4–2   The Peer Paradigm for Organizations, Information, and Accomplishments.

- Synergy between missions of various organizations.
- Synergy between people sharing information, enhancing each others' skills, and working as teams.
- Synergy between components of information resources.
- Synergy between information systems.
- Synergy between technological components of information systems.

The Peer Paradigm recognizes that this growing synergy is needed to serve the increasing interdependence among elements of society.

THE PEER PARADIGM IN ACTION

All organizations participate in alliances over common goals. The Persian Gulf War demonstrates that a complex alliance can be put together quickly and can achieve its purpose. This war provides a rich example of the Peer Paradigm.

More than two dozen nations formed a coalition to pursue the goal of driving Iraqi forces out of Kuwait. There was unity over the intended result.

The challenges involving people included assembling a military force and an integrated command structure. There had been varying degrees of cooperation in the past among some groups of the coalition's countries, but there was no preexisting structure for managing the situation at hand. Of course, no one language was shared by all troops.

Within the war effort of the United States alone, there were many organizations to bring together. Coordination among the Army, Navy, Marines, and Air Force was destined to exceed that of the past because of experience in having a general or admiral in charge of all U.S. forces in a region and because of changes, made after the Vietnam War, strengthening the role of the Chairman of the Joint Chiefs of Staff. Within the Department of Defense, there were also, of course, many other participants besides those in the military services.

Outside the Defense Department, there were yet more groups. For example, the General Services Administration provided telecommunications support; delivered supplies, including fulfilling emergency needs for sand-colored paint for military vehicles; contributed computer systems consulting services that expedited the preparation of maintenance manuals and the development of medical computing systems; and gave first priority to the Department of Defense for spare computers from other federal agencies. Many other parts of the government also participated, as well as private industry, which contributed support essential to the government's use of systems and other equipment.

The Peer Paradigm applied also to individuals working together. For example, physicians in the field and specialists in the United States jointly reviewed medical X rays. The X-ray images were sent to the United States via satellite telecommunications. Patients received timely treatment based on information-proficient, peer-to-peer consultation between the care provider and a specialist.

*   *   *

Sometimes peer alliances build potential, transcending the original goals of the partners.

In the 1980s, several U.S. federal agencies fostered advances in supercomputers, supercomputing software, and telecommunications. Some advances occurred because of sponsored research in technology, others through the development or acquisition of technology to support federal operations. Research sponsors included the Department of Defense Advanced Projects Research Agency, Department of Energy, National Aeronautics and Space Administration, National Science Foundation, Department of Commerce National Institute for Standards and Technology, Department of Commerce National Oceanic and Atmospheric Administration, Environmental Protection Agency, and Department of Health and Human Services National Institutes of Health National Library of Medicine.

In the late 1980s and early 1990s, these eight agencies developed the High Performance Computing and Communications Initiative, a single initiative embracing their sponsorship of progress in supercomputing and high-capacity telecommunications. They developed an interagency budget, with each agency determining what it would do if the total budget were set at various amounts. By working together on this ostensibly bureaucratic effort, people laid groundwork for sharing results and avoiding duplicate research.

Bringing together into one publicized initiative the various projects called public and federal attention to the potential implicit in this work. The telecommunications portion, known as the National Research and Education Network, provided impetus for the development of the concept of the "information highway," or "information superhighway." The overall program provided impetus for the concept of a National Information Infrastructure.

*   *   *

The following example features one company's consistent emphasis on synergy and modularity throughout the Peer Paradigm.

This corporation supplies software tools through which customers develop software systems. For example, one customer used the tools to build systems that support coast guard officers as they make and implement command decisions.

The company's mission statement centers on ensuring customer success. Many customers find that the software tools embody unfamiliar systems development techniques. The company has expanded its services into successively broader areas: education about how to use the tools most effectively, consultation on systems analysis and design, and advice on how to manage systems development projects. Expanding the services upward in the Information Age framework (Fig. 2–1), from providing *technology* to supporting customers' *systems* development and *people,* represents one step toward accomplishing the mission.

Another step features aggressive synergy building, based on the Peer Paradigm (Fig. 4–2), both within the company and between the company and customers.

Customers are served by account teams. A typical team has one salesperson and four technical staff members. Team members do not report to sales or technical services managers; instead, the teams report to customer service managers. For both team members and the managers of groups of teams, the company grades performance in terms of contributions to five measures of team success:

- Revenue production.
- Customer success.
- Development of business within the sales territory.
- Operations of the team or group, including internal teamwork and contributions to the company as a whole.
- Business basics:
   Prudent use of resources.
   Stability in methods of doing business.
   Adding value for customers without sacrificing corporate objectives such as profitability.

In building peer synergy among employees, between employee groups, and throughout the corporation as a whole, the company also recognizes four objectives that working for the company should help an employee achieve:

- A degree of financial security.
- Opportunities for personal and professional growth.

- Opportunities to make real contributions, both for customers and within the company.
- Realizing the first three objectives within a sustainable lifestyle—for example, without burnout.

This well-articulated internal emphasis on synergy includes and extends to relations with clients. The commitment to client success, as articulated in the mission and personal performance standards, builds *goals* and *results* synergy between the customer's mission and the company's mission.

Corporate commitment to achieving effective *people* synergy is so strong that the company:

- Has fired a top salesperson who excelled at the first of the five account team objectives but did poorly with regard to some of the other four.
- Has recommended to customers that they remove certain people from their project teams.

Making recommendations about customer personnel generates both business risk and detractors for the corporation; however, securing the interpersonal and interorganizational synergy needed to satisfy the company's perception of customer needs is felt to be in the long-run best interests of both customers and the company. The true client is a customer corporation, not a customer corporation's project team member.

The company also recognizes Peer Paradigm opportunities regarding *information proficiency* and *information*. The company believes that an account team and its client normally have the best information available for making and implementing the decisions necessary to accomplish their mutual goals. The corresponding empowerment for account teams is based on the concept that the company's manager to whom an account team reports does not have, and is unlikely to be able to obtain, as good a base of information as the team has. Indeed, the nuances of vocabulary and communications used within the account team may differ significantly from those used when communicating with the manager. "Upward delegation" of a decision is undesirable and symptomatic of problems beyond those inherent in making the decision itself. Although upward delegation is discouraged, Peer Paradigm sharing of information and techniques is encouraged by managers and the performance-grading criteria.

The rigorous modular definition of the internal and external responsibilities for account teams parallels principles and methodologies the company teaches regarding *systems* design and employs within its own *technology* products. Each systems component and each technology product component must have a well-defined function, be shielded from untoward external demands, and add to the value of its peers, both currently and in the future.

Thus, this company recognizes opportunities for building synergy in each layer of the Peer Paradigm. The company also emphasizes modularity and responsibility. This company has an unusually consistent interpretation of these principles—modularity, responsibility, and synergy—throughout the layers of the Peer Paradigm.

* * *

The following example illustrates how an international firm providing financial auditing, tax advice, and information technology consulting services has embraced the Peer Paradigm to build its competitive advantage.

The firm provides advice on the impact of taxation. For example, a client wants to know how to minimize taxes worldwide as it acquires and manages a new subsidiary. The firm's success requires marshaling and integrating the expertise and information proficiency of tax experts worldwide. The traditional approach, using isolated national tax consulting practices, is not appropriate. Knowledge flow and utilization must follow the Peer Paradigm.

More generally, the firm considers that its business is based on intellectual property. The key resources are people and knowledge.

Although the importance of people is indisputable, individuals can provide only so much effort per day, and their knowledge and expertise are lost when they leave the firm.

The company looks to its knowledge as a resource that can be leveraged for competitive advantage. According to the traditional paradigm (Fig. 4–1), information, whether data or a technique, might be created, used once, and lost, only to be reinvented elsewhere in the firm.

The firm has made a concerted effort to leverage information by encouraging employees to contribute to the resource, capturing knowledge for long-term use, developing an extensive information resource, and making the resource available to employees. Success depends on implementing the Peer Paradigm (Fig. 4–2) at all levels. Beyond synergy between goals and between people, such as is evident in the tax practice, the firm develops a synergistic resource of knowledge. Standard technological tools facilitate building the information resource and providing services to clients, as well as employees, working together as teams on projects and while visiting offices worldwide.

Readily useful information includes thousands of items: data and other aids for performing consulting work, guidance from management, support services for external customers using software supplied by this firm, data that can be provided to clients, marketing information, ongoing global intrafirm dialogue on important evolving issues, information brought in from outside the firm, information about employees, survey forms, vendors' prices and company procedures for ordering technology, software for internal use, and advice on using the firm's technology.

For organizations that use it, the Peer Paradigm provides an appropriate Information Age framework guiding the formation and operations of alliances within and between organizations.

VIRTUAL ORGANIZATIONS

An ancient tribe engaging in barter with other tribes exhibited characteristics of a virtual organization. It chose to acquire goods rather than make them.

Today's family is a virtual organization. It grows little to none of its food. It employs repair services to fix mechanical and electrical problems in its home. It hires an accountant or buys software to prepare its income taxes.

Automobile manufacturers buy parts from other firms and require "just-in-time delivery." Aircraft manufacturers acquire, rather than build, fuselage segments as well as smaller parts.

While you are familiar with such examples, it is a good idea to explore the limits to which this concept can be taken and identify what is required to ensure success at those limits. Consider the following examples.

One part of the General Services Administration's Information Resources Management Service provides services to federal agencies, including software programming, computer systems planning, and computer facilities planning and operations. On average, for each government employee, there are 17 private-sector employees supporting this IRMS program. Federal employees conduct competitive bidding to select private-sector contractors. Government employees also market the services to federal agencies; negotiate statements of work, taking into account clients' needs and suppliers' capabilities; administer the projects; and oversee transfers of funds from clients to suppliers. The contractors' employees do the programming and other work. This federal business unit is a virtual organization.

The advantages of being a virtual organization are clear. With 17-to-1 leverage and with minimal guarantees of business to contractors, this federal business unit scales its operations up or down much more flexibly than if it directly employed a complete staff. As business changes, the skill mix and geographic locations are adjusted more easily.

The challenges of any service business remain. Coping with business changes does not vanish. The contractors pick up much of the risk, although they can have the advantage of abating the risk by having nonfederal clients. Maintaining competitiveness requires concerted effort to minimize project management overhead because both government and contractor personnel oversee each project.

In another part of the IRMS, 60 employees run a "virtual store," through which federal agencies annually acquire approximately $2 billion in computing and telecommunications products and services. Negotiating contracts with about 1000 suppliers each year consumes most of the staff's time. Almost all the other activities are "virtual." The suppliers print and distribute their own catalogs, worded to link the catalog to this GSA Schedules program. Federal agencies shop using the catalogs and place orders directly with the vendors. Vendors send goods and invoices directly to their customers. The "store" learns how much business it conducts through quarterly reports from the suppliers.

This high degree of employee leverage requires support from other sources. For example, GSA's Office of the Inspector General reviews some of the proposed prices to help determine if they meet the government's "fair and reasonable" standard.

Even such a low-overhead operation faces Information Age needs to modernize. Customers want to browse through electronic catalogs. Making the catalogs available electronically through one source not only reduces the vendors' and government's burdens related to physical catalogs but also facilitates comparison shopping. An electronic store for browsing has recently been built. It remains to be seen whether it will turn into an electronic store for ordering.

In any event, this development holds out hope of setting a new standard of "fair and reasonable pricing." In the past, the government has negotiated prices based on a vendor's best prices available to comparable commercial customers. Direct competition in the electronic marketplace could supplant this time-consuming practice. Vendors will not have to supply so much information so often to justify their prices, negotiations will be simpler, there will be fewer needs for price reviews and audits, and prices will adjust rapidly, presumably to the advantage of the government and taxpayers.

The entirety of the Information Resources Management Service exhibits characteristics of a virtual organization. It remarkets telecommunications, systems integration, and other services. Most of its work force is virtual. Even its management education services rely significantly on outside instructors. While companies in the information technology services business earn revenues of about $100,000 to $150,000 per year per employee, this federal business unit's ratio is between $400,000 and $500,000, not counting virtual revenue, such as that from the virtual store.

The entirety of the General Services Administration earns $10 billion per year by providing services to other federal agencies. With nearly 20,000 employees, the annual revenue per employee, $500,000, is similar to that for its computing and telecommunications business unit. Other parts of GSA are highly leveraged. For example, the Federal Supply Service resells paper, pens, tools, and other goods acquired from nonfederal manufacturers.

Unlike GSA, the government as a whole is not perceived as a business, but it is a virtual organization. Less than 4% of the American workforce spends a budget several times that percentage of the gross domestic product. Some other examples of the government's role as a leveraged virtual organization are evident. Veterans and other citizens receive "federal" mortgage loans; however, banks provide the loans while the government provides loan guarantees and standards for the lending programs. Federal grants sponsor scientific research done in universities and the private sector. The Department of Defense and the National Aeronautics and Space Administration fly airplanes and launch spacecraft built by private-sector companies. The director of one state's computer center estimates that half of the center's workload is devoted to federal programs. State and local governments, companies, and individuals spend countless hours and dollars in order to comply with federal regulations.

Businesses striving for "virtual" leverage confront challenges similar to those faced by government agencies. Contracting out work requires successful contract negotiation and administration. Contracting to several suppliers with the expectation they will produce a coordinated result requires even more skill. Changing goals or specifications in midstream leads to delays and cost increases. Entrusting funds to others entails risk.

ADDITIONAL PERSPECTIVE ON THE INFORMATION AGE TRANSFORMATION

Humankind has gone through at least two previous radical transformations based on improvements in knowledge and communications.

First, when people learned enough about agriculture, civilization supplanted tribal living. People developed towns and government. Manufacturing arose in the form of crafts. Commerce and trade developed.

Second, when knowledge of mechanical and electrical phenomena grew, machinery catalyzed the Industrial Revolution. The fraction of the population devoted to growing food decreased again. Mass production replaced craft work. Commerce and trade took a step forward based on improved transportation of goods and communication of information.

In both cases, the fraction of society devoted to traditional activities decreased. Today, we have disparate attitudes toward reduced needs for labor. With a long tradition of ever-increasing efficiency in food production in the United States, many people take for granted the fact that a small fraction of the population grows almost all the food the nation produces. With a shorter history of change in manufacturing, there are many reactions to decreases in manufacturing jobs. Some people view these changes favorably, based on the premise that increased efficiency leads to competitiveness, which prevents even further loss of this type of work. Others wonder whether the nation is losing a base of skill. Others, of course, focus on the loss of jobs.

Questions remain. As the Information Age progresses, will society transform its endeavors and achieve new vitality as it did when it developed civilization? If so, how long will the transformation take? How much turbulence will occur along the way? What will be the outcome? Or will society simply run short of useful work as the supply of labor and automation outruns the demand for goods, traditional services, information services, travel, and interpersonal communication?

*   *   *

The Information Age represents a new era in the evolution of society. It develops new avenues of human progress. It extends progress made during previous eras. Similarly, the Information Age itself consists of stages, each drawing on, reinforcing, and extending previous stages.

Our Information Age journey (Fig. 4–3) starts at a ground floor of human progress from the electromechanical age and all that occurred before that time. The first step in the Information Age was the creation of promising technology. Early applications automated traditional clerical and analytic work. These steps focused on improving work specific to the relatively narrow endeavors associated with the traditional paradigm for organizations (Fig. 4–1). With increasing experience, know-how, and better technology, we now reengineer broader processes, thereby supporting and driving the evolution to the Peer Paradigm (Fig. 4–2).

Each of these strides has increased the information proficiency of the organizations and individuals who have taken that step. Each step remains a focus for future opportunities. The next steps are:

- Building ubiquitous knowledge bases, as the audit, tax, and technology consulting firm is doing.
- Enhancing our capabilities for making and implementing all types of decisions (Fig. 1–1), including nonrepetitive ones.

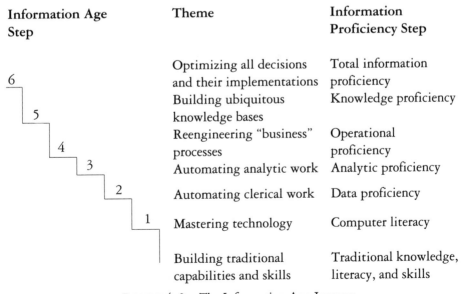

Information Age Step	Theme	Information Proficiency Step
6	Optimizing all decisions and their implementations	Total information proficiency
5	Building ubiquitous knowledge bases	Knowledge proficiency
4	Reengineering "business" processes	Operational proficiency
3	Automating analytic work	Analytic proficiency
2	Automating clerical work	Data proficiency
1	Mastering technology	Computer literacy
	Building traditional capabilities and skills	Traditional knowledge, literacy, and skills

FIGURE 4–3   The Information Age Journey.

These steps characterize the future of the Information Age and of society's growing information proficiency.

REFERENCE

Personnel Research and Development Center, 1994. *Report on the Survey of the Information Proficiency of Federal Employees (draft)*. U.S. Office of Personnel Management, Washington, DC.

CHAPTER 5

Understanding Information Proficiency

The products of all individuals and groups are decisions and their implementations. Enhancing those products depends on understanding and improving the information proficiency of people and organizations.

"IF ONLY . . ."

"Why did they do that?" This frequently asked question is useful—to do well in the present and future, we need to learn from history. But this can also be a loaded question, expressing criticism of a less than optimal action.

When decision makers admit that their decisions could have been better, they are likely to offer such explanations as these:

- "If only we had known . . ."
- "If only we had remembered . . ."
- "Evidently, that idea got lost; it never reached us."
- "We thought of that, but by then it was too late."
- "If only there had been more time."
- "We thought there were more important issues to concentrate on."
- "We started out with a specific goal, but . . ."
- "That idea was considered, but not well researched, so we could not . . ."
- "We got mired in details."
- "Halfway through the project, the team changed."
- "The idea seemed good, but too hard to accomplish."
- "We never thought that the other party would accept . . ."
- "We never thought that this decision would affect . . ."

And, of course, other people, especially those affected by the decision, also have reactions:

- "If only we had been involved, they could have considered . . ."

Each of us knows of decisions that could have been better: for example, money spent on an item seldom used, a poor choice between employment offers, or a purchase of stock at a high price. Or you might recall the decision that led to the disastrous last launch of the space shuttle *Challenger.*

Each of us also knows of reasonable decisions for which the implementation fell short. Perhaps you remember an instance in which the management of an organization made a decision but did not tell enough people about it . . .

- "If only there had been good follow-up . . ."

These "if only" quotations point to problems arising in making and implementing decisions—problems that include missing information, less than adequate attention to the matter at hand, improper focus, less than optimal judgment, inadequate communications, ill-advised changes in direction, and unintended consequences.

Twenty/twenty hindsight makes it easy to learn from past mistakes. Your challenge is to do better in the future.

SOCIETY AND DECISIONS

Society and its components (Fig. 2–2) make many types of decisions (Table 5–1). A convenient characterization of decisions (Fig. 5–1) emphasizes three categories: empowered, complex, and dramatic. (Today, society is rethinking and reshaping how it makes decisions.)

In business, government, and other organizations, one current trend is toward empowerment, that is, allowing and encouraging individuals, small groups, and automated systems to make decisions with minimal review. This trend applies to decisions that are suitable for individuals, small groups, or systems.

For more complex decisions, the trend is toward involving many people. Recognizing that a few people will not be able to foresee all the consequences of a decision and that modern societal practice and communication techniques facilitate collecting needed inputs, decision makers seek broad background and, if desirable and possible, near consensus. Regardless, however, of how close constituents come to a consensus or how far away they may be, decision makers need to act in a timely manner.

TABLE 5–1   EXAMPLES OF DECISIONS

Entity	Defined Decisions	Open-Ended Decisions
Society	Two camps of nations declaring "world war" on each other	Society saving tropical rain forests
Macroentity	A country bestowing a "national medal"	A democratic country enacting national legislation
Amorphous group	A mob "deciding" to riot	A regional coalition taking a step toward enhancing air quality
Focused group	A family buying a car	A corporation deciding to acquire other companies
Individual	An empowered worker deciding to approve an application for insurance coverage	A person setting up a personal investment strategy
Automated system	A computer system processing a credit-card transaction	A computer system making automated investment decisions

These two trends can be viewed as opposites or as part of a single, broader picture, depending on whether we want to emphasize differences or similarities.

One difference is apparent. The involvement of fewer people for an empowered decision contrasts with the involvement of more people for a complex decision.

One similarity lies in the attempt to find the most appropriate method and parties to make a decision. Another lies in the attempt to utilize an adequate amount of "collected wisdom." Even in an empowered decision, the people or systems are not acting in a vacuum; they should have learned enough from other people, other systems, and other societal sources of norms and information to make a sound decision.

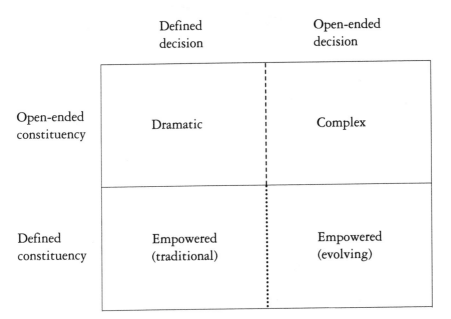

FIGURE 5-1   Characterizing Decisions.

So, it is fair to say that there is broad participation in both types of decisions. Perhaps the fundamental principle behind seeking broad participation in decisions is a belief that, by working together, two or more people can produce a result that is more beneficial to each of them than decisions that would be made singly.

*   *   *

How do we make decisions? One key practice in making decisions is to look for similarities and differences between alternatives. We just did that in contrasting two trends in decision making. We found differences, such as growing individual empowerment in one case, and growing mass involvement in another. Recognizing that both cases lie on a spectrum of styles of decision making, we found similarities.

Similarities are powerful. In relations between nations, between businesses, or other entities, there seems to be a growing appreciation for the search for common goals, similar interests, and opportunities to work together. Differences need to be well understood and dealt with, but there is an increasing willingness to try to reconcile differences rather than letting them stand in the way of success.

Looking first for similarities has been essential to successes over a relatively few years in furthering peace in the southwestern Middle East and in political change in South Africa. Finding similarities also catalyzes the growing synergies between information sources and between information-delivery technologies needed to support the Peer Paradigm for organizations (Fig. 4–2).

A pattern emerges. Look first for similarities and ways to cooperate. Next, recognize differences. Then, look for similarities to overcome the differences or, if you cannot find enough similarities this time, recognize quickly that the differences cannot be reconciled. And so on, alternating attention between similarities and differences until enough issues are resolved and the opportunity at hand is captured or abandoned.

It is interesting to observe our attitude at each stage. When we are looking for similarities and common interests, the presumption is that the opportunity can be captured. When we are looking for differences in goals, the attitude of the moment may shift toward a presumption that the opportunity cannot be captured.

Think of an important decision involving or affecting you in which the similarities and differences among alternatives were not well understood. Perhaps this decision came to mind when you read the "if only" statement, "We got mired in details." Focusing too narrowly on details often means that we think alternatives are more similar than they actually are. Hence, we try to resolve minor issues while missing key points.

Consider another example of perceived differences. Some people believe that society is dividing into two groups, an "information-literate" group and everyone else. Perhaps it is appropriate to replace this two-camp hypothesis with a continuous scale of capability. Such a scale would incorporate several factors, including sense of purpose, skills, knowledge, and personal contacts to make and implement decisions. In short, points on the scale represent degrees of information proficiency.

Undoubtedly, you want to find out where you are on that scale and then move to a more advantageous spot on it.

INFORMATION PROFICIENCY AND QUALITY

Information proficiency denotes effectiveness in defining and achieving goals (Fig. 1–1). It includes making good decisions and implementing them effectively (Fig. 5–2). Decisions and their implementation are essential to all conscious human endeavor and accomplishment.

Picture yourself making an important decision affecting yourself, your family, a business, or a community organization. Think of a decision you face now or one that you recall in some detail from the past. What are some of the major questions? Perhaps they are similar to the following:

- What decision are you actually trying to make? How will the topic, your frame of reference, or the scope of the decision change as you explore the issue?

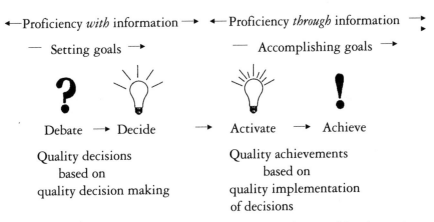

FIGURE 5–2 Information Proficiency: Quality in Making and Implementing Decisions.

- To what extent will the decision be driven by urgency or other factors besides overall importance?
- Who will be affected by this decision?
- Who should be involved in making this decision—because they may have useful information or insight, because it is expected that they participate, or because you will need their support in implementing the decision?
- What information would you like to have?
- How will you obtain it?
- What information are you likely to have when you make the decision?
- How accurate will the information be?
- How consistent will it be with itself and with other knowledge you have?
- How will you appropriately involve other people in making this decision?

Consider each of the preceding questions in the context of the important decision you've chosen. Formulate and address other useful questions. By taking yourself out of the decision-making process momentarily, you can monitor your own behavior and develop a context in which to define success in making the decision.

Think of society's movement toward quality. Programs such as *total quality management* stress enhancing the products and services provided by businesses and other organizations. These programs encourage measuring, analyzing, and improving those products and services and the processes that produce them. Quality applies equally to decisions: quality in making decisions and quality in implementing them are the major components of information proficiency.

The quality movement stresses that successful planning, measurement, and early attention to difficulties save considerable work later. So it is no surprise that the list of questions to be asked about implementing your decision is shorter than the list of questions about making the decision. Indeed, your plans for implementing the decision should have been outlined while you were making the decision.

Recall the decision you made or, if it is still pending, settle on a plausible outcome. Apply the following questions about carrying out that decision:

- Who needs to know about this decision?
- Who is supposed to act based on it?
- How will you persuade these people to take the desired actions?
- What follow-up will be needed to ensure that the decision is implemented properly?
- How will you know when to close or to reopen the issue?

* * *

Operationally, information proficiency (Figs. 1–1 and 5–2) consists of two major components:

- Proficiency *with* information to make decisions.
- Proficiency *through* information to implement decisions.

Proficiency with information is quality decision making. It is based on coping successfully with the "who, what, when, why, where, and how" questions pertaining to a decision and the actions that lead to making it.

Similarly, ensuring appropriate results depends on the "who, what, when, why, where, and how" of implementing a decision. In short, proficiency through information, or quality communication, causes actions to be taken.

* * *

Today's decisions are made by individuals, groups, software, and electromechanical systems (Table 5–1). Information proficiency applies throughout the spectrum of decision makers—human and automated.

Think of your credit card and your monthly bill. Software has been entrusted to generate that bill, based on data collected during one month. The credit-card billing corporation uses that software to make what should be the last determination of the amount you owe, based on credit transactions, payments posted, and current rates for finance charges. There could be errors in the data or the software. The processing organization's processes do have quality checks, such as authorizations and data capture at the time of purchase, but the processes do not eliminate the possibility of errors.

The ultimate quality control is determined by individual cardholders and merchants. Cardholders complain about being overcharged for purchases, being charged for purchases never made, or not being credited for payments sent but not posted. Merchants complain about sales for which they have not been paid or about supposed credits that have been posted but not actually given to customers.

Mechanical designs and computers incorporated in automobiles illustrate decisions that, while not made directly by people, are made based on principles formulated by people. In designing older cars, people determined through mechanical principles how pressure applied to a brake peddle translated into braking power. Today, sensors and computers provide antilock braking. Quality in mechanical and electromechanical systems depends on design, testing, manufacturing, and maintenance.

As society's needs become increasingly demanding, more sophisticated systems will be required that react to external stimuli and internal change. Automation applies best when the breadth of issues is relatively narrow and the depth has been fully explored. While entrusting more decisions to people who design software, mechanical systems, and electromechanical systems, society also demands higher quality in decisions made directly by people.

For decisions based on well-developed rules and good data but not yet automated, one person should be able to make a good choice. Such empowerment can pertain, for example, to people making insurance underwriting decisions. Only if a case has a unique issue or the employee is not familiar with an aspect should the employee seek help.

Empowering individuals can include considerable authority to decide based on principles or guidelines instead of rules. For example, a hotel desk clerk decides, based on a personal estimate of the best interests of the hotel, how much to reduce a bill, or what other compensation to give a guest, because of a verbal claim of poor service. Management's advice in preparing its staff for such situations may have been as vague as "pretend that you own the hotel."

Instructions and training that stop at "pretend that you own the hotel" are too imprecise to generate optimal decisions. Much more knowledge and information proficiency is needed to ensure quality in decisions.

Individual empowerment handles decisions involving greater uncertainties than are found in automated decisions. This distinction correlates with the difference in the degrees of automation between credit-card billing and insurance underwriting. Further understanding in an area's breadth and depth can lead to increased automation or to increased individual empowerment.

Toward the other end of the decision-making spectrum are found complex decisions affecting diverse interests (Fig. 5–1). Should tax rates be decreased? If so, which ones and by how much? How can we reform the financing of health care? How should a country respond to the possibility of armed conflict on another continent?

All the subtleties of information proficiency come to the forefront in these complex decisions. Why, for example, might a nation consider lowering tax rates? To stimulate the economy by allowing individuals and businesses to spend and invest more money more freely? To increase governmental revenues by broadening the taxed base sufficiently to more than compensate for the reduced rates? Both economic stimulation and increased governmental revenue might be desired goals; however, some people will argue that increasing the same tax rates, coupled with targeted government spending, will facilitate those ends.

What are the "real" issues? What are the most meaningful questions? What are the best decisions to make? What are the best alternatives to choose for those decisions?

Broad issues with broad constituencies generate much tension. We need to deal with such issues in a broad context, even when we cannot fully understand that context. No one fully grasps history and today's world. We cannot predict tomorrow's world or all the effects of a proposed decision. Practicality drives us toward narrowness and specificity, thereby sometimes excluding visionary solutions.

Many people may be affected by a broad decision. Many will want their views heard before action is taken. Current practice invites decision makers to seek broad input to develop a "best" solution. No matter what the decision, implementation depends on cooperation, or at least lack of resistance, from those affected. People's support often depends on knowing that their views have been heard; yet listening to many people takes time, mental stamina, and other resources that could be invested otherwise.

The most difficult decisions can be made by a single person, such as a corporate chief executive, or by a combination of groups and individuals. For example, enacting a U.S. federal law depends on a joint decision requiring agreement between the Congress and the President.

Your most important Information Age opportunity is to improve decision making and decision implementation. You must measure your information proficiency and take steps to improve your effectiveness. You should focus on the decisions and implementations for which improvement will generate maximal advantage.

6

Measuring and Analyzing Information Proficiency

Measuring and analyzing how proficient individuals and organizations are at making and implementing decisions points to opportunities for improvement.

This chapter presents a method for measuring and analyzing information proficiency. More specifically, the chapter takes you through steps to measure and analyze an organization's or individual's proficiency at making and implementing any one type of decision. The steps include choosing an organization or individual and a type of decision; using the first part of a questionnaire, thereby measuring proficiency at making that type of decision; analyzing measurements obtained through that part of the questionnaire; constructing and using the second part of the questionnaire, thereby measuring proficiency at implementing the type of decision; analyzing measurements of implementation proficiency; using the third part of the questionnaire to measure general aspects of information proficiency; and determining an information-proficiency improvement plan.

MEASURING INFORMATION PROFICIENCY

You can measure the level of information proficiency (Figs. 1–1 and 5–2) of an organization, an individual, or yourself.

Use the rating procedure presented in this chapter to measure information proficiency and provide thought-provoking ideas for improvement. The rating procedure is based on a three-part questionnaire comprised of multiple-choice questions. Most of the multiple-choice options provide images of possible behavior. Determine which images best characterize how the organization or individual handles a particular type of decision. Later, you can use other choices to set improvement goals.

Choosing an Organization or Person

You can use the questionnaire to rate the information proficiency of an organization or individual. Choose an organization or person. If you are considering an individual, use this questionnaire as if it applies to an organization consisting of one person. In any event, recognize that you will be considering roles and contributions of people, such as customers or peers, outside the chosen group.

Stay with your choice. Do not change to a smaller or larger organizational component as you go through the questions.

Choosing a Type of Decision

An organization's information proficiency varies based on the type of decision. Generally, organizations are more information-proficient with routine decisions than with one-of-a-kind decisions. You can rate the organization for its handling of a specific type of routine decision. You can rate it for a specific type of decision that is important but not routine.

Select one type of decision, preferably one for which improved decision making and implementation are likely to generate significant benefits. Stay with that choice through the first and second parts of the questionnaire.

The Questionnaire

The questionnaire consists of three main parts. The first part provides a way to measure your organization's proficiency *with* information to make decisions (Fig. 5–2). The second part deals with proficiency *through* information to implement decisions. The third part emphasizes general information proficiency. Use the rating form (Fig. 6–1) to summarize your measurements.

Rating Your Organization for More Than One Type of Decision

You can use the questionnaire more than once to measure information proficiency for different types of decisions. After completing a

---

Information-Proficiency Rating

Organization or person rated: _____

Type of decision rated: _____

Range of marks (circle all that apply)	Most typical rating	Topic
1 2 3 4 5	____	*Proficiency with Information to Make Decisions*
1 2 3 4 5	____	Anticipated Results
1 2 3 4 5	____	Participants
1 2 3 4 5	____	Process
1 2 3 4 5	____	Information
1 2 3 4 5	____	Achieved Results
1 2 3 4 5	____	_____ *
1 2 3 4 5	____	*Proficiency Through Information to Implement Decisions*
1 2 3 4 5	____	_____ *
1 2 3 4 5	____	_____
1 2 3 4 5	____	_____
1 2 3 4 5	____	_____
1 2 3 4 5	____	_____
1 2 3 4 5	____	*Other Aspects of Information Proficiency*
1 2 3 4 5	____	_____ *

Recommendations:

Value of improving information proficiency:

Endeavors needed to improve information proficiency:

Recommendation as to how to proceed:

Rated by: _____   Date: _____
*The rater is invited to add topics.

FIGURE 6–1   The Form for Summarizing an Information-Proficiency Rating.

rating for your first chosen type of decision, consider applying the first and second parts of the questionnaire to other types of decisions.

Drawing Conclusions

Consider the "opportunity" questions following the questionnaire as you design an information-proficiency improvement program for your organization.

MEASURING PROFICIENCY *WITH* INFORMATION TO MAKE DECISIONS

Score your organization's proficiency at making a specific type of decision. The first part of the information-proficiency questionnaire follows immediately. For each item, consider the options. For this type of decision, select the numbered option 1–5 that most typically applies.

Wording for each item is structured around a hypothetical decision that your organization makes. Taken literally, the multiple-choice statements can be used to analyze how a particular decision is being or was made. To rate your organization for your specific type of decision, interpret the words "this decision" to denote your type of decision.

A "participant" can be a person, organization, or automated system that can support making the decision. Do not overlook participants from outside the organization on which you are focusing.

Anticipated Results

The organization's objectives related to this decision are:

1. Unknown or ignored.
2. Known and used by a fraction of the people involved in making the decision.

3. Used by each participant in doing that participant's part of the work.
4. Used to guide the decision-making process, as well as in the performance of tasks leading up to the decision.
5. Reviewed and refined, along with the definition of the decision to be made, appropriately during decision making, as well as being used to guide process and activity.

Participants

Use the following five numbered options for each of the eight "choices of participants" listed after the five items.

1. Is haphazard or based on convenience.
2. Is tailored to the decision.
3. Optimizes making the decision.
4. Optimizes making and implementing the decision.
5. Optimizes, in the context of all relevant concerns of the organization, making and implementing the decision.

The choice of participants.
The choice of participants who make the decision.
The choice of participants to coordinate the decision-making process.
The choice of participants to advise on the decision.
The choice of participants to provide specific information.
The choice of participants asked to provide useful but unspecified information.
The choice of participants whose "buy in" or support will be needed.
The choice of participants whose participation is "expected."

Process

The process for making the decision is determined:

1. Haphazardly.
2. Intuitively, based on familiarity with previous decisions.
3. By reviewing prior decisions to find a similar, successful case.
4. By synthesis, based on at least a few other cases.
5. By optimal methods ingrained in the practices of the organization.

The decision-making process is characterized by:

1. "Just do it."
2. Finding a good process and staying with it.
3. Determining a good process and staying with it until a problem arises.
4. Evaluating the effectiveness of the process and making needed changes while making the decision.
5. Appropriate midcourse evaluations and changes, along with conveying procedural lessons learned for use in other decisions.

Management of the decision-making process, while making the decision, is:

1. Ignored.
2. Given occasional attention.
3. Active and beneficial.
4. A beneficial part of the process itself.
5. A beneficial part of the process and of the culture of the organization.

Progress will be paced by:

1. The perceived urgency of this decision.
2. The uncoordinated setting of priorities by individual participants.
3. The coordinated setting of priorities within the activities of the participants.

4. The setting of priorities within overall organizational objectives.
5. A concerted effort to optimize the performance of the organization.

The key issue that is decided on is likely to be:

1. First discovered late in the decision-making process.
2. The one first imagined or defined.
3. Stated early in a list of issues and better understood or modified as information is received.
4. Stated early as the likely key issue and better understood or modified as part of the decision-making process.
5. Targeted early and better understood or modified based on exploration of its relations to the goals of the organization as well as to information received.

Coordination among participants is:

1. Haphazard.
2. Stylized.
3. Ingrained procedurally and optimized for this decision.
4. Optimized for this decision and ingrained for the organization's overall work.
5. Ingrained and optimized for this decision and the organization's overall work.

Changes, such as in the process for making the decision or in the definition of the decision, are:

1. Made without adequately communicating them.
2. Made available to people as they continue to participate.
3. Communicated clearly and quickly to all who need to know.
4. Communicated appropriately for this decision and evaluated for applicability in other decisions.

5. Communicated appropriately for this decision and evaluated for relevance to improving decision-making processes.

The decision is made:

1. "When it gets done."
2. When it has become urgent.
3. When it is scheduled for completion.
4. When appropriate within a managed process.
5. At the time of optimal impact.

When decision making is complete or abandoned, the results are:

1. Unavailable or imprecisely stated.
2. Documented in language that is clear to some people.
3. Stated well for all immediate constituents of the decision.
4. Stated well for all constituents of the decision, including those who may need to refine the results later.
5. Stated well for all constituents of the decision and for further analysis for improving decision making.

The decision is:

1. Not sent to some people who need to know it.
2. Sent to most people who need to know it.
3. Appropriately communicated to all who need to know it.
4. Appropriately communicated, and also conveniently available for postdecision process reviews.
5. Appropriately communicated, and also used appropriately in improving decision making.

The decision is reviewed:

1. If the issue comes up again.
2. If there is a review of related decisions.
3. No later than at a time set when the decision is made.

4. At an appropriate time.
5. At an optimal time and, if appropriate, in a review aimed at improving the organization's overall information proficiency.

Information

The context for making the decision is:

1. Unknown or ignored.
2. Known and used by a fraction of the participants involved in making the decision.
3. Used by each participant in doing that participant's part of the work.
4. Used to guide the decision-making process, as well as in performing tasks leading up to the decision.
5. Reviewed and refined, along with the definition of the decision to be made, during decision making, as well as being used to guide process and activity.

While the decision is being made, plans to implement the decision are:

1. Barely considered.
2. Developed late in the decision-making process.
3. Developed and considered as a normal part of the decision-making process.
4. Developed and considered to maximize the impact of the decision.
5. Developed and considered in the context of optimizing the organization's achievement of its goals.

Learning from past decisions and other history:

1. Occurs if someone calls attention to the opportunity.
2. Features attempts to find parallel cases before getting too far into the current decision.

3. Is ingrained in the context of decision-making processes.
4. Is ingrained in the context of continuous organizational improvement.
5. Is ingrained in the context of optimizing the organization's performance.

The information considered is:

1. That which is easily obtained.
2. That which is felt to be needed.
3. Determined procedurally.
4. Determined procedurally, including refinement of the selection process while making the decision.
5. That which is needed, with little extra.

The quality of the information is:

1. Unchecked.
2. Verified, if possible.
3. Verified routinely.
4. Verified if the information is important to the decision.
5. Verified to the extent it is important, and also used to review the effectiveness of the decision-making process.

Metainformation, that is, lists of information people want; estimates of the likelihood of getting information; status of the pursuit of information; references to hypotheses, deductions, and tentative conclusions; and statements about the quality of information, is:

1. A concept little considered.
2. Known and used by a fraction of the participants involved in making the decision.
3. Used by each participant in doing that participant's work.
4. Used to guide the decision-making process, as well as in the performance of tasks leading up to the decision.
5. Reviewed and refined appropriately during decision making, as well as being used to guide process and activity.

(For the following list, start with a score of 1, and increase it by up to $\frac{1}{2}$ point for each attribute.) Information used in making the decision is appropriate with respect to:

a. Accuracy, including enough definition of what the information actually represents.
b. Consistency within itself and with other information.
c. Completeness in scope.
d. Timeliness of availability.
e. Degree of detail.
f. Convenience for those needing the information, along with security against inappropriate use.
g. Knowledge of sources of the information.
h. Trustworthiness.

Achieved Results

The decision, if reviewed later in the context of possible outcomes that could reasonably have been achieved, is most likely to be found:

1. Toward the lower end of the range of quality that could have been achieved.
2. Acceptable in the context of the question posed.
3. Acceptable in the context of the questions that could have been posed.
4. Reasonable in the context of the goals of the organization.
5. Optimal in the context of the organization's goals.

ANALYZING PROFICIENCY *WITH* INFORMATION TO MAKE DECISIONS

Review your organization's scores regarding the type of decision you considered and determine the most typical score: 1, 2, 3, 4, or 5.

Each numeric step features certain behavioral characteristics (Table 6–1). Higher scores within the range of Novice (a rating of 1), Experimenter (2), and Implementer (3) denote greater ability to deal with a specific decision within its own context and greater ability to learn from the past to support a specific decision. Scores of Innovator (4) or Master (5) indicate sophistication beyond a score of Implementer, including active use of overall organizational goals and attention to strengthening processes.

TABLE 6–1   THE INFORMATION-PROFICIENCY RATING SCALE

Rating	Stage	Characteristics
5	Master	Optimizes and extends processes and effectiveness; tailors environment. ■ Optimized, self-optimizing, rational within the broadest appropriate context.
4	Innovator	Tailors processes to changing needs and conditions. ■ Guided, managed, self-guiding, self-controlling, self-improving.
3	Implementer	Follows a path to success; communicates to colleagues, who follow the path. ■ Procedural, planned, organized, rational within the context of a specific endeavor.
2	Experimenter	Tries varied approaches; when finds a success, provides a path for others to follow. ■ Stylized, patterned, intuitive.
1	Novice	Searches randomly; can succeed by trial and error. ■ Haphazard, ad hoc.

Novice (1), Experimenter (2), or Implementer (3):
   The focus is on a specific opportunity within its own context.
   Higher scores within this range indicate a greater ability to learn from the past.
Innovator (4) or Master (5):
   There is a broader focus on capturing current and future opportunities, including more active use of overall goals and attention to strengthening processes.

MEASURING PROFICIENCY *THROUGH* INFORMATION TO IMPLEMENT DECISIONS

Score your organization's proficiency at implementing your chosen specific type of decision. Determine whether the organization is typically a Novice (1), Experimenter (2), Implementer (3), Innovator (4), or Master (5).

When implementing this type of decision, the organization's list of questions similar to the ones above for making decisions:

1. Does not exist.
2. Exists and is used occasionally.
3. Exists and is routinely used.
4. Is used routinely and refined occasionally.
5. Is ingrained, along with a process to improve it, in organizational culture and behavior.

Find or develop such a list, and rate the organization using it and the information-proficiency rating scale (Table 6–1). Alternatively, you can make overall judgments based on the choices presented by the rating scale: Novice, Experimenter, Implementer, Innovator, Master. The following are some topics that should be covered:

- Understanding the audiences for the decision.
- Articulating the decision, including:
  Contexts.
  Goals.
  Principles and other rationales used in making the decision.
- Measures and goals pertaining to successful implementation.
- Implementation planning and plans.
- Communicating the decision, implementation plans, and goals.
- Programs, steps, schedules, and choice of participants for the implementation.
- Carrying out the implementation plan.
- Feedback on success.

- Adjustments based on feedback.
- Successful implementation of the decision.

ANALYZING PROFICIENCY *THROUGH* INFORMATION TO IMPLEMENT DECISIONS

Review your organization's rating regarding proficiency *through* information and determine the most typical score: Novice, Experimenter, Implementer, Innovator, Master. Compare the rating for implementing decisions with that for making decisions.

MEASURING OTHER ASPECTS OF INFORMATION PROFICIENCY

Rate your organization on the following items that address the organization's climate with respect to information proficiency.

In devoting people, funds, and other resources to make and implement all the decisions the organization faces, the organization:

1. Virtually ignores the relative importance of the decisions to be made and implemented.
2. Assigns priorities to important endeavors.
3. Balances its use of resources across current decisions and implementations so as to achieve maximal advantage.
4. Balances its use of resources across current decisions and implementations so as both to achieve maximal advantage and to improve its skills at resource allocation.
5. Optimizes the making and implementing of decisions and the future enhancement of information proficiency.

A person receiving some new, probably useful information is likely to:

1. Review it when there is free time.
2. Review it if it seems urgent or of immediate use.
3. Review it promptly to keep up to date.
4. Review it promptly and remember it for use in discussions with others who may need to know it.
5. Review it promptly and communicate it to other people who may need to know it but won't unless action is taken.

Attention to the organization's perspective on the world around it:

1. Is haphazard.
2. Can be characterized as active in some parts of the organization.
3. Is adequate and beneficial in all parts of the organization.
4. Is a part of all the organization's endeavors.
5. Is optimal for the future of the organization.

People's attention to the quality of information:

1. Is not evident or focuses on timeliness.
2. Focuses on attaining accuracy.
3. Includes providing adequate information on the accuracy and consistency of information.
4. Meets all needs of people who use the information.
5. Meets all needs of people who use the information and involves minimal extraneous work.

Attention to the organization's development of its capabilities:

1. Is haphazard.
2. Can be characterized as active in some parts of the organization.
3. Is adequate and beneficial in all parts of the organization.
4. Is a part of all the organization's endeavors.
5. Is optimal for the future of the organization.

The organization's effectiveness in dealing with information in all contexts outside of specifically making and implementing decisions is:

1. Toward the lower end of the range of quality that should be achieved.
2. Often acceptable in the context of specific endeavors.
3. Acceptable in the context of each specific endeavor.
4. Reasonable in the context of the goals of the organization.
5. Optimal in the context of the organization's goals.

If asked to improve this questionnaire, the organization would:

1. Have difficulty comprehending the task and its value.
2. Produce some useful results related to making and implementing decisions.
3. Produce a good result regarding processes for making and implementing decisions.
4. Produce good results regarding both processes to do work and methods to improve those processes.
5. Produce good results, regarding both processes to do work and methods to improve those processes, mainly by comparing this questionnaire with practices the organization already uses.

ANALYZING THE OPPORTUNITY TO IMPROVE INFORMATION PROFICIENCY

Use the following questions to draw conclusions from your measurements of how your organization makes and implements decisions. The form for summarizing information-proficiency ratings (Fig. 6–1) contains headings for summarizing your conclusions for any one type of decision.

- How much value would your organization place on making and implementing these decisions more effectively?

- What action will be needed to improve your organization's information proficiency?
- Considering the goals of your organization, does the value of improving information proficiency for this type of decision outweigh the efforts needed, and any opportunities that it would have to forgo, to make the improvements?
- Will your organization undertake a program to improve its information proficiency?

7

Implementing Information-Proficiency Enhancement Programs

Implementing successful information-proficiency enhancement programs is facilitated by using information-proficiency measurements, organizational climate assessments, knowledge of existing proficiency-improving processes, and All A's improvement techniques.

THE ALL A's PROGRAM TO ENHANCE INFORMATION PROFICIENCY

Now that you understand and can measure information proficiency, you are able to implement a program to improve your organization's information proficiency (Figs. 1–1 and 5–2). Your goal is to design a successful program to enhance your organization's quality in making and implementing decisions.

Envision your group making and implementing decisions. Recall examples. Think about procedural improvements that can be made and how can you effect them.

Here are some elements to consider for your program (Fig. 7–1). Envision how each will work for your organization.

One element is *awareness*. You want all members of your organization to embrace the need to improve. It is much easier to effect change if people know that there is an issue or opportunity. You can . . .

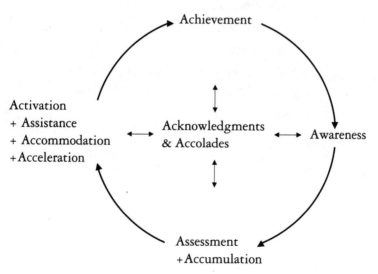

FIGURE 7–1   Elements of the All A's Program to Enhance Information Proficiency.

- Encourage each member of the organization to become capable of convincing others of the need to improve quality in making and implementing decisions—we truly know something if we can teach it to someone else.
- Tell people about the situations you evaluated in measuring your organization's information proficiency.
- Encourage people to apply the "who? what? . . ." questions regarding information-proficient behavior.

The goal of your program is improvement. Improvement should be measurable. People need to understand the current situation and how their future can be enhanced. Here *assessment* comes into play. You can . . .

- Use your information-proficiency measurement criteria to rate your organization.
- Ask employees and customers to rate the organization.
- Discuss the types of routine and nonroutine decisions they considered and the ratings they developed.
- Share the ratings with everyone in the organization.
- Discuss behavior typical of the next higher rating to identify what constitutes more effective behavior and how to promote it.
- Make choices as to which types of decisions to improve and what improvements to pursue immediately.

Accumulate all the ideas for improvements. It may not be appropriate to pursue all of them at once, but your organization can keep a list for future reference.

Activate people and projects to work on the best opportunities to improve the organization's information proficiency.

Ensure *assistance* to foster beneficial results. Assistance is likely to involve education, formal or informal. Your measurements and goals will point you to opportunities for relevant education. Learning is likely to focus on communications skills, empathy, teamwork, negotiating, process or project management, or working with statistical data and other forms of information. Informal teaching can be very effective, especially if provided by colleagues and applied to normal work challenges in the usual work setting.

You may have thought of *accommodation*—redefining some of your organization's goals or processes, or employing new tools, such as a new software package.

Accelerate progress through sharing success stories between people and groups.

Ultimately, you want to foster *achievement*. Be alert for opportunities. Again, measurement is needed, this time to ensure that there has been improvement.

Acknowledging progress and people's contributions to it is essential to maintaining both progress achieved and momentum for the future. You can provide *accolades* at every step along the way.

These elements of the All A's program form a continuous cycle (Fig. 7–1). Your step into the cycle consists of an achievement—your decision to improve your organization's information proficiency. Give yourself an accolade. Each achievement spawns new awareness of opportunities to improve. With this awareness, you are poised for the next assessment of opportunities and for further improvement activities and achievements.

As you employ your All A's program, you can *augment* it by adding other elements to the ones that comprise the figure.

USING THE ALL A'S PROGRAM: TWO EXAMPLES

After an information technology services business unit published its first strategic and tactical plans, its leader made speeches about the plans at the unit's offices throughout the United States. Time was reserved for general discussion at the end of each speech.

People spoke up. Through this discussion, the leader became *aware* that employees were spending too much time on the mechanics of financial management for their projects and programs. Every month, administrators reconciled revenue and expense transactions with those reported in printed listings from the accounting system that served this and peer business units. Employees had to read and correct data from the central system. Furthermore, every month these people reestimated revenues and expenses for each project and program for several months in advance. While anticipating future cash flows is a reasonable expectation of staff responsible for financial performance, getting the new numbers into the system and backing out the old estimates proved burdensome.

Employees had already *assessed* the opportunity. There was no trouble *accumulating* ideas and previous work to expedite progress. People in regional offices had already devised automated procedures to ease their work. A California-based group had developed software to generate reconciliation data automatically for the central system. Employees in Washington, DC, had built automated procedures for themselves. Pennsylvania-based staff working for a different business unit had developed techniques facilitating computerizing financial data.

The business unit assembled a small group in its central office to *activate* a nationwide improvement project. It was easy to capture the enthusiasm of employees nationwide and build on the work that had already been done. As well as formally justifying and managing the project, the coordinating team ensured that the procedures and systems to be produced would serve as broad a need as reasonably possible and would conform to relevant standards.

The main form of *assistance* was the help that each of the participants provided to others. *Accommodating* the needs of the program and its participants included hiring a consultant and deploying new computers and networks.

The *achievement* became evident with the first uses of the system. Project managers in field offices were better served, and the business unit's controller's staff also benefited.

Accelerated progress was also evident. Although designed for this business unit, the system was scheduled to be used by others. Perhaps the most prominent *acknowledgment* and *accolade* came from the overall organization's chief financial officer, who talked of spreading the system throughout the organization and possibly earning revenues by selling the system, or services based on it, to other organizations.

As well as exemplifying the All A's approach to improving an organization's information proficiency (Fig. 7–1), this project shows a good approach to a widespread Information Age challenge. Modernizing the central corporate computer system was not practical within this project. People wisely settled for an arrangement in which current data is transmitted to a new computer as often as daily. The project built its procedures and software to run in employees' individual computers, which exchange data with the new computer. Reconciliations and reestimates are posted electronically for automated input into the corporate system.

*   *   *

Recall the example of the citizens who preserved parkland by establishing a shoreline preserve. This history of sticking to a preservationist principle includes repeated use of All A's techniques to enhance information proficiency.

The first achievement was the original coalescing of a citizens' group to work against the first development proposal. The group went through an awareness-assessment-activation-achievement cycle each time it blocked a proposal. During each cycle, it gained core members, lost core members, and activated support from other concerned citizens.

As awareness of the wildlife preserve strategy developed, new assessment and activation resulted in placing people on the planning commission and the city council. The coalition's core group sought candidates, encouraged them to stand for office and supported them based on two criteria: general fitness for the job and commitment to preserving the land. At no time did the coalition stray into other criteria or broader issues; the focus was on advancing the one cause. Filling each position represented another achievement—another successful traversal of an All A's cycle.

Each round of the cycle built further awareness of opportunities and techniques for success through practical politics. This awareness was essential for obtaining and implementing the legislation that led to the climactic achievement of the shoreline preserve.

INFORMATION PROFICIENCY AND ORGANIZATIONAL CLIMATE

The information-proficiency paradigm can be a vital driver when an organization takes steps to improve its decision-making and decision-implementing capabilities.

In catalyzing an improvement program, it is important to assess the competitive posture of an organization (Fig. 7–2). The higher up an organization is on the chart (Fig. 7–2), the more successful it currently is relative to other similar entities. For a business, profitability and marketplace standing are measures of success. For a nation, the measure can be economic wealth. The further to the right an organization is on the chart, the more intently it works to improve itself.

The figure suggests a progression over time for organizations and institutions. Consider, for example, the history of the United States

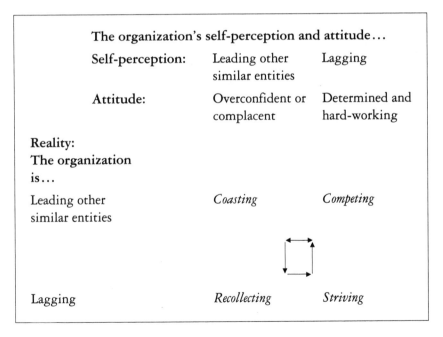

FIGURE 7–2   Competitive Posture.

as a nation. In the late 1700s, this country is found in the lower right Striving quadrant—lagging Europe economically and working hard. For more than a century, it moves upward, generating wealth by "conquering" a continent and capturing the benefits of electro-mechanical technology. By the 1960s, the United States achieves world economic leadership—the top of the chart. The nation also has, by then, moved toward the left on the chart. Industry ignores foreign competition—for example, cars and consumer electronics—and foreign markets. Government attempts to tackle many problems and capture many opportunities, including sending people to the moon, maintaining Cold War readiness, fighting a war in Vietnam, and adopting the Great Society agenda of social programs. The upper-left Coasting quadrant is one of instability, with two ways out. During the 1980s and early 1990s, American business realizes its plight and moves itself back to the right; focused leadership, attention to customers and quality, cost control, and innovative use of information technology all contribute. You might consider whether American government will now move down the left column of the chart, following past overextended governments, or across to the right, following current American enterprise.

Take a moment to think of other organizations and institutions of which you are aware and to place them on the chart. Your placement should be made relative to similar entities, not on a perceived absolute scale. Adding detail to the chart (Fig. 7–3) suggests for each quadrant both an assessment of the current situation and a vital use for an information-proficiency improvement program.

For example, a business in the upper-right, or "ideal," quadrant is poised for continued success but will need to adopt new competitive techniques before its competition does. A competing company should use information-proficiency improvement as a guide when capturing the benefits of focused leadership, attention to customers and quality products and services, reengineering repetitive processes, and right-sizing. Additionally, the competing company needs an information-proficiency improvement program to suggest vital new ways to stay competitive (Fig. 4–3), including better ways to make and implement "executive" decisions.

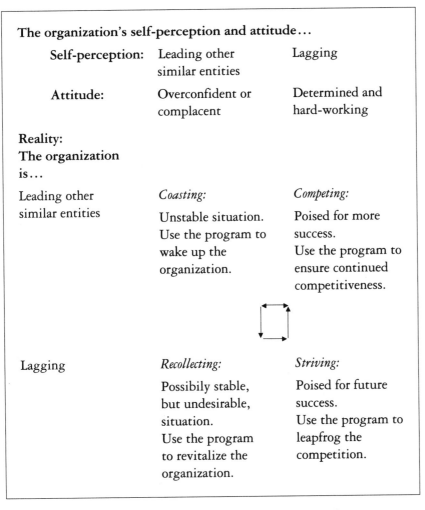

The organization's self-perception and attitude...

Self-perception:	Leading other similar entities	Lagging
Attitude:	Overconfident or complacent	Determined and hard-working

Reality:
The organization is...

Leading other similar entities	*Coasting:* Unstable situation. Use the program to wake up the organization.	*Competing:* Poised for more success. Use the program to ensure continued competitiveness.
Lagging	*Recollecting:* Possibily stable, but undesirable, situation. Use the program to revitalize the organization.	*Striving:* Poised for future success. Use the program to leapfrog the competition.

FIGURE 7–3   Sharpening Competitive Posture Through an Information-Proficiency Improvement Program.

Enhancing information proficiency is also essential for organizations elsewhere on the chart. If your organization is in the lower-right Striving quadrant, it needs an immediate leg up on its competition, which information proficiency can provide. If it is in the upper-left Coasting corner, the organization needs an information-proficiency wake-up call and a program that will save it from falling down the left side of the chart. Organizations in the lower-left Recollecting quadrant need an even harder jolt—survival depends on recognizing the situation and moving quickly to the lower-right Striving quadrant.

Understanding the climate and strategic purpose for improving information proficiency is key to contributing to your organization's future success.

MEASURING EXISTING POTENTIAL TO IMPROVE INFORMATION PROFICIENCY

In planning an information-proficiency improvement program, you will also want to know and take advantage of existing proficiency at improving processes.

Just as you can measure information proficiency itself, you can evaluate ongoing improvement processes and the potential to use and improve them. The following questionnaire uses the same five-step Novice through Master rating scale (Table 6–1) that is used for measuring information proficiency. Again, the ratings apply to a specific type of decision. You should focus on a type of decision for which you measured the information proficiency.

Use the rating form (Fig. 7–4) for summarizing, for one entity and one type of decision, measurements of both information proficiency and improvement processes.

Proficiency at Improving Decision-Making Processes

This section explores the organization's program to improve the means by which it makes decisions.

The processes, choice of participants, and information used to improve decision making are:

Information-Proficiency Process Improvement Rating

Organization or person rated: _____

Type of decision rated: _____

Range of marks (circle all that apply)	Most typical rating	Topic
1 2 3 4 5	____	*Proficiency with Information to Make Decisions*
1 2 3 4 5	____	*Proficiency Through Information to Implement Decisions*
1 2 3 4 5	____	*Other Aspects of Information Proficiency*
1 2 3 4 5	____	*Proficiency at Improving Decision-Making Processes*
1 2 3 4 5	____	_____ *
1 2 3 4 5	____	_____
1 2 3 4 5	____	_____
1 2 3 4 5	____	*Proficiency at Improving Decision-Implementing Processes*
1 2 3 4 5	____	_____ *
1 2 3 4 5	____	_____
1 2 3 4 5	____	_____

Recommendations:

Value of improving information proficiency:

Endeavors needed to improve information proficiency:

Recommendation as to how to proceed:

Rated by: _____ Date: _____

*The rater is invited to add topics

FIGURE 7–4   The Form for Summarizing a Rating of Processes for Improving Information Proficiency.

1. Toward the lower end of the range of quality that could be attained.
2. Acceptable in the context of individual decisions as they are being made.
3. Acceptable in the context of individual decisions as they could be made.
4. Reasonable in the context of the goals of the organization.
5. Optimal in the context of the organization's goals.

Understanding of the organization's processes for improving decision making is found in:

1. Some people in the organization.
2. Most people in the organization.
3. All people in the organization.
4. All people within the organization and some external constituents who need to know.
5. All people within the organization and all external constituents who need to know.

Records of processes used to make decisions:

1. Are virtually nonexistent.
2. Are found in records related to individual decisions and are reviewed for ideas for process improvement.
3. Include recommendations for process improvement and are used systematically to improve processes.
4. Are consistent across decisions and are used as an integrated body of knowledge to improve processes.
5. Are consistent across decisions and are used as an integrated body of knowledge to optimize future processes.

Review of processes for making decisions:

1. Is nonexistent or occasional.
2. Focuses on analyzing failures.

3. Is aimed at continuous improvement in decision-making processes.
4. Includes continuous improvement in activities that refine decision-making processes.
5. Optimizes decision-making processes within the overall objectives of the organization.

Processes for improving the making of decisions are:

1. Ad hoc.
2. Stylized.
3. Procedural (that is, set out as known, repeatable procedures).
4. Procedural and improved occasionally.
5. Optimized.

Proficiency at Improving Decision-Implementing Processes

The organization's list of questions about improving processes for implementing decisions:

1. Does not exist.
2. Exists and is used occasionally.
3. Exists and is routinely used.
4. Is used routinely and refined occasionally.
5. Is ingrained, along with a process to improve it, in organizational culture and behavior.

You should find or develop a list of topics, produce five-step multiple-choice statements based on the information-proficiency rating scale (Table 6–1), and rate your organization. Alternatively, you can make an overall judgment based on the attributes presented in the rating scale.

* * *

Current capabilities for improving information proficiency seldom exceed and often lag information proficiency itself (Fig. 7–5). You will want to take your organization's position on this chart into account when implementing an information-proficiency enhancement program. You will also want to take advantage of existing mechanisms and traditions that foster information-proficiency improvements.

ACTIVATING YOUR ALL A's PROGRAM

Here are some suggestions for you as you activate your All A's information-proficiency improvement program for your organization (Fig. 7–1). These suggestions are drawn from common sense and the experiences of groups implementing quality-improvement and process-reengineering programs.

Be *aware* of relationships between information proficiency and other fields. Information proficiency relates to, for example, the behavioral sciences, quality and process measurement and improvement, all types of knowledge, education and learning, and communi-

	Extant improvement processes				
Information proficiency	1	2	3	4	5
5	•	•	x	x	x
4	•	x	x	x	•
3	x	x	x	•	•
2	x	x	•	•	•
1	x	•	•	•	•

FIGURE 7–5   Correlating Improvement Potential and Information Proficiency.

cations techniques and technologies. Utilizing expertise, whether yours or that of your colleagues, in these and other fields will pay handsome dividends to your program.

Assess your organization's opportunities. Along with your tools for measuring your organization's information proficiency (Fig. 6–1), competitiveness posture (Fig. 7–3), decisions (Fig. 5–1), and improvement processes (Fig. 7–4), you can use the Peer Paradigm for organizations (Fig. 4–2) for evaluating your organization's effectiveness by asking, for each element in the paradigm, who?, what?, why?, when?, where?, and how? Determine your organization's best improvement opportunities.

Also, assess your own opportunities to be most effective in improving the way your organization makes and implements decisions. There are two ways to initiate change: using the influence that comes with an established leadership role and proceeding without using formal authority. Make your assessment from these two points of view:

- Assess your opportunities based on the leadership roles you play. These roles can be associated with your holding a managerial position or with the respect people have for you because of your expertise, good counsel, and past accomplishments.
- Also, assess your opportunities based on your being one of the group. Informal approaches to change can be very effective.

Accumulate your opportunities. Everyone wonders why things are not better; everybody develops why-not ideas for improvements. All too often, these ideas remain filed in people's minds, never to be used. Encourage people to unlock their mental filing cabinets and recall their ideas. Encourage people to think of new ones. Record the ideas. Ask people to review and prioritize the suggestions based on the value of the improvements and the cost to implement them. Save the results. Update the list as new ideas arise.

Many techniques can be used in this regard. For example, in one group each person was asked to write down three major strengths of the organization and the three most important weaknesses. A small group of staff and managers selected the most promising targets for improvement. This technique focused attention on a few projects and left a list for future consideration.

Activate people and projects to capture the best information-proficiency improvement opportunities. To motivate people, activate your own information proficiency. To the extent appropriate, help people find a good process to select the best opportunities. Help them select those opportunities and get started. Consider why people need to be motivated. Consider who needs motivating and how to motivate them. Implement your decisions by being an effective leader.

Assist people. Assist yourself by ensuring assistance for people needing it. Again, put your own information proficiency to good use. Put yourself in other people's shoes. Determine who will need assistance, in what form, and how it can best be delivered?

Accommodate the needs of your organization and its people. Instigate changes, such as uses of new software or other tools, that will facilitate innovation.

Achieve the objectives of your improvement program. Using your information-proficiency assessment tools, measure the improvements made throughout your organization.

Accelerate progress. Encourage people to share improvements they have made, and help people develop the habit of looking for opportunities to share. Reusing progress surpasses reinventing the wheel.

Acknowledge achievements and give *accolades* to the people who contributed to them. A little extra appreciation goes a long way. Tangible appreciation can include a cash bonus. A certificate reinforces memories of successes and, when displayed, encourages passersby to ask and learn about those successes. Also, use intangible appreciation. Congratulate people. Describe a success story in a newsletter or speech. You recognize the people who made it happen. You make it easier for other people to use the improvement. You build momentum for the overall improvement program.

Consider *adding* other elements to your program. Also, consider that you can *adopt* and *adapt* All A's techniques for other uses.

INFORMATION PROFICIENCY AND YOU

Here is a technique you can use day-by-day to determine how well you are doing at making and implementing decisions.

From time to time, pull your attention away from the context of the activity in which you are involved. Imagine that whatever you are doing is part of a play on a stage. Place yourself both on the stage and in the audience. Watch yourself and the other people in the play. Be critical. Look for new insights. Review your perceptions of other people's objectives and roles. Look for new similarities in people's interests and new ideas about the seeming differences that are impeding progress. Review and consider changing your own tactics.

Athletes employ a similar technique. Visualization is an oft-used training technique that can also be used during competition.

An extension of this technique is to pretend that someone you respect is in the audience. Ask yourself how that person views what you are doing on stage and what suggestions that person might have for you.

*   *   *

You are positioned to improve the information proficiency of groups with which you work. You do not have to be in charge of a group to influence its behavior. Leading by example contributes significantly. Adding explanations of what you are doing helps. Providing advice and coaching for others adds another dimension. All of these techniques are readily available and easily applied—none requires changing laws, rules, or organizational structure. All of them promote sharing among people and finding common interests on which to base progress.

Change can be an informal movement. Informal changes of culture can be as, or more, effective than change sponsored by formal programs. Individuals and organizations that will thrive and compete in the 21st century need the advancements that accompany increased information proficiency. There are perceived risks for both innovators and traditional leaders, but your challenge includes helping other people find the commonalities of interest that lead forward toward enhanced information proficiency, as well as helping to build the human infrastructure that is the fabric of society.

CHAPTER 8

Optimizing Organizational Learning

*U*sing information-proficiency measurements and
improvement programs solves the riddle of choosing
appropriate general-purpose education. The Just
Ask . . . approach to education enhances learning.

INFORMATION PROFICIENCY AND EDUCATION

The information-proficiency paradigm can have considerable impact on the field of training.

If you have been a part of a business or governmental organization, the following overview of training should be familiar.

The organization has established ways to deal with education for *specific* needs. For individuals pursuing career paths, the organization recommends sequences of classes. The career paths emphasize a profession, such as engineering, finance, or computer programming. The recommended classes emphasize specific knowledge.

When there is a current organizationwide emphasis, such as a change in product line or production technique, there is corresponding training. Instruction emphasizes how to sell the new products or operate the new equipment. For an emphasis on total quality management, classes teach how to measure results and inputs while emphasizing the need to improve quality and reduce costs.

As comfortable as the organization may be in dealing with specific training, it seems uncertain regarding nonspecific organizational improvement and *general* education. The organization recognizes the necessity for learning that is not specific to a career path or timely emphasis, but there is little structure in which to evaluate training needs and related opportunities. Catalogs and advertisements indicate many courses on topics such as interpersonal communications, team building, negotiating, running effective meetings, time management, managing groups, working with statistical data, and using information technology. Making choices—topics, depth and breadth of coverage of those topics, timing, and which people will receive education—is difficult.

Providers of general training have the corresponding challenge. With potential customers feeling uncomfortable in deciding on their own needs, trainers find their own uncertainty in designing courses and marketing them.

The information-proficiency paradigm provides a context in which a potential customer chooses the right education for the right time and vendors sharpen their offerings to match customers' demands.

Through an information-proficiency assessment and improvement program (Figs. 6–1 and 7–1), an organization chooses education to match current opportunities for general improvement. The choice is made based on measurements of organizational information proficiency (Fig. 7–4), specific knowledge of what behavior would be like at the next higher step on the information-proficiency scale (Table 6–1), and a plan to improve information proficiency (Fig. 7–1).

Of course, when customers have a framework within which to choose education programs, training vendors have a framework within which to market effectively. For the providers of training, information proficiency offers the opportunity to modify existing courses and develop new ones to match clients' needs comprehensively.

Information proficiency will catalyze improvement on both the demand and supply sides of the training marketplace. Indeed, it makes formerly *general* education *specific* to an organization's needs.

EDUCATION—JUST ASK . . .

Effective learning need not be formal learning. Consider as an example how an organization should teach its employees to use a new computer system or software package.

Consider the obvious approach. Each person goes to class. Conscientious instructors cover as much material as possible. The class proceeds through the capabilities of the system or software, general capability by capability and specific feature by feature. There are many capabilities and features. People return to work knowing that there are many nuances in the successful operation of this new technology but not remembering all the details. For those people who have an immediate need to use the technology, there is some progress. For others, the training is mostly lost.

Whether featuring instructors, books, or recordings, this nearly universal training approach appeals to the instincts to be thorough. But it is time to take another look and to consider alternatives.

There have been successes in which most people received little formal training. Consider two examples of such success.

First, a well-designed information system that is built specifically for the mission of an organization obviates needs for formal education. Such a system is a tool that addresses the needs of people already skilled in their work. This tool uses familiar vocabulary to display information and is based on procedures that are already familiar to its users or that have been carefully designed to improve on traditional methods. The tool introduces capability and flexibility but not confusion into the workplace.

The training strategy can be both complete and minimalist. In one case that took place before the development of personal computers, the workers had no previous acquaintance with computing. They were, however, experts in their workers' compensation insurance claims adjudication work. The work consisted of deciding whether their employer would pay a person for a claim based on that person's inability to work because of an injury and whether their employer would pay a doctor for treating such an injured person. The information needed was the history of the case and the basis for a specific claim. The new system had been carefully designed.

Clustered around a desk on which sat a newly installed terminal, ten adjudicators from one work group received an informal introduction to the system. After five minutes, these people were asking questions and trying to use the system. After half an hour, the people returned to their own desks and started performing work using their own terminals. People from other work groups came by out of curiosity. Some of these employees had terminals, but none had received any instruction. The first users taught their colleagues.

Within a few days, one hundred adjudicators became more effective at their jobs. Within a few months, the typical time between receipt of a claim and issuance of a payment had decreased from eight weeks to two weeks. There was also a significant decrease in telephone calls from injured workers and their doctors.

The previous example illustrates how a Just Ask . . . approach (Fig. 8–1) to learning works—*just ask* a colleague. Although completely informal, Just Ask . . . education was an integral part of the

Why?
- To facilitate immediate and future work

When?
- "Just in time" to learn to do work better

Where?
- In the workplace

How?
- Using work as examples
- Using the work vocabulary
- Learning by applying what is being learned

From whom?
- Familiar colleagues or computer systems, or...oneself

What?
- Learning new techniques and reinforcing that learning through immediate, relevant use
- Accomplishing current work and enhancing potential to accomplish future work

FIGURE 8–1.   Characteristics of Just Ask...Learning.

program that increased the information proficiency of that workers' compensation insurance organization.

As a second example, consider the introduction of a new general-purpose personal computer software package into an organization.

Consider a software package that your organization is about to install or that you have seen introduced in the past. Perhaps it is a word processing program, a spreadsheet, data manager, graphics tool, publication tool, statistics package, project management tool, or tool for capturing procedural knowledge about work.

Your challenge is to maximize the effectiveness of your entire organization based on an education program you design and implement for the organization.

Your situation is perhaps more difficult than that of the insurance claims processing office. A general-purpose software package is not designed specifically for your organization's work. The software is based on vocabulary that may not match the work and may have been chosen by computer specialists. The software has a multitude of features, perhaps many that will seldom be used in your organization.

As you consider your approach, you can ask yourself whether anyone you know has encountered such a challenge before. This is one of the best questions to ask when confronted with any challenge. You can learn from previous experience, both yours and that of other people. For this example, you may know of several sources of useful perspective. Here is one. The story of the insurance claims adjudicators provides a useful clue. The clue is in the behavior of those individuals who *just asked* their peers.

If you choose this approach, you can find employees who fit a pattern: perceived leader, able to communicate, self-starter, enthusiastic about work and about helping colleagues improve their work, willing to try something new, willing to stay at least one step ahead of those colleagues. If employees helped in selecting the software package and proving that it can improve their work, you may already have identified some of people you need.

Once these employees are motivated, word of mouth, plus the Just Ask . . . principle that all people know, takes over. Your challenge may then be to identify isolated employee groups and key people in those groups so that the new technology and its benefits take hold as soon as possible. If parts of the organization still have no familiarity with this or similar software, you might consider postponing introduction of the package there until some people in these groups try to apply the software to sample work or receive some training.

The Just Ask . . . approach worked well for teaching the use of general-purpose software throughout a company with tens of thousands of employees. The company found that people learn well from colleagues who share work foci, speak similar work-related vocabulary, work near one another, and are usually available for questions. Several general-purpose software packages were introduced this way.

Many benefits were derived from their use. Also, time that might otherwise have been spent in classes was put to better use.

This approach is needs-driven, not technology-driven. People's focus during the informal training remains on their work. Their proficiency with technological tools grows as a consequence of taking advantage of practical opportunities to improve job performance. Learning the technology is secondary, as well it should be. For anyone's work, the supporting technology should serve as a tool, not a distraction or a primary focus.

As you may have observed, Just Ask . . . training is also just-in-time training.

You can even apply the Just Ask . . . principle to classroom or other traditional education. Focus the training on examples drawn from people's work. Use familiar vocabulary.

For example, the previously mentioned large company that applied the Just Ask . . . principle so well decided that formal training for some secretaries would hasten development of people key to the general informal training strategy. Classroom training emphasized typical secretarial work, with word processing, spreadsheet, and database software as tools.

Learning should emphasize principles. For example, for word processing, students can be encouraged to think of the activities needed to prepare a document. The people who designed the software should have done the same thing. Therefore, for each needed activity, there should be a way to accomplish it. More important than learning all the software's capabilities, students should gain the confidence and ability to learn on their own. Gaining the insight and confidence to teach oneself represents a significant achievement: Just Ask . . . yourself!

Just Ask . . . learning is effective. The federal Office of Personnel Management survey (Personnel Research and Development Center, 1994) indicates that employees find Just Ask . . . training to be the most effective method of learning skills essential to managing and using information. Traditional classroom training ranks fourth behind three Just Ask . . . techniques.

The Office of Personnel Management survey studied the types of training most effective in developing information skills. The training methods, with the percentage of employees finding each to be effective, are:

- On-the-job training, 81%.
- Assistance from co-workers, 60%.
- Self-teaching, 44%.
- Classroom training prior to using a new technique, 42%.
- Classroom training after some use of a new technique, 31%.

Just Ask . . . techniques provide for very successful training. They match many important guiding principles for organizations: empowerment, effectiveness, efficiency, and just-in-time delivery, to name a few.

Recall that the All A's principles (Fig. 7–1) apply to improving information proficiency and to any other organizational or personal improvement program. Similarly, Just Ask . . . training applies well when people learn to use tools and techniques other than computer systems and software.

REFERENCE

Personnel Research and Development Center, 1994. *Report on the Survey of the Information Proficiency of Federal Employees* (*draft*). U.S. Office of Personnel Management, Washington, DC.

Information and Information Resources Management

CHAPTER 9

Understanding Information

*I*nformation proficiency depends on processes to make
and implement decisions and on the information used.
Understanding information and the processes that generate it is crucial to success.

INFORMATION—RANGE AND QUALITY

Our senses and information systems gather information from many sources. Some information comes from formally recorded data such as printed articles, motion picture images, or motion picture sounds. Other comes in less formal, but reasonably stylized forms, such as the words in a conversation. Appreciated, but less well understood, are sources such as "body language." Of course, each of us has available considerable information in our memories and perceptions of past events and thoughts. And, we create new information through imagination and thinking.

Information can be roughly divided into two categories, data and procedures. While such a division is helpful, it is neither complete nor perfect. For example, the decisions and actions one uses to drive a car can be thought of as procedures; however, if someone writes down instructions for driving, the procedures become data.

The contents of a spreadsheet or a software program are data from the viewpoint of other software that is used to edit, store, or interpret the spreadsheet or program. To the person creating the spreadsheet or software program, some of the material represents data—for example, numbers for this year's and next year's budgets. For that person, however, much of the material represents procedure—steps that a computer is directed to take to compare the two budgets.

You must do well with both data and procedures. Information proficiency depends on the data you use and on process, that is, actions you take to make and implement decisions.

*   *   *

An important issue regarding information, whether data or procedure, is that of quality. When we think of the quality of information, we often emphasize accuracy. Accuracy is important, but considering only accuracy leaves some questions about quality unanswered. What if the information is not precise? What if it is precise, but you cannot understand its context well enough to use the information?

Much of your use of information depends more on context than on precision. "Big" or "many" requires a context. Even in working with numbers, there are many examples in which people focus on consistency at the expense of accuracy.

Here is an example in which people are required to choose explicitly between accuracy and consistency.

Many engineering studies were done based on some software that simulated a variety of physical phenomena. Dozens of engineers had used the software over a period of years. These people learned how to interpret the results of simulations in order to explain and even predict the results of experiments.

Eventually, someone discovered that one physics equation had been incorrectly implemented in the software. A factor of 2 was missing from one of the terms in that equation.

The software is changed so that engineers must specify the factor, with a choice of 2 or 1. An engineer who is working on a new experiment and who has never done a simulation can be expected to choose 2, the accurate choice. Another engineer, who is designing the last in a series of related experiments and who has used the simulation tool successfully to design and interpret the previous experiments, can be expected to choose 1, the consistent choice. The latter engineer chooses inaccuracy in order to complete the series of experiments with satisfactory results, timeliness, and cost.

Consider another example, one in which the choice between accuracy and consistency is not as precise as that between 2 and 1. An organization is developing a budget for next year based on a goal to cut expenses by 3 percent. The goal itself is one of consistency. By starting with the numbers for a prior year, the group is emphasizing consistency. The focus is on changes between years, not on the total budget. In contrast, a complete review of each activity generating revenues or costs would force thoughts toward accuracy.

These two examples have dealt with trade-offs in quantitative work between accuracy and consistency. In situations in which information is not entirely numeric, considerations about the quality of information are more complex.

*   *   *

"I'm sorry, but that's what the computer says." How many times have you heard such a statement? And how many times has the computer "been wrong"?

Today, there is a movement toward quality—quality products, quality services, even measurable standards of quality for processes for the development of software. But software programs are no better than the data to which they are applied.

Traditionally, improving the quality of information has focused on errors.

Sometimes, errors are easy to spot. For example, consider the case of one large error in the data in a computerized corporate accounting system. A purchase order for one item of considerable cost had been entered incorrectly into the system. Some of the digits of the corporate-standard part number had been put into the quantity field. The multiplication of a large quantity by a large unit price resulted in a computed total cost that came close to, or exceeded, the maximum monetary amount for which the accounting system was programmed. Corrections were made, but the system could not complete the appropriate reversal. The problem proved irreversible for the relevant fiscal year.

Budget analysts and financial managers learned that, when they received a very wrong result, they should try adjusting by a particular large dollar amount. If the adjusted result looked reasonable, it was acceptable. Fortunately, the problem did not spill over into subsequent fiscal years' data.

This is not the only mistake that has ever been made. Indeed, laws were passed to ensure individuals' access to credit databases in the hope that errors would be found and corrected.

*   *   *

The most important person in the life of information is the person who uses the information or relies on summaries or deductions based on the information. Today, systems tend to leave this person with inadequate information and little recourse. Missing for that person are estimates of the quality of the information presented, audit trails to follow for clarification or correction, and more attractive alternatives than the standard fallbacks, "It's in the computer" or "I can transfer you to my supervisor."

The time has come to design information-proficient organizational and technological systems that present qualification along with information. Consider the trends. More decisions are based on summarized information, information that itself is often based on historical estimates and future projections. There are fewer middle managers, the people who traditionally provide assurances of data's reasonableness or find sources to confirm information. People realize that quality is a never-ending quest and that, therefore, neither data nor anything else can be assumed to be 100 percent correct.

For makers of strategic decisions, the qualification of information must be adequate to provide knowledge of the confidence that people can have in the information. These people need to make quality decisions and deserve the basis to do so.

The same is true for a worker handling one client case or telephone call. Empowerment to make decisions and the capability to make them well demand that information, including associated confidence levels, qualification, and audit trails, be readily available.

The imperatives are there, including the quality concept that a well-spent unit of up-front planning, testing, or other work saves many units of work later. The opportunity is also there as the costs of designing and building information systems decline, based on better software development tools and declining costs of hardware.

"Black Box" Information

Traditional mechanical systems can be designed satisfactorily for quality. Consider a mechanical automobile braking system. There should be a list of design goals. For example, the system cannot fail under the maximum force or impulse that can be applied by a person. The designers and testers pick margins of error. For example, the system must hold up under a certain multiple of the maximum force that people can exert. Prototype systems can be tested for such criteria. They can also be tested after simulated aging of the component parts. If a system performs under extreme conditions, as well as normal ones, it is assumed that it will perform under all reasonable conditions. After testing, the challenge shifts to manufacturing the system within appropriate tolerances.

The output from computer systems can be much more difficult to trust. Consider some examples.

One of the early heldheld scientific calculators produced erroneous arc-tangents for a range of numbers. Arc-tangents were calculated differently for various ranges of numbers. Evidently, the formula for one range was incorrect.

This example points out the desirability of testing algorithms in all ranges into which the underlying calculations are divided. There are, however, limits. Even in administrative computer applications, it is impossible to test all cases. For example, suppose that a programmer puts software into an accounts payable program to issue an extra check on one certain day if certain conditions are met. Testing the software is unlikely to find this "feature" or prevent such fraud before it happens.

Recall the example of an error in software used for engineering simulations. The example of a missed factor of 2 illustrates only one of the potential problems in using simulations.

Simulations are used to design buildings for structural integrity under normal conditions, during windstorms, and during earthquakes; airplanes for safe flight and fuel economy; molecules for biological applications; electrical transmission networks for appropriate capacity and for stability during periods of rapid change in electrical supply or use; and telecommunications networks. In such cases, the basic science underlying the simulations, such as laws of physics and chemistry, is reasonably well known, though some properties of materials and some varieties of earthquakes or weather phenomena may not be.

Simulations are also applied to subjects for which theories of behavior may not be as well verified: tactics for military battles; economic phenomena; automobile crashworthiness, including effects on passengers; and population dynamics.

* * *

To illustrate some issues that confront developers and users of simulators, consider an example. Suppose one wants to develop a simulator to predict the positions of planets in a solar system. This software can answer a question such as: Given the masses, positions, and velocities of the planets and sun in our solar system today, where will these objects be at any time during the next 10 years? The results of such a simulation are essential in choosing a trajectory for a spacecraft that will travel from Earth and pass by several planets.

A simulation presents a number of challenges regarding utility of results:

- Does the input given to the simulator describe the problem that one wants to explore?
- Is the problem within the scope of problems the simulator can handle well?
- Do the software renditions of the equations produce accurate solutions to the equations?
- Is each equation the correct one for the phenomenon it purports to represent?

Consider these four questions in reverse order, using the example of a simulator for solar systems.

First, is an equation suitable to the phenomenon simulated? In the solar system example, the two fundamental equations are among those taught to high school physics students. In the simulator, these two equations are combined into one, which computes the rate of change of velocity of an object at a given time.

For some simulations of some solar systems, that equation is suitable. In other cases it is not:

- If the solar system is large, effects of the time it takes gravity to "propagate" need to be considered.
- If any of the objects are moving rapidly enough, effects of special relativity must be included.
- If at least one of the objects is sufficiently massive, like a black hole, effects of general relativity need to be incorporated.

In a simulator, some effects, small in the originally intended uses, may have been omitted or approximated. The user of the simulator must run only problems within the range of relevance.

Second, does the software match the equation? Having the correct mathematics does not necessarily guarantee useful results. Assuming no collisions, a planet moves along a curved path; its position and velocity change instantaneously and smoothly. The simulator, however, produces paths composed of straight-line segments. Using the initial positions and velocities the simulator calculates accelerations and then derives new velocities and positions for a short time in the future. For the time interval between the start and finish of a time step, a planet's path is assumed to be a straight line. The process repeats until the 10 simulated years are completed. Thus, the problem is not solved continuously in time. Instead, an approximate solution is estimated for the time at the end of each time step. Thus, care must be taken in implementing the emulation to ensure that results adequately approximate the true curved paths.

Third, is the problem within the scope of problems the simulator can handle well? A problem can escape the bounds of a simulator for evident reasons. For example, the solar system simulator may not be able to handle collisions between objects.

There can be other, more subtle limits. Consider the implication of the choice of time steps in this example. If the steps are too long, the line-segment approximations to planetary orbits will be inaccurate. If the steps are too short, the computer does too many arithmetic calculations, each with a potential rounding error, and the simulation is again inaccurate. Many simulators adjust the time step automatically during a simulation in order to avoid these two problems as best they can. Nevertheless, no such simulation should be carried on indefinitely; the effects of discrete calculations and approximate arithmetic eventually take hold.

Another question regarding the limits of a simulation is whether the problem being attempted actually fits within the capability of the simulator, or perhaps any simulator. For example, recent mathematical research suggests that no matter how "accurately" our solar system is simulated, the predicting of positions cannot be carried indefinitely into the future. This conclusion has little to do with physical assumptions, such as that no new objects enter the solar system, that the sun does not explode, and that other physical changes do not apply. This result comes from the mathematics of chaos.

Assuming that the simulator is used within its limits, one of the four questions remains: Does the input given to the simulator match the problem being studied? In this example, the simulator would not make up for the user's leaving out a planet.

*   *   *

Learning to cope with simulators and other black boxes is important. How much should you trust the results of a simulation or of any computerized process? If you want to build something that varies from a design that has been simulated, how much variation is acceptable?

More generally, how much proficiency with and through the results of simulations is appropriate? This question has several aspects.

Knowing and communicating the end results from a series of simulations may not suffice. You may need to understand key aspects that determined the results. Analysis of the evolution of conditions during the course of a simulation can be essential in order to develop a feel for the matter. Communicating this insight may be needed.

A simulator can help you develop such insight. Many simulators provide options to request details about a simulation, for example, at regular intervals of simulated time or if particular types of events occur. Some simulators produce error matrices estimating how much the results would change if the initial conditions were slightly different. Human review of such information can be important, not only to develop a feel for the trustworthiness of a result but also to be able to estimate the results of simulations of similar problems without having to run those simulations.

In using simulators to design objects or processes, people often run several simulations to try to find an optimal solution. Each run tests a different design. The designer who takes the time to analyze the runs can minimize the number of simulations needed. This strategy contrasts with "dartboard design" in which the designer, in effect, throws darts at a "map," the points on which denote different designs. By simulating the design "chosen" by every dart, the designer hopes that one simulation will identify a point near the peak of a "tall mountain," that is, a nearly acceptable design. The designer needs to make appropriate trade-offs regarding how much reliance to place on each of the two strategies.

Finally, consider again the issue of how much to trust the laws of behavior incorporated in a simulator. The equations used may be deterministic, but society may not know how well they represent appropriate behavior. In the solar system example, the applicable laws of nature are thought to be well established; however, had such a simulator been built in the 19th century, it could not have included effects of relativity because the appropriate theories had not been developed. As another example, a simulation of global economics depends on assumed behaviors that have not been verified against experiment. Unlike scientific work in laboratories, history may not produce enough similar starting situations with controlled variations for people to develop verifiable laws of behavior.

In the preceding examples, the inputs, software, and accuracy of hardware arithmetic fully determine the outputs. One can trace the logic that develops an answer. In effect, the black boxes have definitive "black-and-white" insides.

BLACK BOXES WITH GRAY INSIDES

There are also black boxes with indeterminate "gray" insides. Some such black boxes do not produce exactly repeatable results. As for others, nobody can explain how they work.

*   *   *

Consider, for example, simulating the flow of automobile traffic toward a group of toll gates. The input to a simulator specifies a profile of incoming traffic, say, eight cars per minute during one quarter hour and ten the next.

During any such quarter-hour period, the cars do not arrive at equally spaced intervals. This simulator introduces variability by picking "randomly" the intervals and initial speeds for the cars. It adds more variability in treating both the propensities of drivers to tailgate or change lanes and the time it takes individuals to pay tolls.

Unless the user directs the simulator to duplicate the "random" choices, subsequent simulations based on the same inputs will generate and use different arrival times for individual vehicles. Results, such as the average time spent waiting to get through the toll booth area, will not be repeatable.

Developing confidence in results from such simulations may involve experimenting to observe the variations in results.

*   *   *

Another type of black box with gray insides "learns" through training. Some of these systems are based on the principles of neural networks.

Neural networks are patterned after a model of the brain. In the brain, memory and thought patterns depend on the strength of chemical and electrical connections between neurons. A neuron has one input area at which it can receive electrical impulses from the outputs of many other neurons. Chemicals help transmit the pulses between neurons. Each neuron has many output strands and thereby can influence many other neurons. Learning establishes, and practice reinforces, patterns of ease of electrical conductivity in the connections.

One application of systems that learn, and of neural networks, involves scanners that recognize typewritten characters. You can build a prototype scanner that knows nothing about the shapes of characters. An input is generated when the scanner "looks at" a part of a piece of paper and records a measurement of light intensity for each rectangle in a grid, superimposed by the design of the scanning mechanism, over that part of the paper. The scanner uses the pattern of light intensity to guess which character it is seeing. A trainer, human or machine, provides feedback as to whether the guess is correct. A correct guess reinforces the pattern of neural connections. An incorrect guess leads to changes in an attempt to find a pattern that improves the accuracy of subsequent guesses. This "pattern of neural connections" is represented by numbers in a computer memory used by the prototype scanner rather than as physical, chemical, or electrical attributes, as in the brain.

Every character is used many times as input. After many tries, each with appropriate feedback, the scanner increases its chances of being correct. The device learns to recognize patterns of black and white representing the letter *a,* even if some characters are off center in the grid or somewhat misshapen.

If all possible output characters have been tried as input enough times during the learning period, the scanner becomes quite accurate. You can record the pattern of neural connections and proceed to mass-produce scanners based on those connections.

Your prototype is a potential product, but no one knows how it works. It is a black box with "gray matter" inside.

How will the scanner react to an as-yet unseen character from a foreign alphabet? At best, all you know is that the device will call it one of the characters it knows, but which one? The results are unpredictable. Probably, such a product would not sell well in the marketplace.

The designer of such a device must include at least one more output, "undetermined," and make sure that the prototype learns to produce this result for many inputs outside the otherwise intended range of outputs.

*   *   *

To go a little farther, you could design a neural network system that learns to pick stocks. For example, the system could guess the one-year attractiveness of each stock at the end of each trading day. The attractiveness might be a return ratio: price one year hence, plus dividends during the year, divided by current price. The system could "learn" from the entire past ticker tape history of market trades and the records of dividends for all stocks. Guesses would be graded for a stock that had traded, say, for at least one year. Learning, that is, adjusting based on the grades given to the guesses, could begin with decades-old data and proceed daily through data from one year ago.

If some of the predictions for the most recent decade looked reasonable to you, you might invest based on current and future output from this system. Among millions of trades, the system might have discovered patterns. If it did, however, it would be impossible to determine what the patterns were. In any event, it would be up to you to consider which past predictions seemed convincing and to decide to what extent to follow the system's "recommendations."

Some people today pick investments with the aid of advice from neural-network-based systems.

*   *   *

To what extent will black boxes with gray insides approach or surpass the functioning of human "gray matter"? If you use such systems, you may be discovering answers to this question.

STEPPING INTO THE BOX: SIMULATIONS WITH COLORFUL INSIDES

Video games provide many examples of simulators featuring personal involvement. The simulation software features a model of a real situation, such as piloting an aircraft during a landing, or a model of an artificial situation, such as an adventure in an imaginary world. Video games can provide a player with education, excitement, and relaxation.

The sophistication of a game depends on the insight provided by the people who programmed it and on the capabilities of the devices with which the game is played. A flight simulator running on a home computer emphasizes visual information. Commercial and military pilots train using more elaborate simulators that allow the pilot to experience sensations beyond sight and sound. The pilot sits in a mock-up of a cockpit and uses real controls. The mock-up tilts.

Some games are used to train business managers. For example, in one game, a group of people pretend to be running an electric utility. The team is provided with a summary of the company's condition at a particular time, including a financial statement and a list of key decisions that may need to be made. The team may want to set a medium- to long-term corporate strategy that might include a major decision about a nuclear power plant. The team must make various choices about corporate emphases and expenditures for the next year. The simulation then provides results for that year, including financial statements, results of customer satisfaction surveys, the condition of the company's plants, and statements made by regulatory bodies.

Some of the results are heavily influenced by the team's decisions; for example, a reasonable investment in customer outreach programs will increase the utility's customer satisfaction ratings. Other results, such as an increase in summer use of electricity for air conditioning because of unusually hot weather, do not depend on the team's decisions, unless, of course, the team decided not to acquire enough means to meet such demand. The annual cycle is then repeated. At the end of several cycles, the team receives feedback on how well it did. When several teams play the game at the same time, each starts with an identical company; the feedback includes a report on how well a team performed in comparison with its rivals.

Games are not limited to single-entity simulations. War games allow teams to play directly against each other. Such a game may simulate overall battle strategy or can involve teams pretending to use individual tanks. When using current simulation technology, the members of a tank team see on televisionlike screens simulations of what they would see from inside their tank. They develop a useful feel for battle without leaving the room.

Simulation technology and historical records make for realistic reconstruction of events. Based on tape recordings of conversations during battle and interviews afterward, the U.S. Department of Defense reconstructed, using a simulator, the events of a tank battle fought during the Persian Gulf War. It has been claimed that this battle is the most accurately documented battle in the history of warfare. Using the simulator, soldiers who participated in the battle have verified the authenticity of the reconstruction.

As we learn more about patterns of behavior and how people sense their surroundings, and as information-handling techniques improve, simulators become more realistic. You may have noticed advances in the delivery of sound to movie audiences. Corresponding advances are being made in visual techniques, especially for home or office use. The term *virtual reality* conveys images of a person experiencing realistic sight, sound, and some touch.

The future for interactive simulators is bright. Applications can combine education, decision making, and entertainment. Perhaps eventually small-screen "glasses," earphones, "smart gloves," and a communications and simulation system will provide an expansive window for communicating with other people, exploring the world as we know it, and imagining other worlds for academic pursuits or entertainment.

Even Pros Make Mistakes With Statistics: The Hunt for the Kappa Meson

It has been said that it is easy to "lie with statistics." Statistical data is everywhere: results of opinion polls, scientific studies on the effectiveness and side effects of proposed medicines, census data, data on the quality of items being manufactured on assembly lines, ratings of the popularity of television programs.

How are you to know how much you can rely on such information? Here is an example that indicates that even professionals make mistakes.

One of the goals of elementary particle physicists is to find new subatomic particles. This activity has parallels with the desires of scientists in an earlier century to find new chemical elements. A new element might be useful by itself or in compounds. There was personal satisfaction and potential recognition for having discovered something new. After the formulation of the periodic table of elements, there was even a road map suggesting properties for elements that, once found, would fill in blanks in the table.

In the 1960s, there was rapid growth in the number of known or suspected elementary particles. The era paralleled the search for elements at a time when the periodic table was not quite formulated. People saw patterns among particles, somewhat akin to the similar chemical behaviors of elements in what would become columns in the periodic table. Any of a wide range of experiments might turn up a new particle. A new particle might provide a clue to the structure of all matter in the universe. Finding a new particle might lead to a Nobel prize.

To find a new particle, one shoots, from a particle accelerator, a beam of particles toward a target. (Today, in some experiments, one shoots two "colliding beams" of particles head-on toward each other.)

The energy of the particles in the incoming beam is controlled, and a "cross section" is measured. The cross section represents the fraction of incoming particles that do not travel unimpeded through the target. The cross section is expressed as an "area," in effect, the fraction of the area across the beam that is blocked to free transit. This blockage is interpreted as the sum of many small areas, each being the effective area presented by a single object in the target.

The experiment is repeated, with the energy of the incoming beam varied. If there is a range of energies over which the cross sections are significantly greater than for the neighboring lower and higher energies, one has found a resonance. If the resonance meets certain criteria, it is a particle. If the particle has not been detected before, the experimenters have found a new particle.

In the late 1960s, there were a number of experiments that seemed to provide evidence of a new particle. It received the name "kappa meson." Many groups of physicists performed experiments that could produce evidence of this particle. Some reported finding the particle.

Eventually, one physicist performed "statistics on the statistics" of how many relevant experiments were being done per year, how many incoming particle energies were likely to be tried in an experiment, how readings were made at each energy, and what criteria were being used to decide whether one had observed a particle.

Assuming that there is no such thing as a kappa meson and that the normal statistical procedures were used in interpreting the experimental data, the physicist estimated that there would be about six reports that year of experiments confirming the existence of the meson.

This physicist reported this estimate at a conference. Later in the conference, another physicist withdrew a paper that would have reported evidence for the existence of kappa mesons.

WORKING WITH INFORMATION

Doubtless, you have, at some time, read a newspaper or magazine article and come away with the impression that the writer's approach was very clever. Perhaps you read the article because it dealt with a topic about which you have read a great deal. You recognize the author's creativity. How did the writer find that new "angle?"

Part of the creative process involves testing concepts in pairs. For example, we compare a person's behavior with attributes of animals. "He is a tiger." "He is a pussycat." "He is snake."

Pick any two subjects—each one a person, thing, event, or concept. You probably can easily find a plausible theme linking them and outline a short essay, using that theme, about the two topics. For example, suppose your subjects are "cow" and "moon." You can write an article based on the nursery-rhyme theme of a cow jumping over the moon. You can write an essay about the fact that cows give milk and the myth that the moon is made of cheese. If you want a scientific theme, you can talk about how the methane emitted by cows alters the composition of moonlight as it passes through the Earth's atmosphere.

We value such cleverness and the insight it can produce. We appreciate writers who find useful juxtapositions of concepts upon which to base articles. Ultimately, however, the usefulness of such creativity is determined by the reader (Figs. 3–1 and 3–2). Filtering and interpreting information are among our most frequent activities. Here is an experiment to try occasionally.

Take an item of "important" news from a normal news source, for example, an article on an international incident in today's newspaper. Read the headline and the article. Carefully reread the first few paragraphs.

For the adjectives used in those paragraphs, how many are objective and verifiable as true? "Heroic," "tragic," "ill-conceived," or "important" may express commonly held views of something but are probably not statements of hard fact. "Liberal" and "conservative" are oft-used terms, but it may be hard to picture what is meant in a specific use. Both "landslide victory" and "narrow majority" can characterize the same election result if the newly elected majority party in a legislative body won 51% of the seats and no one other party won more than 20%.

Keep going. How about the adverbs, for example? After you have weeded out these and other kinds of phrasing "ambiguities," review each sentence as a whole. To what extent does the sentence appear to be factual? To what extent does it appear to be the opinion of the writer, of an "unidentified source," or of a "school of thought?" Is it presented as fact or as opinion? Whether fact or opinion, is the sentence plausible? To what extent does it seem verifiable? Does the writer make claims about how it has been verified? If written from another point of view, how different a "slant" could there be?

Review the first few paragraphs and then the entire article, comparing the material to your first impression, evaluating links between topics, and determining significant facts or explanations that seem to be missing.

Try to put yourself in the writer's shoes. Evaluate to what extent it appears that the author was motivated by factual reporting, competing to get the article published, helping to sell more newspapers, and espousing a point of view.

Analyzing articles and other sources of information should add value to the information for you.

*   *   *

In this the Information Age, society relies more and more on the opinion poll, a blend of fact and opinion. No matter how the people or organizations asked to respond to the poll are chosen and no matter how opinion-oriented, emotionally worded, or ambiguous the questions are, the results of a poll are, indeed, facts.

What does it mean for someone to say, in response to a poll, that he "approves" or "disapproves" of how a political leader is handling an issue or job? What does a question as to whether a governmental body should provide more service or "benefits" mean if the question does not suggest costs or other consequences?

Furthermore, there is always the possibility that poll respondents will choose answers that "send a message" rather than reflecting the respondents' true opinions.

No matter what the questions are, to whom they are addressed, and how they are answered, the results are facts. If the poll is reported fully, you can learn the exact questions; the percentages of respondents who chose each option, including "no opinion;" how the respondents were chosen; and the number of respondents and corresponding statistical accuracy of the poll.

You may observe how often, however, reporting about a poll obscures some questions or does not state them completely; does not cover the sequence of the questions, which could affect the responses; does not discuss how people were chosen to be polled; or ignores the issue of statistical accuracy.

A poll can be done well from the standpoint of asking questions significant to the audience for the poll's results and taking precautions to poll an appropriate cross section of the population. Yet the results can still be misused. How often, for example, with polls of preference among political candidates, does one find it reported that a particular candidate is gaining when, in fact, the change in the difference in the poll results between the two leading candidates, say 2 percent, is less than the statistical accuracy, say 3 percent, of either of the two polls being compared?

*   *   *

Enhancing your information proficiency depends on how you work with information. You need to understand the information you use well enough to know how much confidence you can place in it and, consequently, in your decisions.

10

Managing Information as a Resource

*I*nformation is more than an amorphous collection of data. It is a resource to be managed, understood for its quality, and used to build information proficiency and competitive advantage.

INFORMATION AS A RESOURCE

Pieces of information have value. Investors subscribe to information services to check at any moment on the prices of individual stocks. Similarly, collections of information have value. Businesses buy rights to television series and movies; corporations amass or buy access to information about their marketplaces, customers, and competitors; university archives collect rare books.

Information constitutes a resource. In some ways, information is like a physical resource. It can be accumulated. To preserve its value and extend its usefulness, it needs to be maintained. Preserving an information resource may require capturing useful information from people who are changing jobs or leaving an organization, as well as carefully combing computer systems before they are phased out. In some ways, information is different from most physical resources. Often, sharing it does not require giving up its use.

Organizations have many repositories for their information resources. A corporate law department, for example, manages documents pertaining to the company's litigation and maintains a library of precedent-setting cases. Also, the department's personnel have memories of the corporation's legal proceedings, allies, and adversaries, memories that also constitute resources. The corporation's tax department is another repository for information. So is the shareholder relations department. So is every other group and each employee.

Segments of an organization's information resources can be identified by:

- Information subject.
- Group maintaining the content of the information.
- Group storing and helping others retrieve the information.
- Technological system used for storing and retrieving information.

Such divisions of labor place responsibility for maintaining a portion of an organization's resources with people who have expertise and incentive to do so. These vertical divisions, however, have built barriers impeding access to information by people who may not know it is available or have no convenient ways to retrieve or enhance it.

Such division of information traditionally extends to various sectors of the communications and information industries. Until recently, there was little overlap between the entertainment industry, with its libraries of movies and television programs, and the computerized database services industry, with its libraries of economic, demographic, and other data. Information industries were isolated from each other.

Information Age advances are closing the gaps between traditional information industry segments. New products contain audio, still visual, moving visual, numeric, and textual information, all synergistically packaged on an optical disk for use with a personal computer. Companies in one field are buying rights to information traditionally associated with other fields. Service-providing companies are crossing traditional lines.

A new paradigm is emerging. The traditional paradigm (Fig. 10–1) associated information with its storage and delivery mechanisms. *Television* denoted both the programs and the TV sets. The traditional paradigm for information resources has also reinforced the traditional paradigm for organizations (Fig. 4–1).

Today, we anticipate an application (Fig. 10–2) of the Peer Paradigm that supports the Peer Paradigm for organizations (Fig. 4–2). Consider the four layers (Fig. 10–2), starting from the bottom:

- Basic information *technology* falls into one peer class. Just as it was not long before television stations showed movies, overlaps will grow and distinctions will wane among computing, various forms of telecommunications, broadcast television, cable television, radio, movie theaters, videoconferencing facilities, and so forth.
- All *general information* falls into a peer class that mixes many forms of information, including television programs, computerized databases, movies, and the contents of publications such as magazines and newspapers. This class also includes automated and manual procedures for selecting general information and for

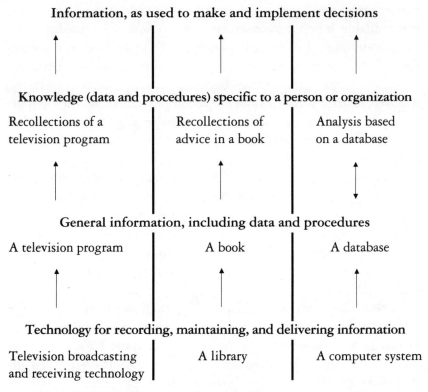

Information, as used to make and implement decisions

Knowledge (data and procedures) specific to a person or organization

| Recollections of a television program | Recollections of advice in a book | Analysis based on a database |

General information, including data and procedures

| A television program | A book | A database |

Technology for recording, maintaining, and delivering information

| Television broadcasting and receiving technology | A library | A computer system |

FIGURE 10–1   The Traditional Paradigm for Information as a Resource.

using this information to generate information specific to a person or organization.

- Above these two peer layers is a third, namely, *knowledge*, both *data and procedures, specific to individuals and organizations.*
- On top of the third layer lies synthesized *information used to make and implement decisions.*

This change in the information resources paradigm will not happen overnight, and it will not happen without costs to all organizations. It does, however, present opportunities, not only for purveyors of general information and technological systems but also for consumers of those services and systems.

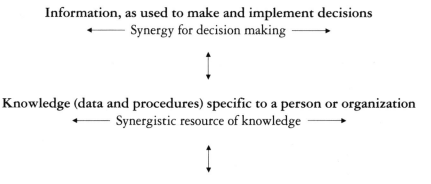

Information, as used to make and implement decisions
◄——— Synergy for decision making ———►

Knowledge (data and procedures) specific to a person or organization
◄——— Synergistic resource of knowledge ———►

General information, including data and procedures
◄——— Resource of generic information ———►

Technology for recording, maintaining, and delivering information
◄——— Peer-linked technological systems ———►

FIGURE 10–2   The Peer Paradigm for Information as a Resource.

Organizations can develop information resources strategies around the new paradigm. These strategies tear down historic barriers between parts of an information resource and untangle the snarls left from having managed information sometimes on the basis of subject, sometimes of "content owner," sometimes of "media owner," and sometimes of delivery mechanism.

Here are the principles for one strategy, based on the Peer Paradigm (Fig. 10–2) and the information-proficiency paradigm (Figs. 1–1 and 5–2), for managing information as a resource. All parts of an organization share a common infrastructure of technology for recording, maintaining, and delivering information. General information is universally available through use of that infrastructure. People from throughout the organization specify the generally available information they need. If some such information is not yet available in the organization but exists and is affordable in the general marketplace, the appropriate access is acquired, and everyone in the organization can use the information. As for knowledge that has been specific to individuals or groups, the persons or groups are urged to make information available to others in the organization. Finally, people are encouraged to involve appropriate participants in their decision-making and decision-implementing processes, thereby taking advantage of and enhancing the total pool of information and wisdom.

In this strategy, all people are responsible for maintaining the information they affect. Also, all people are able to specify general information, such as demographic data available from outside the organization, needed by the organization. Most people are spared the burdens of maintaining general information and providing general information technology and services. Information resources specialists enhance the utility of the organization-specific and general information by cataloging it for easy access; these specialists also ensure the currency of generic information, provide for the technological storage and delivery infrastructure, and suggest new sources of information that people might find useful.

No matter what strategy an organization chooses, including the passive one of not having a strategy, there will be costs for keeping up with useful Information Age advances. But having an appropriate information resources strategy avoids excessive cost and maximizes the value of those resources, thereby contributing to the organization's information proficiency and overall success.

MANAGING INFORMATION RESOURCES

Everybody is an information resources manager. Each individual and each organization manages information resources by:

- Acquiring new information.
- Maintaining the current resources.
- Cross-linking pieces of information to gain new insights, which themselves become new pieces of information.
- Discarding materials.
- Communicating with other people and with information systems.

Successful information resources management is key to information proficiency. Treating information as a resource raises many issues, including how to decide how much you are willing to invest to develop or acquire a new component for your information resources. Information Age developments add both challenges and flexibility to meet the challenges but do not change the fundamental issues.

Here are some characteristics on which people rely regarding the information they use (Fig. 10–3). You can consider these attributes, for example, when conversing or when preparing a speech or memo; your audience will appreciate the enhanced usefulness of what you say or write. You can also use these characteristics when you plan a change to an organization's long-term information resources.

Completeness

Simply stated, people want all the information they need. This means that an information resources manager must somehow anticipate what those needs will be.

Traditionally, demands arise because information users come up with lots of why-not desires: "If only we could know. . . ." Building information resources costs money and time; information managers

- Completeness
- Timely availability
- Convenience
- Security
- Degree of detail
- Consistency
- Accuracy
- Knowledge of sources
- Trustworthiness

FIGURE 10–3   Quality Attributes for an Information Resource.

cannot satisfy everybody's wish lists. Also, some desired information may not be available anywhere or may be proprietary to another organization.

As the Information Age progresses, the balance shifts from information scarcity toward information overload. Inside an organization, information systems keep much detailed data. Outside the organization lies a wealth of information sources, including newspapers, magazines, television news broadcasts, and numerous services providing on-line information ranging from current securities prices to last year's purchases by the United States federal government. The growing international infrastructure of telecommunications and data services allows people to find and use even more information.

Completeness will always be an issue for information resources, but information consumers and resources managers will find the focus of concern shifting toward filtering, understanding, and combining information (Figs. 3–1 and 3–2).

Timely Availability

Information that arrives too late is of little use—"If only we had known . . ."

Even with the press of modern business, Information Age advances are obviating some concerns over timeliness. For example, once located, information can be moved very quickly.

Timeliness depends more and more on anticipating users' needs, enabling users to locate information readily, and preparing to combine knowledge from disparate sources into timely, useful information.

Convenience

Customers of information have a right to excpect convenience just as the customers of any business do. Anyone supplying information to someone else needs to make that product convenient for its audiences.

Some experiences that information clients prefer to avoid include receiving a lengthy, perhaps even specially prepared, report when only highlights are needed; listening to a speech in which the details drown the main points; receiving a large printout from which only a few individual items or summary numbers are needed; having to type computer-printed data into their own computer systems instead of transferring it electronically; and being unable to obtain information from the office while traveling on business.

Security

Most organizations have restricted information such as personnel records and plans for new products. Information managers must guard against inappropriate distribution of information.

It is necessary to avoid corrupting an information resource through the acquisition of detrimental material. Inaccurate data can ruin analytic work. A software virus can cripple both one's information resources and one's technological infrastructure.

Also, information managers must help organizations avoid untoward use of information. Recall, for example, that it is easy for people to make mistakes in using statistical data.

Degree of Detail

Different clients have different needs. For example, a report must satisfy both a reader who wants only highlights and a reader who needs details. Traditionally, writers include in such reports executive summaries, chapter summaries, chapters with a moderate degree of detail, and appendices with supporting data.

Newer Information Age techniques, such as "hypertext," add flexibility by facilitating browsing through information, top-down, bottom-up, or outward from an instance of a specific word or concept. It is becoming easier to find and, if needed, extract appropriate degrees of detail on various aspects of a topic. One use of this technique will allow consumers to shop electronically, focusing sometimes on products' pictures and prices and, perhaps moments later, on details of design and construction.

The challenge for the information resources manager is to develop techniques and systems that provide the flexibility for people to obtain just the degree of detail they need.

Consistency

We all depend on the consistency of information. Often, we are more interested in whether the unemployment percent or a stock market index increased or decreased than in the number itself.

Consistency is difficult to maintain. Some economic data is seasonally adjusted in an attempt to present a consistent framework in which to view the latest month's figures. The stocks that make up a market index change. One measure of unemployment gives way to another.

Consistency is also a broader concept. For example, people comparing price-to-earnings ratios for stocks of United States businesses with stocks for Japanese businesses need to remember that accounting techniques, and therefore earnings calculations, vary by country.

Challenges to information resources managers include developing information sources that explain how consistent their information is to those who need to know and, of course, encouraging recipients of information to pay attention to the issue of consistency.

Accuracy

How many times do people read numbers and wonder what they mean? An accurate number or sentence may be useless if its reader cannot place it in a meaningful context. No wonder we tend toward judging information based on consistency. People deserve to be able to find out what a number or other piece of information means. Enabling them to do so can be quite a challenge.

People also deserve to know how accurate a number is. Opinion polls often publish a "margin of error." For statistical data, there are measures of uncertainty, such as the standard deviation, from which a person can learn about the accuracy of numbers reported. Even for supposedly precise information, there is room for inaccuracy—today's summary of yesterday's sales may not include some transactions for which the reporting was delayed.

Similarly, people deserve to be able to verify the accuracy of text, sounds, and pictures. Language is not precise. You may recall having heard or read a sentence carefully crafted to encompass two disparate positions on a political policy. Sounds and pictures are routinely altered.

Knowledge of Sources

When you read mail from an organization that you have never heard of before, you probably don't feel satisfied with judging the content—you want to know who wrote the letter.

For the most part, people trust information based on their knowledge of its sources. How was the data originally collected? Who compiled it? Whose interpretation are you reading? What are the writer's biases? How reliable has his or her information been in the past? How useful was it?

In short, the information resources manager will find increasing demands to supply audit trails, not only for transactional numeric data but also for other types of information.

Trustworthiness

Issues such as consistency, accuracy, and knowledge of the sources all add up to the key concept of trustworthiness. The challenge of anyone making information available is to help the recipients understand to what extent the information can be trusted. This is not easy—the trustworthiness of information depends on its intended use.

*   *   *

The preceding characteristics constitute a useful list of attributes to keep in mind in managing an organization's resources. Generally, your challenge in managing information is to recognize the values and costs of managing information resources, make good decisions, and develop a used and useful resource that helps optimize its constituents' information proficiency.

QUALITY AND COST

It costs effort and money to provide quality information resources. Consider, for example, just the issue of convenient public access to U.S. federal information. There is much information—millions of employees cannot help but generate and collect copious amounts of data each year. How easy should it be for people to obtain federal information and to what extent should they have to pay for it?

One school of thought has it that taxpayers have paid for the collection of information and that access should therefore be easy and free; another notes that it costs effort, time, and money to fulfill citizens' requests for information. As might be expected, the federal government provides varying degrees of access to information. Pricing also varies.

There is general agreement that release of some information, such as national security secrets or personnel data, is not appropriate, with opinions varying on the matter of disclosing vendors' bids for government contracts. Security secrets are off-limits to most people but are provided free of cost to contractors needing to know them. Access to vendors' bids varies by circumstance. Some agencies provide this information, with the bidders' proprietary specifications and prices expunged, after a procurement is complete and only if the requestor files a Freedom of Information Act request. While reviewing and blacking out information are time-consuming, the government charges only for the cost to copy the material. This use of the Freedom of Information Act has generated some controversy and is thought to inhibit some vendors from bidding on federal business.

Some government information is available free, for example, from the Consumer Information Center or from various agencies. The Government Printing Office charges for publications. Some government databases can be accessed on-line, at no cost to the user. The Catalogue of Domestic Assistance is a compendium of grants for which organizations may want to apply. People can use it on-line from many public libraries.

Sometimes a government agency gives away copies of a database but charges the full cost of producing a custom report. The Information Resources Management Service's Federal Procurement Data Center essentially gives away complete copies of its annual database of federal purchases. Some companies add data and processing procedures, thereby producing and selling information products and on-line services. These products and services compete with the custom reporting services provided by the government.

*   *   *

There can be many policies regarding dissemination and pricing. One job of the information resources manager, whether in government or the private sector, is to find the ones that best meet the needs of each situation.

COMPETITIVE ADVANTAGE

An organization continues to exist to the extent that it proves worthwhile for its members. In the realm of business, this means performing well enough and having enough promise for the future to provide incentive for owners, employees, creditors, and suppliers to keep the company running. The term *competitive advantage* is applied to the potential of the company in its marketplaces. More generally, consideration of competitive advantage should also take into account competitive posture (Fig. 7–2) and potential in the overall marketplace because the company's products actually compete against the entire range of customers' potential uses of money.

Numerous examples have been documented of companies deriving competitive advantage through innovative use of people's time and information resources management techniques. Examples include:

- A financial institution that offers each customer one point of contact for all the company's services.
- A pharmaceutical distributor that provides technology-based services so that customers can easily determine their needs for and order new stock. The distributor packages each shipment to match a stock clerk's optimal route through the customer's store.
- An airline reservation system thought to be more valuable as a business than the airline operations portion of the same company.
- An auto manufacturer offering lower-cost cars because of just-in-time manufacturing and purchasing.
- A credit-card issuer that offers rates and payment dates tailored to the needs of individual cardholders.
- An aircraft manufacturer that designs an airplane without using paper and is set up to customize easily the interior of each plane made.

In the Information Age framework (Fig. 2–1), information resources management is found in the middle element, linking technology and systems to information proficiency and results. Information resources management plays a key role is achieving information proficiency. Information proficiency plays a key role in overall competitiveness and success.

Competitive advantage is sometimes characterized as being "external" or "internal." External advantages are apparent to customers: new products, product quality, more choices, ease of doing business, and lower prices. Internal advantages include effective support for externally evident advantages, along with cost savings and efficient back offices. External advantages are usually supported by internal improvements.

While the advantages derived through successful management of information resources are apparent, the appropriate roles for information resources managers in helping an organization achieve its information proficiency potential and getting the most value from information resources management techniques have not been fully worked out.

KEY ISSUES IN INFORMATION RESOURCES MANAGEMENT

What are the most important issues in information resources management? This question arises from time to time, especially among people in the United States federal government. The following issues are felt to be important (Robinson, 1994; General Services Administration, 1994):

- *Goals* and *results*:
  Enhancing effectiveness in supporting governmental missions.
  Measuring that effectiveness.
  Focusing planning on achieving overall governmental goals.
  Emphasizing mission as a driver of change.
- *People* and *information proficiency*:
  Improving processes through the use of information resources management.
  Fostering appropriate relations between the information resources management community and its clients.
  Creating client ownership for information resources responsibilities, including top-level support and long-term commitment.
  Bringing together planning and budgeting processes, including integrating information resources management planning with overall planning.

Managing projects and other endeavors well.

Obtaining substantial customer input for those projects and endeavors.

Coordinating well between organizations.

Ensuring that information resources management groups are full partners in agencies' operations.

Ensuring high-quality staffing and enhancing information resources management skills.

- *Information* and *information resources management:*
  Improving information management.
- *Information systems:*
  Developing and using an overall architecture.
  Building comprehensive systems and services within that architecture.
- *Technology:*
  Using technology appropriately.
  Acquiring technology and services easily.

REFERENCES

General Services Administration, 1994. *Federal Government Business Process Reengineering: Lessons Learned.* U.S. General Services Administration, Washington, DC.

Robinson, Brian, 1994. GAO study may set benchmark for IT management. *Federal Computer Week,* March 21, 1994, p. 6.

11

Energizing the Information Resources Community: Awareness

*O*rganizations have many opportunities to increase the
value provided by their information resources
management practitioners. An example of an
information resources community's catalyzing progress
provides "All A's awareness" pointing the way to
capturing those opportunities.

LEADERSHIP AND SUCCESS—AN EXAMPLE

There is a broad spectrum of possible roles for the information resources management community in an organization. At one end of the range, the community runs information systems. At the other, it generates opportunities that shape the strategic direction of the organization.

Information resources communities can succeed in roles beyond those that are expected. The following example shows the information resources community in the United States federal government catalyzing governmentwide movements, including one to improve governmental services to citizens (McDonough and Buckholtz, 1992; McDonough and Trenkle, 1993).

In the late 1980s, an employee of the General Services Administration (GSA) attends a conference in Europe and learns that some European governments are implementing one-stop shopping, whereby individuals learn, during a single contact with the government, the status of each of their accounts with the government, how to contact a member of parliament, or useful information about any government program.

In early 1990, a group of federal information resources management officials meets at a retreat sponsored by GSA and the Office of Management and Budget. They decide to explore the topic of improving some of the *results* of government, namely, federal services to Americans. Along with the European efforts, the concept of one-stop shopping implemented by American financial services companies provides impetus. If citizens can have, and will demand, that standard of service for one part of their lives, why not for others?

Interest grows throughout the federal information resources management community and among its clients. Federal employees become champions of this cause. In addition to speaking publicly about it, they sponsor projects.

In the Department of Agriculture, leaders of an "Easy Access" program develop several pilot projects to determine how to improve farmers' access to Agriculture's programs. Many farmers have computers, and one project focuses on providing automated procedures through which farmers review the status of their governmental accounts. Another project pilots one-stop contact with all programs represented in a departmental field office.

The Departments of Defense and Veterans Affairs begin work to determine how to provide information about future veterans to Veterans Affairs so that it can prepare to provide benefits expeditiously. Without such progress, new veterans must prove their eligibility for benefits to Veterans Affairs, based on information known to the Defense Department but not to Veterans Affairs.

Along with initiating the entire "service to the citizen" movement, GSA sponsors three specific studies. The areas examined are retirement benefits, mortgage programs, and business loans. Two of the studies are led by people on loan from the Department of the Treasury. In each of the three areas, several agencies provide similar services and other agencies provide information about the programs. The studies conclude that

- Federal agencies are becoming more customer-service-oriented.
- Federal agencies have a vertical paradigm focus with few Peer Paradigm partnerships between providers of similar services.
- Citizens turn to nonfederal sources for information on federal programs.
- Federal agency use of information technology for customer-service improvements have focused on internal improvements to systems and processes.
- External use of technology for customer service is limited.

A report (General Services Administration, 1993) identifies opportunities to simplify and standardize procedures and to explain programs more clearly and fully to the public.

In mid-1993, more than 150 representatives from federal, state, and local governments and corporations attend a service to the citizen conference. The conference's recommendations focus on developing central leadership for improving services governmentwide, encouraging public participation in fostering improvements, and moving toward one-stop shopping for information.

The service to the citizen movement generates public attention when a national magazine cites "Improv[ing] communications among the many agencies whose work overlaps to provide 'one-stop shopping' for citizens seeking information and aid" as a major objective for improving government (Gleckman, 1993). The movement provides momentum to the federal National Performance Review.

The General Services Administration encourages the federal community to explore the opportunity to enhance the skills of all federal *people* and organizations in making and implementing decisions. Paralleling the service to the citizen program to enhance the results of government, an informationproficiency program can provide the internal improvements needed to support better results of any type. As a step in this direction, the Department of Defense Information Resources Management College adds to its Advanced Management Program class sessions devoted to evaluating the decision making that led to two unfortunate results, the last launch of the space shuttle *Challenger* and the shooting down of a civilian airliner over the Persian Gulf. Also, GSA initiates a baseline study of aspects of federal information proficiency (Personnel Research and Development Center, 1994).

The federal information resources management community extends its tradition of upgrading its own information proficiency by creating and providing education programs open to the entire community. The General Services Administration runs a program to enhance the skills of managers of large acquisition projects. It adds one program to educate contracting officers and another to train managers in the implementation of large projects. It also begins a program that encourages colleges to offer graduate programs tailored to the needs of federal employees who lead information resources management endeavors. In the spirit of the Peer Paradigm (Fig. 4–2), GSA fosters personal networking and mutual assistance among graduates of each of these programs. The Department of Commerce starts a series of monthly meetings, each highlighting progress in the development and use of a new technology. The Departments of Defense and Agriculture, along with GSA and others, offer other training in various aspects of information resources management.

The information resources management community makes and supports decisions to move some activities from the realm of *mission-specific,* or *organization-specific, information* to that of *general,* or *generic, information* (Fig. 10–2). The General Services Administration supplies generic software supporting the Joint Financial Management Improvement Project's endeavors to promote standardizing financial management practices. In the Department of Defense, information resources managers sponsor a Corporate Information Management initiative, with objectives, among others, to standardize internal business processes and unify supporting information systems—there seems to be little need to maintain several similar systems for generic administrative functions. The Department of Commerce develops a catalog of federal databases of general interest.

The community takes a number of steps to capture opportunities for deploying *technology* throughout the government. For example, GSA provides a new nationwide long-distance telecommunications service that reduces federal costs by hundreds of millions of dollars per year. Also, agencies band together in a GSA-sponsored endeavor to acquire services for making overseas phone calls from the United States. First, the Department of State leads a task force that determines the government's overall needs. The resulting procurement, accomplished by the Department of Defense, creates price reductions of 20 to 60 percent, depending on the phone call considered.

Another project provides personal computer software allowing people to send sensitive, but unclassified, data securely over normal telecommunications lines. Also, agencies pool resources to acquire backup computing facilities for use in case of emergencies. Another program is undertaken to acquire mainframe computers as commodities that can be ordered quickly and inexpensively by any agency. In addition to fostering projects aimed at satisfying needs governmentwide, GSA encourages agencies initiating acquisitions for their individual needs to structure the procurements so that other agencies can place orders using the contracts that will be awarded. The goals of these "one for all" procurements include lower costs and less pre- and post-procurement overhead for both government and industry.

The federal government takes a leading role in fostering the development and deployment of information technologies for people with disabilities. Many federal agencies, state and local governments, and foreign countries gain practical insight from GSA's practices, seminars, and documents (Buckholtz and Parks, 1991).

This example from the U. S. federal government demonstrates that an information resources management community can not only build appropriate cooperation within itself to support its nominal objectives but can also extend its role to catalyze needed improvements in the attainment of organizational objectives and in the information proficiency of both organizations and individuals.

Unfortunately, this example is not indicative of the roles of information resources communities in many organizations. Often, the information resources community is, at best, reactive to demands placed by constituents and focuses mainly on operating and upgrading technology.

THE CEO'S VIEW OF INFORMATION TECHNOLOGY—WHERE IS THE GOOD NEWS?

Put yourself in the shoes of today's senior business or government executive. Then ask yourself two questions: What do I know about information technology? What do I hear about information technology?

Chances are that the executive has little education in, or feel for, the subject. Compared to finance, personnel, purchasing, public relations, and law, information technology (IT) is a relatively unfamiliar staff function.

Senior executives form perceptions based on material they read in newspapers and business magazines. Much of the news on IT has been negative: volatile financial performance of vendors, including one's own sources of technology and services; vendor rivalries and alliances, formed over seemingly incomprehensible issues; and projects that went awry. Magazines and newspapers feature articles on the "technology of the future," but so often the technology is described in incomprehensible jargon, cannot be verified as representing a sound investment, or is not available in the marketplace. Vendors' advertisements feature technology but seldom show how it improves the performance of businesses that deploy it.

An executive does not have to be an expert on information technology. Leaders delegate and rely on subordinates for recommendations and independent action. Again, the news is likely to be unfavorable. Many corporate IT groups are focused on keeping "backroom" operations running. Often, IT management is more likely to ask for budget to meet tactical demands than to talk with the chief executive about how information resources management can provide a basis for new or improved corporate products and services that will enhance the firm's competitiveness in years to come.

So the executive sees IT as unfamiliar, costly, and fraught with uncertainty and risk of failure for those who trust in its promise. Indeed, while wanting better information about marketplaces and competitors, the executive may be unable even to connect those needs to the potential for information technologists to help fulfill them.

Ultimately, that senior executive will choose between IT-intensive proposals and IT-nonintensive ones. That decision may come during budgeting or during evaluations regarding the potential acquisition of another firm. It may come during preparation for divesting or winding down a division.

With today's knowledge and perceptions, it is all too likely that the executive will discount the potential for IT-intensive investments or operations. That executive will find it easier to choose either to make investments intensive in people or traditional facilities or to earmark additional funds for return to the company's owners.

Yet the ramifications of *not* investing in IT may be lost information proficiency and competitive advantage.

So where is the good news? The good news is locked away in the untold experiences of many past IT bottom-line successes and the true visions of future ones. It is locked away with untold stories of improving the performance and skill levels of employees and groups. Also, it is hidden by the propensity of almost everyone to discuss information technology, not information resources, and certainly not information proficiency.

Society can recognize IT's potential. An important first step is for people to talk about the successes, benefits achieved, and the true potential of IT. Almost everyone has experienced a success—almost no business can compete today without using modern information technology. Individuals know the successes but if people don't talk about them, society does not see the overall picture.

Also, the good news is locked away in the experience of IT professionals. The IT community needs to market its potential. The professional in an IT-using business, the marketeer for an IT vendor, the advertising professional hired to develop commercials for an IT vendor, the consultant, the academic . . . all can steer conversation and writings toward the benefits that can be achieved through IT.

Soon other communities will catch on. For example, people working in the news media can well appreciate their own successes based on IT: regional editions of newspapers and broadcasts, attractive graphics and animation, photographs and video footage received from around the world, and last-minute editing for late-breaking stories. News successes depend on IT successes, and there is common ground from which to begin to obtain news coverage of IT successes. Indeed, business magazines are now beginning to highlight IT success stories.

Eventually, the tide will turn. The IT community will be known for its roles in improving corporate performance; enhancing governmental services to citizens; building the information proficiency and contributions of all employees; and freeing people to pursue the most important, least routine activities, whether in the workplace, community, or home.

These then become the perceptions about, and the roles for, IT. Everyone wins. Corporations and governments enhance products, services, and competitive posture by choosing and benefiting from IT-intensive projects. People lead more attractive lives, at work and away from it. Information technology vendors are more successful, selling appreciated products and services in an expanded market-place.

There is good news about IT. And there is good reason to propagate it.

MAXIMIZING THE VALUE OF THE INFORMATION RESOURCES COMMUNITY*

While the world's *information technology* community works on establishing its worth to chief executive officers and others, there remains the broader opportunity for organizations' *information resources* communities to enhance their value to their clients.

Does an organization's information resources and systems function have a strategic future? Before you automatically nod yes, consider that every information systems activity can be, and is increasingly being, performed by contractors and clients. "Outsourcing" examples abound and encompass selecting and operating technology, maintaining and replacing long-standing information systems, developing new systems, training, and providing information services. Even business reengineering falls in line—consultants and empowered employees suggest and implement change.

Unless something is done, the information systems community is likely to be a casualty of its own success, with information resources managers and technologists destined to be people without whom a business cannot compete but who are perceived as fulfilling a second-class staff function providing commodity services.

Contrast the position of information resources with that of other staff functions such as finance and law. For the CEO, finance retains vitality based on issues such as profitability and the financial aspects

---

*Adapted from T. J. Buckholtz, 1994. Material similar to portions of this section appeared in *ComputerWorld*, February 7, 1994, p. 105. Re-used with permission of CW Publishing/Inc.

of potential business partnerships. Chief executive officers deal with legal issues such as maintaining a favorable regulatory climate. But all too often, information resources practitioners fail to capture opportunities to enhance their work, its value, and people's perceptions.

The products of all organizations are, or depend explicitly on, decisions and their implementation. Information resources professionals can help formulate and solve the who, what, when, why, and how of strategic decisions. They can catalyze improvements in communicating and implementing those decisions.

Can information resources groups achieve line status in their organizations? Can they achieve first-class staff status? Fortunately, the answers are yes.

Information systems groups have become profit centers by developing revenue-earning software products, systems integration services, or telecommunications services.

Achieving first-class staff status may seem difficult, but it need not be. Information resources group members have both great insight into their clients' activities and the potential to add commensurate value. For example, the federal information resources management community sparked a movement to improve governmental services to citizens.

Information resources groups can play key roles in decisions about forming business alliances; much of the value of a partnership lies in its information proficiency, for example, the ability to share information. Or, as noted earlier, information resources practitioners can actively facilitate the making and implementing of strategic, nonroutine decisions.

The information resources community must recognize that its overall contribution is fostering information proficiency (Figs. 1–1 and 5–2). By focusing on business goals and synergy between people and organizations, information resources professionals can become coaches for, and partners in, the most important decisions.

If they prove their worth in fostering improved information proficiency for strategic decisions, information resources professionals will add needed value and can achieve the status of a first-class support function—indeed, they can become an integral part of general management.

The time has come for the information resources community to show its true potential.

REFERENCES

Buckholtz, Thomas J., 1994. Maximizing IS' value to the organization. *ComputerWorld*, February 7, 1994, p. 105.

Buckholtz, Thomas J., and Parks, Judith A., 1991. *Managing Information Resources for Accessibility*. U. S. General Services Administration, Washington, DC.

General Services Administration, 1993. *Service to the Citizens, Project Report*. U. S. General Services Administration, Washington, DC.

Gleckman, Howard, 1993. A productivity junkie takes on fat city. *BusinessWeek* July 5, 1993, pp. 76–78.

McDonough, Francis A., and Buckholtz, Thomas J. 1992. Providing better service to citizens with information technology. *Journal of Systems Management,* April 1992, pp. 32–40.

McDonough, Francis A., and Trenkle, Anthony F., 1993. Emergence of the Service to the Citizen Movement. *THE PUBLIC MANAGER * The New Bureaucrat,* Winter 1993–94, pp. 39–42.

Personnel Research and Development Center, 1994. *Report on the Survey of Information Proficiency of Federal Employees (draft)*. U. S. Office of Personnel Management, Washington, DC.

CHAPTER 12

Energizing the Information Resources Community: Assessment

Assessment *tools provide a basis for analyzing and improving the value added to an organization by its information resources management practitioners and, indeed, by other functional components.*

POSITIONING INFORMATION RESOURCES LEADERSHIP: A HISTORY

For several decades, organizations have grappled with the question of how to organize the people who lead information resources activities. In the 1950s, 1960s, and 1970s, companies recognized centers of information systems activity in administrative and operations-supporting computer centers. The former included programming staffs and dealt with financial, personnel, and other administrative recordkeeping. The latter either included a programming staff or just provided computer capacity used by clients to program and run their own engineering or other work. Other hubs of information resources activity, including libraries, records centers, and office services groups, evolved independently from each other and from computer systems groups.

Recognition of the importance of computing grew. Eventually, many organizations established an officer-level job to spearhead computing. As telecommunications evolved from telephony into a combination of data and voice communications, the administration of telecommunications came under the same officer. The main telecommunications challenges and opportunities featured moving data between computer systems and between systems and terminals on employees' desks.

A question of the perception of this function arose. Work led by a person with a title like vice president for information systems is often perceived as a second-class staff function. In this context, information systems are not information, and information is neither a strategic decision nor a bottom-line result. This "management information systems" function was often seen more as a cost center than as a source of competitive advantage.

In the era of the chief executive officer and the chief financial officer, some organizations began calling the information systems officer a *chief information officer,* or CIO. Advocates of this title want to denote a function that is more encompassing than simply providing technology or even managing information resources. The title represents a vision of a member of the senior management team who participates in the key decisions of the organization.

In some organizations, the deployment of personal computers led to challenges to the need for a management information systems director, let alone a CIO. The new technology seemed to offer an alternative to expensive technology and to long waits for upgrades to be programmed into administrative systems. Individuals in various parts of the organization could "do IT themselves," or at least some of IT for their own work groups. Some people viewed the CIO concept with suspicion, thinking that it represented an attempt to prolong an obsolete function.

Independent of the title and status of one particular job, enhanced information proficiency and improved information resources management represent significant potentials for organizations.

Taking a broad perspective, an organization is best served if it considers at least its entire workforce as its information-proficiency and resources staff. All employees work with and through information; therefore, all contribute in these areas. Employees develop new procedures and systems to improve their effectiveness and, ultimately, that of the organization. Employees use Just Ask . . . techniques to teach each other new skills. It is likely that many outside sources, including contractors and commercial database services, are involved. This entire resource contributes to improving the firm's information proficiency and, hence, its competitiveness.

Employees who develop information systems represent a unique resource for organizationwide improvements. These employees learn extant flows and quality of work and information. They can come together as a Peer Paradigm community (Fig. 4–2) to spot opportunities to reengineer the business by improving existing processes. They can call attention to underutilized value in the organization's information resources, as well as outside sources of data; such value can and should facilitate developing new or improved products and marketing techniques that enhance the organization's competitiveness. They can recognize the next steps an organization can and should take in its Information Age journey (Fig. 4–3). Finally, they can accomplish beneficial change.

The question need not be about a job title; the question is whether information-proficiency and resources activities organizationwide realize their potential to bring about improvement. Each individual can participate, in a local work group or on a widespread project team, in the type of Peer Paradigm leadership role envisioned in the title *chief information officer.*

If there is a CIO, the value of that job is determined by how well the incumbent furthers information proficiency throughout the organization. The same can be said of centralized information resources groups, as well as of dispersed groups of information resources experts.

ASSESSING THE OPPORTUNITY

Most organizations view information resources management as a staff function. A hypothetical chief executive's perceptions of various other staff functions (Fig. 12–1) are based on personal interactions with those functions and their leaders, as well as knowledge of the functions' contributions to the organization's and executive's success. Some functions and their leaders coach the executive frequently on key matters; others suggest new ideas or provide information from time to time; yet others are seldom found in the executive suite. The executive takes an interest in a function to the extent that it contributes to personal information proficiency, that is, the executive's setting and achieving of organizational and personal goals.

Each of the staff functions listed has great importance. Most contribute bottom-line successes; for example, innovative purchasing saves much money. A failure in any one function can lead to severe problems for the executive and the entire organization; for example, a facilities failure cripples work. Some of the functions, such as legal, add considerable value directly for the executive, perhaps even daily updates and advice on crucial matters. Others come to the fore under certain circumstances; for example, human resources may achieve "coach" status when the executive is filling a key position. Still others

Executive: Autonomously takes strategic action on my behalf
- None (applies to some line functions, but no staff functions)

Coach: Understands the game; facilitates my doing the "right thing"; rehearses me for important endeavors
- Finance
- Legal
- Public affairs
- Executive assistant

Analyst: Generates new ideas independently; responds to my general questions
- Corporate planning
- Human resources
- Tax
- Treasury
- Internal audit

Librarian: Provides expected and unexpected useful information, on request
- Administration
- Corporate secretary
- Administrative assistant

Clerk: Processes transactions; provides useful data
- Purchasing
- Accounting
- Shareholder relations
- Correspondence control

Technician: Keeps things running
- Facilities
- Physical security

FIGURE 12–1   A Hypothetical Executive's Categorization of Staff Functions.

run virtually out of sight for long periods of time. Yet none of the functions listed earns the "executive" rating achieved by some of the organization's business units.

There is a rating method (Fig. 12–2) you can use to assess the values added by the leader of an organization's information resources community for its various constituents within the organization:

- Superiors, such as the chief executive.
- Peers.
- Subordinates working in the leader's group.
- Clients not falling into one of the previous categories.
- Other constituents.

Patterned after the characterization of staff functions (Fig. 12–1), this method can be applied to determine perceptions of value added within an organization by any individual or group, including people and units that are not information resources management practitioners. No matter to what group or individual you apply the methodology, use the ratings tabulation form (Fig. 12–3) to summarize results.

With an assessment in hand, an individual's or group's challenge is to move upward toward executive for most, if not all, of its constituents. For an information resources leader or community, various functions pertain at each level from "technician" to executive (Fig. 12–4). The functions and levels can be correlated (Table 12–1) with their closest matches in the Information Age framework (Fig. 2–1). The challenge is to provide new, higher-value-adding contributions while ensuring continued improvement in traditional services.

THREE LEADERSHIP ROLES

People typically spot two contributions for a staff function: *regulation* and *service*.

Consider a purchasing department. Its regulatory role includes set-

Function or person rated: _____

My relationship to the function or person being rated is (check the first one that applies):

_____ Superior: The function or person reports to me
_____ Peer: The function or person works with me
_____ Subordinate: I work for the function or person
_____ Client: The function or person works for me
_____ Other: _____

For my needs, the function or person is a/an (rank all those that apply, with 1 for "most typical"; provide examples for each that applies):

_____ Executive: Autonomously takes strategic action on my behalf

_____ Coach: Understands the game; facilitates my doing the "right thing"; rehearses me for important endeavors

_____ Analyst: Generates new ideas independently; responds to my general questions

_____ Librarian: Provides expected and unexpected useful information, on request

_____ Clerk: Process transactions; provides useful data

_____ Technician: Keeps things running

Remarks:

Rated by: _____ Date: _____

FIGURE 12–2   Rating a Chief Information Officer (or Other Leader or Function).

Function or person rated: _____

Number of ratings by each of the following:
- _____ (sup)   Superiors
- _____ (per)   Peers
- _____ (sub)   Subordinates
- _____ (cli)   Clients not falling into one of the above three categories
- _____ (oth)   Others, typically _____

Their views of the function or person being rated:

(ex) Executive: Autonomously takes strategic action on my behalf

(co) Coach: Understands the game; facilitates my doing the "right thing"; rehearses me for important endeavors

(an) Analyst: Generates new ideas independently; responds to my general questions

(li) Librarian: Provides expected and unexpected useful information, on request

(cl) Clerk: Processes transactions; provides useful data

(te) Technician: Keeps things running

Summary of ratings by how typical (1 = most typical) is a type of behavior (circle all that apply):

Ratings by:

	(sup)	(per)	(sub)	(cli)	(oth)
(ex)	1 2 3 4	1 2 3 4	1 2 3 4	1 2 3 4	1 2 3 4
(co)	1 2 3 4	1 2 3 4	1 2 3 4	1 2 3 4	1 2 3 4
(an)	1 2 3 4	1 2 3 4	1 2 3 4	1 2 3 4	1 2 3 4
(li)	1 2 3 4	1 2 3 4	1 2 3 4	1 2 3 4	1 2 3 4
(cl)	1 2 3 4	1 2 3 4	1 2 3 4	1 2 3 4	1 2 3 4
(te)	1 2 3 4	1 2 3 4	1 2 3 4	1 2 3 4	1 2 3 4

Remarks:

Tabulated by: _____   Date: _____

FIGURE 12–3   Ratings Tabulation for a Chief Information Officer (or Other Leader or Function).

Executive (ex): Executive Vice President and Chief Information Officer

- Earns suitable profits through external sales of information services.
- Leads successful development of the information proficiency of the entire organization, including the senior management team.

Coach (co): Senior Vice President and Chief Information Officer

- Contributes general perspective and wisdom, commensurate with those of other officers.
- Fosters opportunities to create products and services enhanced by information proficiency.
- Provides a full spectrum of information-proficiency enhancement services to most components of the organization.
- Catalyzes organizationwide integration, growth, utility, and shared use of the organization's information resources, including data, processes, and wisdom.
- Fosters synergy between groups within the organization and between the organization and its customers and suppliers.
- Initiates and leads endeavors to reengineer operations outside the CIO's own jurisdiction.
- Ensures corporate flexibility to affect mergers, acquisitions, reorganizations, and divesting of business units; participates in decisions leading to such; and has an active role in effecting such.

Analyst (an): Senior Vice President, Information Resources

- Suggests ideas for the reengineering of operations outside the CIO's own jurisdiction.
- Ensures corporate flexibility to reengineer operations, reorganize divisions, and divest business units.
- Provides advice, before a merger or acquisition, regarding the state of the other organization's information proficiency and how the two entities will merge data and processes after the take-over.
- Finds and reports new opportunities for the overall organization, based on the organization's information and outside trends.

FIGURE 12–4   Functions and Images of a Chief Information Officer.

Librarian (li): Vice President, Information Resources

- Ensures that the organization's information is easy to use.
- Supplies the information from internal and external sources.
- Ensures the security of the organization's information.

Clerk (cl): Vice President, Information Systems

- Ensures that business transaction data and other types of information are handled well.
- Develops software to meet specifications provided by clients.

Technician (te): Manager, Information Technology and Services

- Ensures that the organization uses appropriates, cost-effective information systems and services and that those systems and services perform well.

FIGURE 12–4   (Continued)

ting standards for purchases made by the organization. The standards define procedures for managing competitive bids and the circumstances under which individual groups can acquire something on their own. The purchasing department also has a service role. Typically, it handles most "large" or complex acquisitions and conducts acquisitions for supplies and equipment needed by many components of the organization.

A human resources department has two similar roles. As a regulator, it sets standards governing such personnel practices as hiring and promoting. It may also set the maximum number of employees that each organizational component can have. As a service provider, a human resources department supports or conducts searches for new employees and ensures that the organization has employee health and retirement plans.

People readily spot two similar roles for information resources departments. As a regulator, an information resources management function may set standards regarding topics, such as the following,

TABLE 12–1   CHIEF INFORMATION OFFICER FUNCTIONS AND THE
INFORMATION AGE FRAMEWORK

Chief Information Officer Function	Information Age Framework Element
Executive (ex)	Goals and results
Coach (co)	People and information proficiency
Analyst (an)	Information and information resources management
Librarian (li)	Information and information resources management
Clerk (cl)	Information systems
Technician (te)	Technology

throughout the Information Age framework (Fig. 2–1) and Peer Paradigm (Fig. 4–2):

- Results standards for people who produce information-based products such as analyses and reports.
- Procedural standards to raise people's skill levels, govern developing spreadsheets and other "informal" software, and protect sensitive information.
- Data standards regarding the content, quality, and handling of information.
- Standards for managing information systems.
- Technology standards, such as types of equipment the organization will use.

As a service provider, an information resources function typically emphasizes providing and maintaining technology and providing data processed and stored by information technology.

The apparent mismatch between setting standards at all five levels in the Information Age framework and providing services mainly at three levels presents both a problem and an opportunity. Clients seldom want to be regulated by a group that does not visibly provide services in areas it regulates.

The information resources organization has the opportunity to expand its services in the areas of results and people. As an initiator of information-proficiency improvements, the information resources community can:

- Catalyze improved processes, both for repetitive work and ad hoc decisions.
- Foster development of human potential throughout the organization, including:
  Enhancing the capabilities of individuals and groups.
  Building synergy between groups.

Thus, there are natural roles to take with respect to *people*. There are also strong, beneficial opportunities with respect to overall organizational *results,* including:

- Generating bottom-line benefits through improvements in the organization's products, services, and internal operations.
- Catalyzing, through support and participation, information-proficiency improvements in decisions strategic to the organization and its components.
- Earning profits through external sales of information services.

An information resources management department or community that captures these opportunities is creating a third area of endeavor. Beyond regulation and service, it is engaging in *catalytic leadership*. Also, it is earning the designations of coach and executive (Fig. 12–4).

There is also a perceptual opportunity. Too often, people engaged in regulatory activity miss the opportunity to behave as if their work is a service and to market their activities in the same spirit. Beneficial regulation is a service, especially in the field of information resources management. Most clients focus on getting their jobs done and do not want to spend much time selecting technology and developing standards governing information and technology practice. Most clients want to be provided with beneficial standards and to adhere to them when they are reasonable. If a standard seems inadequate, at least it provides a basis for evaluating change.

Today, the successful information resources management department or community treats its regulatory responsibilities as opportunities to provide beneficial service to its clients. Tomorrow, the successful information resources community will provide catalytic leadership key to enhancing and achieving the missions of its clientele.

13

Energizing the Information Resources Community: Activation

Activating *a program to enhance the value contributed by an information resources community focuses on planning and initiating specific projects, as well as uniting that community.*

SELECTING OPPORTUNITIES

On top of assessing the "supply side" potential for information resources communities to provide new, value-adding services, it is crucial to plan around appropriate "demand side" client opportunities in which improved information proficiency and information resources management will add maximal value.

Using information-proficiency assessments (Fig. 7–4), considering opportunities throughout the Peer Paradigm (Fig. 4–2), and having knowledge of competitive posture (Fig. 7–3), you should be able to identify good candidates for improvement projects.

Validation of candidate projects can also include assessment of client leadership. Use the following rating technique to sharpen your estimates of the chances of success for each potential project and, therefore, to help in setting priorities for tackling opportunities.

RATING A MANAGER REGARDING INFORMATION RESOURCES MANAGEMENT

The behavior of any manager regarding a support function is crucial to the success of that function and to the overall success of the organization the person leads. Information resources management is a support function performed by all people in an organization. Most organizations also receive information resources services from outside groups.

You can rate any manager and thereby understand how that person's attitudes and behaviors influence the success of information resources management within the person's jurisdiction:

- You can use such a measurement to determine the likelihood of success of an information-proficiency or information-resources-management improvement project involving that person's group.

- Also, possibly in other circumstances:

    You can use such a measurement to advance your understanding of the climate of an organization in which you work.

    You can rate a leader to determine how to maximize your effectiveness if you are marketing information technology services to that person's organization.

    If you lead an organization, you can rate yourself.

    If you work on your own, you can rate your leadership of your one-person organization.

If you apply the following questionnaire to a leader of an organization producing products or services based on computers, telecommunications, or other information technology, take care to distinguish behavior related to managing the organization from behavior related to the external customers for the organization's products and services. The focus here is the former; the manager's behavior may be quite different regarding the latter.

Choose an organization and think about the leader. Consider the following multiple-choice statements. For each, select the option that best applies. The manager's familiarity and comfort with information technology:

1. Are low.
2. Are moderate but less than those with accounting, contracting, and other support techniques.
3. Are good and on a par with those for other support techniques.

The manager's familiarity and comfort with the concepts of information resources management:

1. Are low.
2. Are moderate but less than those with finance, procurement, personnel, and other support functions.
3. Are good and on a par with those for other support functions.

The manager's perspective toward information systems emphasizes:

1. Cost.
2. Operational necessity.
3. A balance of value added and cost.

The information the manager receives about information resources management and information technology from within the organization:

1. Is full of jargon.
2. Emphasizes operational necessities.
3. Is visionary with respect to the future of the organization.

Upon seeing a vendor's newspaper or magazine advertisement that emphasizes new computer technology with enhanced "power," the manager is likely to:

1. Clip the ad and send it to subordinates.
2. Ignore the ad.
3. Wonder when vendors' advertisements will more often feature the role of technology in business successes.

The manager's reading about information technology:

1. Emphasizes technology and products.
2. Emphasizes negatives, such as failed projects and volatile financial performance of vendors.
3. Provides a balanced perspective of business and technological opportunities and risks.

In evaluating news reports of volatile financial performance by information technology vendors, failed information technology projects, shifting vendor alliances over potential technological standards, and prototype technology not available in the marketplace, the manager:

1. Views using information technology as unquestionably risky.
2. Views using information technology as likely to be a risky venture.
3. Seeks and uses perspective that includes other organizations' successes and the potential for success within the organization through information technology.

Formulate the picture you are developing about this manager. Use the rating matrix (Fig. 13–1) to help clarify your thinking. The rows represent the manager's knowledge. The columns represent actions

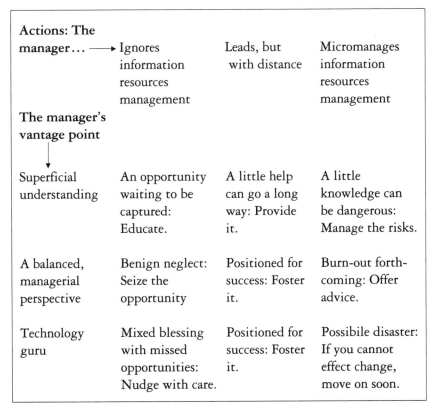

Actions: The manager... ⟶	Ignores information resources management	Leads, but with distance	Micromanages information resources management
The manager's vantage point ↓			
Superficial understanding	An opportunity waiting to be captured: Educate.	A little help can go a long way: Provide it.	A little knowledge can be dangerous: Manage the risks.
A balanced, managerial perspective	Benign neglect: Seize the opportunity	Positioned for success: Foster it.	Burn-out forth-coming: Offer advice.
Technology guru	Mixed blessing with missed opportunities: Nudge with care.	Positioned for success: Foster it.	Possibile disaster: If you cannot effect change, move on soon.

FIGURE 13–1. Rating a Manager on Information Resources Management and Finding the Best Opportunity.

the manager typically takes. The nine elements provide advice to you as a current or potential provider of service to the manager's group.

UNITING THE INFORMATION RESOURCES COMMUNITY

Aside from the support that information technologists supply to other staff functions, organizations typically have yet to build synergy between their computer and telecommunications organizations and their other information resources groups, such as librarians, records managers, legal researchers, and marketplace researchers.

While effective information resources management is crucial to an organization's success, today there is often little likelihood that a chief executive will pay special attention to the details of this function. The executive agenda is dominated by other topics such as profitability and financial survival, changes in customers' wants, impending mergers and acquisitions, and legal proceedings (Fig. 12–1).

Thus, the agenda for the information technology community lies not so much in the hands of the chief executive as in the hands of various clients and itself. Pursuing a strategy of "out of sight, out of mind" may be easy, but it is fraught with risks. Short tenures for chief information officers are but one aspect of that risk. Divesting essentially all the computing and telecommunications function is a real possibility.

The future, therefore, lies in actions taken by the systems, computing, and telecommunications group itself.

The information technology community must ally itself closely with the other information resources practitioners. These practitioners should welcome opportunities to maximize their potential through earlier use of new techniques and technology, to learn new fields for future career growth, and to be associated with work and organizations that often draw higher pay than their own.

Also, similar alliances must extend beyond professional information resources practitioners in information resources staff groups.

Everyone in an organization manages information resources. Nonpractitioners will welcome opportunities to link themselves more closely to information technologists in order to serve their customers better and to further their own careers.

To provide maximal value to its clients and derive maximal satisfaction therefrom, an organization's information resources community must develop its own information proficiency, including unity of goals, synergy among its people, and sharing of information.

There is much to be done. The Peer Paradigm (Fig. 4–2) provides guidance. The All A's program (Fig. 7–1) provides a method. Only individual initiative is needed to get started.

OPTIMIZING HUMAN RESOURCES—WHO SHOULD DO WHAT?

Success for an information resources management program depends on attention to many issue areas, among them organizational goals, people, information, and technology. Within each area are many issues to confront and decisions to make. As in any group activity, one of the keys to success in information resources management is to choose the appropriate application of people, their time, and their skills.

Imagine that your job is to design an office automation program for a business with thousands of employees, spread out geographically. The company's work encompasses a number of engineering and administrative fields. Imagine the period during which that business was about to deploy personal computers for the first time.

The company's computing skills and technology are as follows. Some of the engineers can program problems to run on mainframe computers. These and other engineers run these and other programs. Some engineers have no access to computers. Administrative work is done based on printouts and on-line displays; the supporting programming is handled by the then-traditional single administrative programming group. Some secretaries use word processors.

Don't start right in worrying about what types of microcomputers or spreadsheet software packages to choose. Your focus is on who will do what, including who will choose the technology.

Try a broad approach. Who will be responsible for the results, the bottom-line improvement for the organization? Who will be responsible for information? Who will be responsible for technology?

These can be difficult questions. You can start by using the framework for the Information Age (Fig. 2–1). By considering the information resources management community as a support, or staff, function to all other activities of the organization, you can divide the work of the organization into two categories: line and support. Any person can do some of each type of work; nevertheless, for most employees, the preponderance of work emphasizes only one of the two categories. You can call people dedicated mostly to line work "clients," clients of information resources projects. You can call "practitioners" those people who spend most of their time providing and maintaining information tools and information technology. Of course, information resources practitioners may work in client groups.

While all employees should contribute to setting an organization's goals and while technology can contribute opportunities, the responsibility for setting and accomplishing the broad goals of the organization lies on the client side of the "divide."

In the example, there is not yet a statement of corporate mission and goals. Does this mean that the information resources management leadership should postpone making a statement about corporate office automation goals? Even if it does not make a statement about goals, that leadership can make a statement of principles for office automation endeavors.

What about information? The responsibility lies with clients. Practitioners can make the job easier by providing reliable, helpful systems but, ultimately, the clients must provide, review, accept, use, and rely on the information. Practitioners can also add value by setting standards for information, especially information shared among groups in the organization.

In the example, some information standards have been set for the existing mainframe- and minicomputer-based systems. The standards include "data definitions"; for example, the systems use a standard number of characters to store employees' last names. The standards also include quality control for the information. Personal computers will not be attached to those systems for a few years. Clients will be developing their own spreadsheets and databases.

You might choose a strong policy involving a concerted attempt to standardize data elements and information quality.

Or you might choose a hands-off policy. In this scenario, clients are responsible for their own work and must continue to support the quality and value of the information and processes of the traditional systems. Because there is little automated transfer of data between the traditional systems and the new ones, you can expect inconsistencies. Perhaps the best you can do is to encourage the clients to share their work, thereby avoiding some inconsistencies and simplifying conversion work in the future, when the local computers will become part of a network connecting most of the organization's computers.

What about technology? At one end of the technology spectrum is the special-purpose software developed or acquired by one group to meet a unique need. In this case, the most practical solution may be to let the clients take responsibility, with the understanding that practitioners are available to consult.

At the other end of the spectrum is off-the-shelf technology that will be used throughout the organization. The issues include potential benefits to be derived, the quality of the technology itself, and relations with vendors—each in the near term and potentially for years into the future. The topic of benefits involves real anticipated uses, ease of learning, and ease of use; these are client issues for which practitioners can add insight. The external quality of the technology is also a client topic. The internal quality, the potential for subsequent improved products, and the potential to work well with other products are practitioners' issues, for which knowledgeable clients may add insight. To the extent that the organization seeks technology standardization and coordinated purchasing, the vendor relations topic is best left to the practitioners.

In the specific example, it is reasonable to assume that some of the clients are enthusiastic about generic technology suitable for widespread use. These people want to learn how to use the technology, may have computers at home, and have ideas for immediate benefits in their work groups. The organization should benefit from that enthusiasm without losing the benefits of the practitioners' desires to ensure the best long-term automation program. That program depends on the eventual working together of many current and future technological systems and subsystems in order to facilitate widespread teamwork and consistency.

No matter how significantly your thoughts differ from the ones described here, there probably is still a pattern: The more specific an issue is to a mission of the organization, the higher will be level of client involvement.

CHAPTER 14

Energizing the Information Resources Community: Achievement

*E*xamples of information resources management community achievement demonstrate that successful practitioners catalyze information-proficiency improvements for their clients and themselves. These practitioners create opportunities by appropriately raising their constituents' expectations.

LEADERSHIP AND SUCCESS—A SECOND EXAMPLE

Information resources communities can significantly enhance the effectiveness of the organizations they serve. Here is an example involving the introduction of personal computers and other forms of office automation into an energy utility with tens of thousands of employees. As well as enhancing information proficiency and producing significant tangible results, this office technology project beneficially changes aspects of the culture of the company.

When this example starts, the company has some word processors but no personal computers. A computer department runs the company's mainframe computers, providing complete systems for administrative use and programmable systems for engineering clients. This department has the corporate authority and budget for office automation; it also has a small "office technology project" *group*.

The time has come for the company to consider using personal computers. Software and hardware are proving useful for businesses. People in various parts of the company envision how automation projects can make improvements in their departments.

Several steps launch the office automation program into the era of personal computers. The steps address key focal points: goals and results, people and information proficiency, information resources, mission-specific information and technology, generic information and technology, and the roles of the computer department and its office automation group (Figs. 2–1, 10–2, and 12–4).

To encourage a focus on *goals and results*, the office automation group publishes a simple form to be used to request technology. The form calls for a short project description, a simple estimate of quantitative benefits, an optional statement of qualitative benefits, and a description of technological needs. Requesters must describe technology in terms of needed numbers of systems and general features, not specific products. Use of the form assures all parties that the company can benefit from a project. The information on a form provides a focus around which the group can work with a client to capture the particular opportunity, understand the potential for office automation throughout the company, and deliver technology appropriate to both opportunities. Requests are made sometimes by a line department and sometimes by a staff department on behalf of its line constituents. The discussion of requests establishes cooperation and mutual understanding between the computer department and its clients.

The group does not make an overall statement about anticipated results; it does, however, issue a statement of principles. The computer department publishes and speaks with its clients about these principles:

1. Meet individual and departmental needs, both those needs that are common throughout the company and those that are specialized.
2. Deploy easy-to-use systems.
3. Encourage self-sufficiency for organizations and people using technology.
4. Foster integration of processes and technology.
5. Foster flexibility for accomplishing and sharing work and for taking advantage of changing technology.
6. Integrate office-automation-based information into the company's overall information resources.
7. Promote proper sequencing and timing of progress.

The principles stimulate dialogue and understanding. They are also used to resolve differences. For example, some departments try to formulate their needs in terms of specific technologies outside the standards that are developing within the company. The principles serve to focus discussion on exploring a need in terms of corporate benefit, not specific technology, and in terms of eventually linking systems and processes together. In some cases, agreement is reached to deploy special technology; in others, standard technology is used.

Regarding *people and information proficiency*, the group notices employees throughout the company volunteering to champion office automation. Some have specific visions of how to enhance the performance of their work groups. Others have general ideas and want to experiment. The company adopts the informal designation "office technology coordinator" to recognize the role these people play in helping their own departments and in sharing techniques and locally developed software. Peer Paradigm synergy and sharing is encouraged through coordinator meetings and informal contact. Initially, serving as an office technology coordinator means taking on this new responsibility on top of a traditional job.

Recognizing the roles of clients and coordinators, the group develops a Peer Paradigm "organization chart" for the company's office automation initiative (Fig. 14–1). The chart emphasizes that clients are the key constituents for office automation. Discussing the chart, along with the seven principles, encourages all employees to seek and adopt vital, appropriate roles in sponsoring corporate innovation.

Needs for education are addressed locally. In championing projects, coordinators provide on-the-job, Just Ask . . . assistance and training for their colleagues (Fig. 8–1). Departments designate other people to be informal sources of support. To the extent needed, these individuals receive training and support from the computer department.

Recognizing the value of innovation and improved information proficiency, organizations decide to formalize the roles of their office technology coordinators. With the help of the computer department, these organizations develop job descriptions and designate full-time coordinators. Some organizations develop staffs of a few coordinators. The computer department makes no move to bring these people under formal centralized jurisdiction. The office technology project group embraces and supports these project participants while avoiding controversy over "turf." Thus, the project wins allies and builds a beneficial "human infrastructure" throughout the utility.

One of the seven principles addresses the importance of corporate *information resources*. Recognizing the importance of local innovation, the company encourages development of applications and databases; however, no project can lead to an unplanned degradation of centralized systems.

Contrary to the general culture of the time, which focuses on debates as to how much access for reading centralized databases should be allowed to people using office automation, the company focuses on

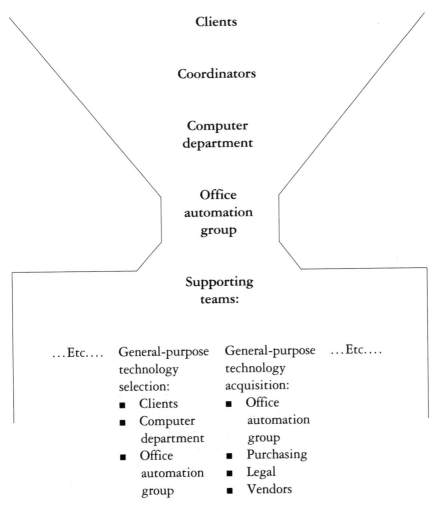

Clients

Coordinators

Computer
department

Office
automation
group

Supporting
teams:

…Etc.…	General-purpose technology selection:	General-purpose technology acquisition:	…Etc.…
	■ Clients	■ Office automation group	
	■ Computer department		
	■ Office automation group	■ Purchasing	
		■ Legal	
		■ Vendors	

Figure 14–1   A Peer Paradigm Organization Chart for Office Automation.

how to move the input of data for central databases away from the centralized systems and onto office automation. Office automation becomes the preferred means for entering data destined for corporate systems. The quality and usefulness of the central databases increases because of enhanced timeliness of updates and decreased incidence of errors in inputs.

Sharing of employee-developed information resources, whether data or processes, becomes commonplace. Office technology coordinators institute a library of company-developed software.

The group encourages individual departments to experiment with and acquire *mission-specific information and technology*, that is software, data, and hardware useful for the work of one function or department but not of much use to the rest of the company. Sometimes such information or technology is bought locally, with central help when requested. If the information or technology promises to have broader applicability, a department and the group determine how best to pursue the broad objectives. Mission-specific acquisitions include networks of early "workstations" and minisupercomputers used for designing and analyzing electric transmission networks.

The group chooses and acquires *generic information and technology*. It optimizes the timing of the company's entering into the use of new software and hardware technologies. Considerations include the ability of the company to take advantage of new techniques and the maturity of the marketplace for a new type of technology. People from client departments lead the evaluation of technology for usefulness and ease of use. Clients sometimes help evaluate the technical characteristics, and the long-term potential evolution, of products. Adding the perspectives of corporate strategies and of the business trade-off between potential deals, the group makes final decisions and conducts acquisitions.

To promote the sharing of mission-specific data and software through the standardization of generic software, and to contain the costs of generic software, the group pioneers the corporate license for personal computer software. Such licenses allow the copying and corporationwide use of the original software, covered by a one-time fee, with use limited to the business of the corporation. The licenses also include future upgrades, provided the company is current in paying the annual fee specified in the original contract.

The news media recognize the emergence of the organizationwide software license. Newspapers covering the computer marketplace interview group personnel and publish articles on this new business practice. The utility seizes the opportunity to publicize the practice, both to facilitate obtaining future software licenses and to enhance the corporation's image as a progressive, cost-conscious organization. News coverage expands. Regional newspapers cover the licensing practice. Computer newspapers feature this company's successes sparked by office automation.

The group takes on some additional crucial roles. Publishing a newsletter helps establish and maintain a corporate perspective. Front-page stories emphasize corporate benefits achieved through the use of office technology and recognize people and departments who effected the benefits. By publicizing successes and crediting the people who contributed to them, the newsletter promotes the sharing of techniques. Other stories provide tips for using technology and feature software new to the company's repertoire.

The group coordinates equipment distribution. Personal computers are distributed as justified by requests. A full complement of basic software is included with each computer; because the cost of including company-made copies of software and manuals is small, there is little reason to spend time determining whether the recipient is likely to need a spreadsheet package. Other software, for indexing all words in a group of documents, for instance, or for helping to manage projects, is available upon request. Software upgrades are handled through requests from departments; timing of the deploying upgrades is a local decision. Within a typical client department, employees with the most demanding applications receive the newest, most capable hardware. Older equipment is shifted to people with less pressing or sophisticated needs. Original combinations of equipment need not be kept intact; a computer may be moved while a printer is left in place. Departments are responsible for maintaining their own inventory records; the computer department needs only to be assured that technology is not lost or left unused.

For general-purpose hardware, maintenance is tailored to each location's need. Any department can swap with the office automation group a defective item for a working one. The group repairs the item or has a contractor do the work. The group keeps the repaired unit for a subsequent swap. This style of maintenance is popular for locations with large offices. Elsewhere, some departments choose to obtain maintenance from local suppliers. Standard maintenance is used for minisupercomputers, workstations, and other special equipment.

The group continues to obtain from the corporation the main budget for office automation. Because of the results being achieved and the cost savings from the corporationwide software licenses, there are always enough funds to meet the needs for requests that estimate payback of less than two years.

Costs and estimated benefits summed over a few years indicate $5 in anticipated annual benefits for each $1 of technology placed.

The specific results achieved via the use of "office" technology are broad-based:

- The cost of reviewing customers' use of energy in homes is reduced to the extent that this energy audit program, which seeks to improve energy conservation, is continued.
- Electronic capture of readings from utility meters, done at the site of the meter, reduces errors, eliminates the need for dozens of data-entry clerks, and facilitates mailing bills one day earlier.
- The optimization of routes for transmission lines saves money on installing new lines and improves, and lowers the cost of, engineering studies, which are done with personal computer software licensed from its developer.
- New techniques for modeling electric transmission networks optimize service and ensure stability in the event of sudden changes in supply or demand; engineers enjoy improved service from systems based on minisupercomputers and networks of workstations and the company avoids acquiring a mainframe computer.
- Computerization of specialized accounting work enhances the effectiveness of the work and allows the controller's department to decrease staff steadily.
- Automation supports the collection of money from customers who pay bills at customer service offices.
- Electronic recording of time-card data at construction sites increases accuracy and eliminates the need for centralized data entry.

- The company automates the summarization of data for corporate income tax preparation.
- A model of utility rates is used during public hearings; the model runs on battery-powered computers.
- Modern tools for local gas and electric engineering design work facilitate the combining of gas and electric work crews.
- There are many instances of informal innovation. For example:

    The legal staff spearheading a general rate case filing devises new techniques for coordinating its work, developing the rate case documents, and preparing cross-examination scenarios for questioning noncompany witnesses at hearings.

    An individual produces a spreadsheet application to estimate corporate losses from a customer's diverting energy to flow around a meter, thereby developing and substantiating a claim for lost revenue.

    The human resources department develops new means for scoring and interpreting surveys and tests.

This example illustrates the potential for an information resources management function to develop partnerships with essentially all departments in a company. These partnerships created significant information proficiency and overall corporate results.

Responsibility for results remained with the clients of the computer department. Development of new techniques was shared appropriately between clients and the computer department. A corporate framework for office automation was developed and coordinated by the central office automation group.

LEADERSHIP AND SUCCESS—A THIRD EXAMPLE

This example features information resources leadership principles within a corporation that engineers, manufactures, and sells high-technology products and provides related services. The example provides one approach to a corporationwide strategy for achieving results and assigning information resources responsibilities.

This corporation consists of a corporate staff and several operating companies. The chief information officer (CIO) is an integral part of the corporate leadership. A small percentage of the staff information technologists in this corporation reports to the CIO. The vast majority report to company presidents; however, the corporate CIO retains the authority to intervene and redirect information resources endeavors.

The information resources emphasis on corporate goals and results includes both quantitative and qualitative objectives:

- Hastening the performance of operational processes is an important goal for this corporation. Information systems have, for example, significantly decreased the average time from receipt of a customer's order to collection of the payment for the products or services provided. The CIO says that "chief time officer" is as apt a title as chief information officer.

- A measure of the success of information resources, beyond properly supporting the corporation's operations, is the decrease in the fraction of corporate revenue devoted to information resources endeavors.

- Another goal is to protect the flexibility of the corporation to reorganize, merge, or sell its business units.

- Functional corporate information systems generate freedom for the corporation and its employees to make progress; however, a possible converse, that client freedom to develop key corporate systems could imply functionality for systems, does not pertain. This is a corporate and personal results-oriented observation: A robust information resource provides people the freedom to do their work. Freedom to invent core systems would imply that there is not enough functionality in the extant systems to support the business. Uncontrolled development of core systems could lead to chaos.

Overall relations between the information resource community and its constituents include several forms of vital communication:

- The corporate chief information officer maintains close communication with the presidents of the operating companies.
- Companies rate information resources management every quarter year based on how well the information resources practitioners performed with respect to plans and how adequate the plans were.
- These ratings are presented to practitioners, along with videotaped presentations, by the company presidents.
- Practitioners are encouraged to distinguish among three roles a constituent can have with respect to information technologists, namely, customer, partner, and user.

  Customers, such as company presidents, pay information systems bills and staff salaries.

  Partners include the clients who participate in developing new applications of information technology. For a typical project, two-thirds to nine-tenths of the participants are partners, not practitioners.

  Users are the people who use the systems and benefit from the data and processes inherent in the systems.
- Practitioners are encouraged to strive for "alignment" between their clients and themselves. Of particular importance is agreement on a vision and budget for information resources for three years into the future.

The CIO's corporate information resources staff focuses on broad issues and opportunities:

- The central group deals with corporate "musts." "Shoulds" are left to the individual companies.
- The central group promotes simplicity as a principle. Saying no to overly complex proposed endeavors is important.
- The central information resources group emphasizes promoting

appropriate practices for managing computing and information resources, not specifying the way people do their computing.

- Corporate rules governing people's conduct and decisions are defined only if they are important enough to cause an employee to be dismissed for breaking them.
- Constituents' voluntary compliance is the goal for effectively implementing corporate rules.

The CIO and overall information resources community work together on their objectives:

- The CIO meets frequently with information resources practitioners.
- Twice a year, the CIO meets with practitioners in an "all-hands" meeting.
- Once a year, the CIO discusses "values and beliefs" with the information resources leaders, about 10 percent of the corporation's practitioners.

Information resources projects are building synergy throughout the corporation. Individually, employees communicate copiously through electronic mail. In one case, three business units have combined forces and funds to maintain and extend a useful software application.

This corporation focuses on corporate and business-unit objectives, with articulated principles and interpersonal procedures to reinforce those objectives.

LEADERSHIP AND EXPECTATIONS

What happens to people's expectations when an information resources management community exercises its leadership potential? How much should the community attempt to influence its clients' expectations? How will expectations change within the information resources community itself?

Providing leadership implies changing people's goals or emphases and, therefore, their expectations.

- When the U.S. federal information resources community initiated the service to the citizen movement, it expanded federal employees' expectations about what they could accomplish. As the momentum generated by this program and other similar efforts produces results, it changes the public's expectations about governmental services.
- The federal information resources community's recognition that it is assuming a new role—catalytic leadership—develops a change in expectations for itself, as well as the government as a whole.
- The utility's office automation group changed the expectations of people throughout the company about how they can do work and how much empowered innovation they can accomplish.
- The high-technology company's successes through operational automation have raised its expectations for exploiting both information resources and the resultant corporate and personal flexibility.

In each of these instances, information resources practitioners created rising expectations among their clients and themselves. In each of these cases, encouraging people to reach for broader goals was entirely appropriate.

There are risks and limits, however. In the past, information technologists have been known to overpromise. Numerous projects have failed to meet schedules or to produce desired results.

For the federal community, the utility office automation group, and the high-technology company's staff practitioners, promoting change and raising expectations were prudent. Characteristics of these examples include:

- Explicit dependence on clients to champion projects and produce results.
- Practical, balanced partnerships between clients and practitioners.
- An agenda appropriate to the organization:

  For the federal government and the utility, this meant an open-ended, opportunistic agenda for capturing opportunities as they arose.

  For the high-technology company, this meant striving for specific strategic changes.

This behavior represents a new style for some organizations. As the behavior spreads, it brings with it changes in corporate culture, including increased empowerment, synergy, innovation, sharing, and risk taking.

Such leadership endeavors can have profound effects on the information resources practitioners themselves, effects such as:

- A shift in focus away from technology and tools and toward organizational mission and information proficiency.
- A new sense of purpose and vitality.
- A closer partnership with clients.
- A more positive image.

For the computer department in the utility, the office automation project propelled that department into some of the roles of a coach (Fig. 12–4), whereas previously it had been a "librarian," "clerk," and technician. There was significant internal change:

- From isolated projects to cooperative ventures.
- From the psychology of a backlogged programming and operations service bureau to that of a forward-looking proponent for innovation throughout the company.

The information resources community that wants to assume a catalytic leadership role must foresee that it will increase expectations among both clients and itself. The community that successfully takes on this role manages its endeavors and those expectations well.

In providing catalytic leadership, an information resources management community:

- Looks for opportunities throughout the framework for the Information Age (Fig. 2–1), the new information resources paradigm (Fig. 10–2), and the functions the community can perform (Fig. 12–4).
- Encourages clients to understand (Fig. 5–2), measure (Fig. 6–1), and improve their information proficiency.
- Uses the Peer Paradigm for organizations (Fig. 4–2) to understand the breadth of each opportunity.
- Uses insight into clients' organizational climate (Figs. 7–3 and 7–4) to understand the subtleties of each opportunity.
- Initiates All A's programs (Fig. 7–1) to capture those opportunities.

The community builds synergy and commonality throughout each aspect, and across all aspects, of the framework. The community creates synergy between the goals of its clients and its own goals. It also creates synergy between client groups, as well as between clients and itself. The community proceeds prudently and enthusiastically, using a Just Ask . . . approach: Just Accomplish!

15

Optimizing Information Resources Education

Individuals and organizations have much to learn about managing information resources. Opportunities also exist, throughout the spectrum of information resources topics, for improving information resources management education and research.

Learning to Use
Information Technology

One day in the early 1980s, a manager wondered how an administrative process could be automated using a certain database management software package. The manager handed a consultant a manual for the software package and asked to see a demonstration the next morning.

The consultant had some feel for the administrative function and had built administrative applications using other software tools, but he was unfamiliar with this particular software. For one thing, the software ran only on microcomputers, which were a relatively new development, and the consultant had no experience with microcomputers. For another, the software manual was sketchy. Nevertheless, the demonstration was successful. With the client looking over his shoulder, the consultant made no errors in implementing a mock-up of the application and in improvising variations.

What was the key to the success in this story? The consultant had enough previous experience and training to know what a database software package should be able to do, to guess which features described in the manual performed which major functions, and to guess how to use those features. Indeed, all that previous training was Just Ask . . . learning (Fig. 8–1), gained by programming other applications with the occasional advice of other people.

The lessons remain current: Learning to use information technology should include developing and exploiting a feel for what technology should be able to do, as well as learning how to use specific features of specific products. In addition:

- Training on techniques and technologies can build the confidence to be able to transfer one's learning to new technologies.
- Training can be informal.
- One needs to be able to overcome the shortcomings of software manuals—shortcomings evidenced by the robust marketplace for how-to books about software packages.

These conclusions lead to follow-on issues and concepts. First, how often do organizations needing new employees think in terms of skills with specific information technology products? Employment advertisements suggest that this is a prevalent practice. This practice can disqualify talented candidates who may not have used particular products but who are well qualified for the mission-specific aspects of jobs and who can become proficient quickly with the products on their own. Also, such ads can convey impressions that jobs provide little opportunity for personal growth because they are too closely tied to specific technological tools.

Second, even if people cannot learn from colleagues, effective informal training can be provided by skilled specialists who are brought into the workplace to train through observation and coaching rather than through formal classroom work.

Third, what happened to "ease of learning" and "ease of use" for information technology products? You do not read a manual before using a rental car, but you do adjust some features of the car, such as the mirrors and seats, and your driving style for the time you use the car. Through their purchases and commentary, customers can push information technology developers to produce products that facilitate self-education rather than require a manual or an extra book.

In the long run, prospects are bright for people to learn to use information technology. Continuing maturity in product design and societal skills will go a long way toward closing today's training gaps. Continued progress in automating repetitive activities will obviate the need to train people to perform those activities. Many of the remaining activities will become second nature for people. Finally, society's impending mastery of computer-based training techniques will allow people to learn on their own with the aid of technology.

THE SCOPE OF INFORMATION RESOURCES MANAGEMENT EDUCATION

Proficiency at managing information resources requires much more than simply mastering the use of information technology. Yet most formal learning in this field today focuses on technology.

This emphasis may seem natural to you. After all, this technology is new, and people need to learn to use it. On the other hand, managing information as a resource is not new, and the major principles were discovered before the invention of the computer. Merging our knowledge of "paper-based" information resources management with our new-found technology skills ought to be enough.

There is a kernel of truth in that reasoning. There are many similarities between yesterday's information resources and today's. One company, when educating first-time users of personal computers, emphasized the similarities between diskettes and file folders, thereby alerting employees to good practices for creating, maintaining, securing, and disposing of computer-based information.

Limiting information resources management training to technology training is not enough. We need to become more proficient in managing information resources. The management challenges are growing with the Information Age flood of data and demands for enhanced competitiveness based on proficiency with and through information. New entrants into the workforce do not have the perspective that comes from years of experience at managing information resources. Further, many other people need updates on this subject, both to reinforce traditional practices and to cope successfully with Information Age issues. For example, people concerned with information security need to learn the relative security of various techniques for encrypting and transmitting data.

More generally, people concerned about personal and organizational proficiency should reevaluate information resources management as a topic in a continuous spectrum of subjects (Fig. 2–1): technology, information systems, information and information resources management, people and information proficiency, and goals and results. Viewed in this continuum, information resources management is a vital link between tools, such as data and technology, and achievements, such as results and information proficiency.

Seen in this pivotal role, information resources management takes on significant vitality. Education should match this importance in both substance and image.

Revitalized education in this field is constituent-oriented education. Everyone manages information resources. Everyone has constituents such as employers, colleagues, and suppliers. All people need to improve their abilities to:

- Support the goals of the organizations with which they work.
- Build information proficiency for themselves, their colleagues, and their organizations.
- Support their colleagues and other information customers.
- Enhance their organizations' information resources.
- Work with suppliers of information and information technology.
- Help colleagues become more proficient with information resources techniques and technologies.

The challenge for all people, as information resources managers and as educators, is to view information resources in this vital context and thereby to enhance their learning and training activities.

IMPROVING ACADEMIC PROGRAMS

The field of information resources management presents challenges for academic institutions.

One challenge involves where to put this subject in the academic curriculum. There are many meaningful questions to consider:

- Because changes brought about by information resources management have ramifications in all fields, should it be taught in all curricula in a college or university?
- With its impact on people and organizations, should the subject be part of a program in organizational behavior? Business management? Public administration?
- Does the topic, with its emphasis on improving processes, fit with industrial engineering? Operations research? Business administration? Public administration? Various branches of engineering?

- Does the emphasis on information overlap with rhetoric? Journalism? Library science? Linguistics? Languages? Every academic discipline?
- Does programming or acquiring mission-specific software fit with every academic field?
- Does the development of generic technology fit with computer science? Electrical engineering? Mathematics?
- Do fundamental improvements in hardware depend on advances in materials science? Engineering? Physics?

The answer to each of these questions can sensibly be yes. Along with the challenge of where to put the topic, or various components of it, comes the question of how much to explore the subject in each academic program.

A particular challenge lies in undergraduate computer science curricula. Enrollment in such programs has declined. Four years of studying fundamentals of hardware and software design can be useful for students desiring careers in research or teaching in this field, especially those who plan to get an advanced degree. Other students, however, gain suitable understanding and practical knowledge by majoring in other fields and taking care to emphasize information technology projects and elective courses. Increasingly, people are learning a great deal about the practical aspects of computer science before college, on their own, from friends, or through classes available from programs that do not grant degrees.

An important issue about undergraduate computer science programs is whether and how to provide a program through which graduates will be able to compete with people who have majored in other fields. Expanding the curriculum to include meaningful coverage of all aspects of information proficiency can help. So can requiring a strong minor in another field.

Also, academic institutions can take a more active research role in information proficiency and information resources management, independently of expanding its research and development roles in hardware and software. More research is needed on deriving benefits from the deployment of technology.

INFORMATION RESOURCES
MANAGEMENT—AN INFORMAL FIELD

The challenges for academic institutions reflect challenges for all of society. You might ask whether these challenges and opportunities result merely from the relative newness of "modern" information resources management and computing. As yet, information resources management is not following the history of similar fields. The field has considerable breadth but relatively little formality and structure.

People find few barriers to entering the field. Having formal education or a degree in the field is not essential. While information resources management professionals provide services similar in many ways to those provided by lawyers and doctors, there is no equivalent of a bar exam or medical degree. For many people, practical experience and common sense suffice. Anyone can gain proficiency in creating and analyzing information or processes. Anyone can learn to program a computer. Also, there are no formal requirements for keeping one's knowledge current.

While there are information resources management professional associations, there is no pervasive equivalent of a bar association or medical association. Aside perhaps from the hardware industry, there is no strong public relations effort or lobbying group.

The field also has much in common with science and engineering until one considers issues of people and organizations. Physicists and chemists develop and precisely test quantitative theories. Engineers apply those theories to develop products and processes. The work of information resources management in dealing with the behavior of people and organizations does not qualify as a science. Indeed, more generally, it has been suggested that managers and employees would be more effective in leading organizations if they used a biological paradigm than if they use a mechanical one. Advocates of the biological paradigm suggest that growth and competition are at least as relevant as mechanical processes.

Academics, and society in general, must look at information resources management for its breadth and depth. The field has much in common with most academic and, in fact, human pursuits. To the extent that people look for strengths in, and possible synergies with, information resources management, society and each individual will take a step forward.

PART 5

Information Systems

CHAPTER *16*

Reengineering Information Systems Projects

*T*he style for deploying information resources
components and information technology is changing to
match the Peer Paradigm and the needs of organizations
and individuals to be more information-proficient.
Understanding the goals of information resources
projects leads to a new paradigm for projects and a
method for categorizing technological components.

CONTEXTS FOR PROJECTS

Improving an organization's information resources management can be seen as a series of projects. Typically, a project starts from one of two roots: a vision for an improvement in the organization or the availability of new technology.

The vision-inspired project targets specific results, such as improving customer service, enhancing the organization's information proficiency, or reducing costs. During the project, people fulfill many needs, including:

- Defining and propagating the vision of the anticipated results.
- Planning, staffing, and managing the project.
- Perfecting the vision, including defining how the organization's work will be done based on the anticipated improvements.
- Building and testing software and databases specific to the vision.
- Deploying generic technology needed to support the vision-specific software and information.
- Training people to use the systems and information.
- Training people to maintain the system.
- Doing the work that the systems support.
- Verifying that the results, whether originally anticipated or deliberately changed during the course of the project, are satisfactory.
- Preparing for further improvements based on this improvement.
- Helping the organization reuse the lessons learned from this project.

A vision-driven project is a top-down effort. The "top" is the vision that, especially in an era of empowered workers, need not come from the top of the organization. The vision-driven endeavor is the traditional way of running information resources management projects. A clear, well-understood vision, backed by dedicated workers, leads to desirable results with a minimum of effort.

Another approach is a bottom-up one. Typically, someone spots a new technology or a local opportunity for process improvement. Rather than formulate and market a broad vision, people experiment. People acquire some of the new technology and determine what can be done with it, or they try a new process.

Neither approach should be discouraged. The results of each should be judged on the merits of the results, not the origins. Indeed, often a project is based on, and handled as, a combination of the two approaches.

For a top-down project, there may be some key procedural or technical unknowns. Even if improvement seems likely, the amount may be quite uncertain. In these cases, people turn to bottom-up approaches to test the main concepts.

The bottom-up approach starts with experimentation and, if the idea continues to be promising, often moves on to a project to prove the main concepts. There may also be a study of the feasibility of extending the new techniques in functional scope or to more portions of the organization. Such work builds a vision and provides a useful basis for marketing it. The bottom-up approach can lead to a well-planned top-down project.

The Paradigm Change for Projects

When technology was more expensive than it is today, the vision-driven project predominated. People not part of the team spearheading an approved project had little direct access to technological tools and, therefore, little opportunity to experiment. Pilot projects did occur, but usually in the context of vision-driven programs.

Further, the visions were narrow (Fig. 4–1) compared to those needed and possible to realize today (Fig. 4–2). With little experience in such projects and limited technology, people could not plan a comprehensive approach to meeting an organization's information needs. For example, developing a system to issue paychecks was difficult enough; organizations were unlikely to try to integrate payroll processing with other personnel systems that supported assigning people to projects or scheduling people for training. Indeed, large organizations often had several payroll systems, as was the case within each of the U.S. military services.

While the visions were narrow in scope, the projects were "deep" with respect to the layers of technology and the skills of employees. Each project required a full complement of technology, from software specific to the project through computer hardware and telecommunications facilities. A full range of human support was assembled, often with emphasis on skills related to technology.

This traditional vertical style of systems deployment (Fig. 16–1) became known as the *stovepipe method*—narrow in scope, deep in effort, and independent of other systems in use, under development, or needed later. This is the vertical paradigm for information resources management projects.

Goals	1	2	3	4	5	...
People	!	>	?	!	>	...
Information used to make decisions	!	>	—	!	?	...
Mission-specific data, processes, and technology	!	>	—	!	?	...
Generic data, processes, and technology	!	>	—	!	?	...

Legend:

1, 2, 3, 4, ...:	Organizational goals
!	Working
>	Being put into place
?	Being considered
—	Yet to be considered

FIGURE 16–1   The Stovepipe Paradigm for Projects.

These projects reinforced the traditional vertical paradigm for organizational behavior (Fig. 4–1). While fostering vertical information flows, they did not support the hierarchical organization well because data did not converge into more useful "executive information" as it neared the top of the hierarchy (Fig. 10–1).

The stovepipe paradigm is much in evidence today, both because of its continued use and because of the legacies left by its use. This paradigm is, however, neither universal for current systems nor desirable for satisfying future needs.

Consider some examples of behavior other than the stovepipe model. A long-standing tradition of the telecommunications industry based on the goal of universal service exemplifies the Peer Paradigm (bottom layer of Fig. 10–2). Anyone can connect into the international general communications network. Little in the network, or the services based on it, is specific to any customer.

Another example is found today in the deployment of computer hardware and some software. Whether mainframes or microcomputers, most hardware can support many types of corporate activity. As commodities supporting a variety of uses, these computers need not be acquired in the context of one specific project. The same can be said of much software for personal computers. Neither word processing packages, spreadsheets, nor database management tools are specific to one use or need be acquired as if they were.

The vertical paradigm is *not* the method of choice for the future. People need information from what is, or would have been, more than one stovepipe. Recall the one-stop shopping concept achieved by some financial services companies. Think of a personnel specialist who needs to synthesize information based on employment histories, training histories, and budget projections. A member of a corporate planning group or an assistant to a chief executive officer may need to draw conclusions by using information from almost any of the company's information sources. Stovepipe systems erect barriers that prevent the information flow people need in order to be effective.

More generally, tomorrow's world is one of alliances, not only within but also among organizations (Fig. 4–2). In business, the corporation whose information systems can support intercorporate partnerships and activities has a competitive advantage. For a national government, pursuing a military war or a war on drugs involves many agencies within that government and probably within other governments as well.

Currently, organizations devote considerable effort to overcoming barriers between stovepipe systems. For example, there are still instances of manual transfer of information—people print information from one system and type it into another. Achieving automated integration across stovepipes can be difficult and often begins with the task of linking generic technologies. After the telecommunications capacity to link computers is acquired, steps must be taken to allow the operating systems in the various computers to communicate. Then, data-translating software may need to be developed so that the data stored under the jurisdiction of one database manager can be processed and stored by a different database manager. On top of this, data definitions are often incompatible. For example, one system might store up to 14 characters for last names, but another might keep only 12; 2 names distinct in the former system might seem to be the same in the latter. After procedures are developed to make sharing data possible, there are still issues that relate to sharing processing techniques and synchronizing information.

These challenges just scratch the surface. Think, for example, of geographic data in one system keyed to a different coordinate system than that used in another system. To combine data from both systems on one map requires accurate translation of coordinates. If that is not bad enough, consider that, after an earthquake, the grid of surveyors' marks may have moved relative to absolute longitude and latitude.

The future demands thinking horizontally and in layers (Fig. 16–2). People will need to employ the Peer Paradigm across the broad contexts in which information resources management systems must serve. Those contexts are specified by the Information Age framework (Fig. 2–1), the need to enhance information proficiency (Figs. 1–1 and 5–2), and the Peer Paradigm for information as a resource (Fig. 10–2).

Goals	!	>	!	?	!	...	
People	>	!	–	!	?	>	!	...
Information used to make decisions	!	>	!	!	?	...	
Mission-specific data, processes, and technology	!	>	>	!	?	!	!	...
Generic data, processes, and technology	!	!	>	!	?	...	

Legend:

!   Working
>   Being put into place
?   Being considered
–   Yet to be considered

FIGURE 16–2   Modular Deployment: The Peer Paradigm for Projects.

Goals (Fig. 16–2) incorporate an organization's visions of desired future results. An information resources project manager needs to consider visions of future organizational capability and flexibility and to anticipate broad, perhaps even unforeseen, goals—goals that may involve other organizations and difficult activities.

People and organizations need to maximize their information proficiency. Projects must support people's broad needs to obtain *information used to make decisions* and to communicate and work together effectively. Thus, project personnel must think across what previously would have been vertical project boundaries. Also, given the many tasks and skills needed to implement projects, and the scarcity in some organizations of staff to devote to projects, project personnel must be capable of supporting several projects at once.

Although an organization cannot design and assemble all its information resources at one time, it can take steps to see that the pieces fit together when needed. Modularity and peer integration are the keys to success. Modularity denotes the ability to add new collections of information at any time. Peer integration denotes the ability to use synergistically all the information an organization has.

Today, *mission-specific data, processes,* and *technologies* emphasize data and software over hardware. While designing and assembling this layer all at once is neither possible nor desirable for promoting flexibility over time, information resources managers can take steps to ensure that the pieces of this layer will work together when needed.

Similar considerations apply to *generic data, processes,* and *technology.* The challenge of integrating stovepipe systems illustrates why peer integration in this layer is essential, even if there are several types of similar off-the-shelf software packages, several types of operating systems, disparate computer systems, and several telecommunications networks.

The new paradigm emphasizes peers and is modular. The organization can add, upgrade, or remove some components within any of the layers with minimal disruption of other layers. For example, a person can move on to a new job. Or an organization can deploy a new version of an off-the-shelf spreadsheet package without changing its other technology; at most, some computers may need additional memory. Generic technology can evolve to meet overall changes in processing, storage, and telecommunications loads almost independently of changes in the mission-specific software and data.

Modularity means that smaller changes can be made in a more timely manner than in the stovepipe paradigm. One can build a resource of information systems that is both capable and flexible. This can be done with little risk, but optimizing behavior in the new modular Peer Paradigm does require attention to standards.

Achieving the full benefits of the Peer Paradigm (Fig. 16–2) depends on meeting challenges at each layer: *goals* and results achieved; *people* and information proficiency; *information; mission-specific data, processes,* and *technology; and generic data, processes,* and *technology.*

CLASSIFYING TECHNOLOGY, USING THE PEER PARADIGM

The framework for the Information Age (Fig. 2–1) features layers such as results, people, information, and technology. The Peer Paradigm for organizational behavior emphasizes similar layers (Fig. 4–2). So do the new paradigm for information as a resource (Fig. 10–2) and the Peer Paradigm for information resources projects (Fig. 16–2).

Technology, the last layer of the framework (Fig. 2–1), divides naturally into two layers: mission-specific and generic (Fig. 16–2). Subdividing the second of these lends clarity to how projects are accomplished.

Consider a person using a spreadsheet software package and a personal computer to develop an organization's budget. The *result* will be a budget. The *people* involved include this person and others in the organization. The *information* used to decide on the budget includes conclusions drawn from the data in spreadsheet applications, as well as other information. The person's input to the spreadsheet package, including the names of activities, projected revenues and costs for those activities, and instructions on how to combine the budget data for individual activities in order to compute an overall budget, contribute to *mission-specific data, processes,* and *technology.*

The remaining technology is not specific to this budgeting work: the spreadsheet package, the computer's operating system, and the computer. These three elements of *generic infrastructure* fall, respectively, into three categories: tools, operating systems, and hardware (Fig. 16–3).

Examples of processing tools include spreadsheet packages, database managers, project management packages, statistical analysis tools, "computer-aided software engineering" tools, and programming languages. Examples of generic data tools include on-line libraries of legal rulings and statistical databases.

Information technology includes telecommunications, as well as computing, technologies. A telecommunications term for capabilities

Goals and Results
   An organization's goals and achievements

People and Information Proficiency
   The organization's employees and other constituents
   Its proficiency in defining goals and achieving results

Information and Information Resources Management
   Information, as used to make and implement decisions
   The organization's use of its information resources

Mission-Specific Knowledge (Data and Procedures) and Technology
   Stored information specific to the organization,
      e.g., records of expenditures
   Computer software specific to the mission of the organization,
      e.g., software that designs the organization's products

Generic Infrastructure: Data, Processes, and Technology
   Tools and features
      Stored information not specific to the organization,
         e.g., a library of legal precedents
      Applications development software tools,
         e.g., an off-the-shelf spreadsheet package
      Telecommunications systems features,
         e.g., "call waiting"

   Operating Systems and Networking Software
      Computer operating systems
      Telecommunications networking software

   Hardware and Networks
      Computer and telecommunications equipment
      Telecommunications broadcast "spectrum"

FIGURE 6–3   The Information Age Framework, Including Layers of Technology.

that customers order and use is "features." Features include "call waiting," "call forwarding," and "speed calling." Thus, one layer within generic technology can be termed *tools* and *features*.

The telecommunications equivalent to computer operating systems is the software that manages telecommunications networks. Computer systems also include software that manages their communications with other computers. Thus, another layer of generic technology is *operating systems* and *networking software*.

The telecommunications equivalent of computing hardware includes switches and links between devices. The switches are computers in their own right. Links include wires, fiber-optic cables, and light-based communications, such as microwaves, for which there is no physical medium. This layer of generic technology is *hardware* and *networks*.

This layering of generic infrastructure provides an insightful framework (Fig. 16–4), for example, by clarifying the tasks required to link disparate systems.

First, it is necessary to make a connection at the hardware and networks level. Otherwise, no communications can flow. The connections must be compatible. It is not enough that two devices use the same physical medium such as copper-wire telecommunications lines. For example, if two computers are linked by telephone lines and one device sends data at a rate surpassing the other's ability to receive it, communications will not work. Or perhaps you have used two computers, one of which did not have a disk reader into which you could insert diskettes written by the other. You could not move information between the computers using diskettes.

Second, synergy must be achieved between operating systems and networking software. When computers communicate, they send the data people need, "mail," and they send directions for how to route and file that information, "addresses." Each device must, in effect, understand the printing on the "envelopes" into which other devices put their "mail." And each device must know the language in which the "letters" are written. Or, returning to the diskette example, perhaps you have encountered two computers that used the same type of diskette but were not programmed to read each other's files.

Goals	!	>	!	?	!	...		
People	>	!	−	!	?	>	!	...
Information used to make decisions	!	>	!	!	?	...		
Mission-specific data, processes, and technology	!	>	>	!	?	!	!	...
Tools and features*	>	!	!	!	?	>	!	...
Operating systems and networking software*	!	>	!	−	?	...		
Hardware and networks*	!	>	>	!	?	!	−	...

*Components of generic infrastructure.

Legend:

!	Working
>	Being put into place
?	Being considered
−	Yet to be considered

FIGURE 16–4   Modular Deployment: The Peer Paradigm, Including Layers of Generic Infrastructure.

Third, synergy is needed between the tools and features. You doubtless have heard a vendor's claims that its off-the-shelf spreadsheet software package can process spreadsheet applications developed using a rival vendor's spreadsheet package or a claim that a word processing package can use the output from a particular spreadsheet package.

This linkage chain does not stop with generic technology. Fourth, synergy is desired between the mission-specific data, processes, and technologies. Perhaps you recall having been forced to rearrange and reprogram someone else's spreadsheet in order to get that information into a spreadsheet you had built. Requirements for synergy continue into the other layers of the general paradigm. Synergy is necessary between interpretations and uses of information; between people, organizations, and their processes; and between the goals of those individuals and groups.

The layering of generic technology provides insight into strategies for acquiring and deploying technology. For example, suppose that a company has a standard set of personal computer tools, such as a spreadsheet package, a word processing package, and so forth. Suppose that there are many operating systems and many brands and models of computers on which those tools run. Suppose that the operating systems and computers have a compatible means of communications. Then, it is of little consequence that the organization uses many of those brands and models of computers; the most important considerations in acquiring new computers may be price and maintenance. On the other hand, if just one essential tool cannot run on a type of operating system or computer, the firm may want to avoid that operating system or computer.

The layering paradigm sheds light on a traditional difference between computing and telecommunications. Mission-specific technology includes data and software but not features of telecommunications systems. The telecommunications industry gained its strength through meeting its goal as a ubiquitous utility connecting everyone. Mission-specific products, such as a telecommunications system for a navy ship, have been limited to clients with specific needs and budgets that could accommodate those needs.

While the telecommunications industry has focused on a horizontal, or peer, paradigm, the computer industry grew initially through a vertical paradigm by supporting specific goals of, and groups within, organizations. Computer systems transform, not just transmit, mission-specific information and contain mission-specific software.

Today, the computer and telecommunications industries are merging. The benefits to society and to the combined information technology industry will be maximized to the extent that the industry both produces useful mission-specific products and achieves universal service.

Just as the layering paradigm accommodates the merging of computing and telecommunications, it also helps clarify the impeding merger of computing and telecommunications, on the one hand, and news, entertainment, education, home shopping, and so forth, on the other (Fig. 10–2). The layering paradigm can help overcome ambiguity in traditional vocabulary. *Television, motion pictures, movies,* and similar terms have come to denote both content, such as a television program, and delivery techniques, such as television broadcasting equipment, signals, and sets. Evidently, *multimedia* is also becoming a term embracing both content and technology.

The layering paradigm provides categories into which to place the various components of the amalgamation of information technologies, information-handling techniques, and information. For example, the "set-top box," or cable box, and other equipment slated to work with a television to provide interactive, two-way video constitute *hardware*. This equipment will contain an *operating system* and *networking software* to support receiving and sending information. There will be *tools* to help the viewer specify what needs to be done. There promises to be plenty of *"generic* programming," including old movies and television reruns. Organizations and people will develop and maintain their own *mission-specific* information, both processes and data.

CAPABILITY? FLEXIBILITY? CAN WE HAVE BOTH?

"Here are the detailed functional specifications. Build a system that allows our employees to work exactly as detailed in the specification, and we will be happy."

These words reflect a core concept for the top-down approach to building information systems. Before the words are spoken, much thought goes into the automation of some components of such work as handling customers' inquiries, processing deposits to bank accounts, or deciding how much to pay on insurance claims. Often, the detailed specification offers some advantages, such as a consensus on a good way to handle work being supported, ease of estimating the costs of building the system, and the ability to know when the system is complete. When such a system is installed, people take satisfaction in providing a certain "capability" that has been carefully designed to enhance the operations of the receiving organization.

Such a system, however, may be obsolete by the time it is installed. At best, it was designed for yesterday's best guess for tomorrow's needs. Today's world features changing marketplaces and ever-improving competitors. Competitive advantage and information proficiency demand flexibility along with capability.

Within the Peer Paradigm (Fig. 16–4), there is ample context to design for both capability and flexibility. One key is the rigorous use of standards: standards that define data, processes, linkages between processes, linkages between data and processes, linkages between other units of technology and, perhaps, standards that apply to those other units of technology.

In the realm of mission-specific information—data and processes—standards promote both capability and flexibility. As the organization's needs and viewpoints change, it is essential to know the definitions of the extant information. With such knowledge, people can make informed decisions about approximations, that is, uses of data and processes in ways not matching their definitions. People can also make informed decisions about putting existing data and processes together in new combinations and about collecting new types of data and developing new processes. Without such standards and definitions, one has both less capability and less flexibility.

Standard interfaces between mission-specific information, whether data or software, and generic technology permit the deployment of elements, singly or in combinations, of mission-specific software and data for widespread use. For example, there is considerable benefit when people share a document, even if their word processing software packages differ. Standard interfaces among units of mission-specific and generic information and technology facilitate meeting changing workloads and taking advantage of new technology because they make it possible to add and redeploy modules easily within the overall information resource.

Technology standards represent only one way to enhance the overall flexibility of systems. Enhancing people's information proficiency and technology proficiency is another.

The real issue is not whether an organization *can* have both capability and flexibility in its systems. Systems issues parallel organizational issues in today's business climate. You cannot maintain capability without flexibility. There is little value in flexibility without capability. You *must* achieve both.

CONTINUOUS SERVICE

Some measures of the quality of information systems and services focus on service delivery times and continuity. Service objectives include minimizing processing and response times, numbers of outages per year, and lengths of outages.

Demands for around-the-clock service increase, as exemplified by worldwide airline reservation systems and credit-card purchase authorization systems. Systems must be designed to operate continuously and to be modified while running. Cost consciousness imposes demands to minimize slack. Given the complexity of the combinations of mission-specific and generic information and technology, these objectives seem especially taxing. Having hardware components that can be expected to run for years without failing helps but does not suffice.

Is there is a theory or academic discipline addressing these issues thoroughly? Much is known about queues and delays, and failures and failure rates; however, these problems constitute only one part of the issue. The overall question could be how to maintain service. But even this may not be enough: The service must change from time to time, and errors need to be corrected and their consequences reversed.

Perhaps a starting point would be a theory of "restorative systems." Life provides many examples of systems that recover from saturation or that need rest. Think of a highway system that clogs during morning rush hours, for which the service level usually returns to optimal a few hours later. Think of your need for sleep; evidently, your brain and other systems need periods to recover from even normal workloads.

The highway system provides an example of a system that needs maintenance and improvements from time to time. Human systems fall into this category, too. Maintenance includes exercise, whether mental or physical. Improvements include learning. Dealing with errors includes "unlearning."

Absent such a theory and the practical application of it, organizations and their information resources practitioners are left, metaphorically, with the problem of changing a tire on a moving car. Mission-specific software and data must be both continually in service and often enhanced. The generic technology must provide continuous, often increasing, service.

Absent a good theory and unlimited staff, an organization can contract out part of the work to people who specialize in keeping systems running. The Peer Paradigm for projects and technology (Fig. 16–4) features a layered model of technology: mission-specific technology, generic technology used for expressing mission-specific software and data, operating systems and network management software, and finally, computers and telecommunications hardware. The farther down that four-item list one goes, the farther removed are the technologies and services from the goals of the organization supported by a system. The services provided may be essential to operations, but the balance of issues shifts from value toward cost and risk. The farther down the list an information resources group concentrates its efforts, the more likely it is to be emphasizing technology and services available from outside the organization and the less likely, except in cases of failure, it is to be viewed as dealing directly with the overall goals of the organization. Therefore, the farther down the list an organization looks, the more attractive it will be to hire an outside group to provide the service.

Also, the farther down the list, the more likely it is that the units of service will be dealt with on the basis of cost and will be paid for on a fee-for-service basis. With fee-for-service billing, clients know how much the support costs. Presumably, they evaluate choices regarding scope and quality of service. Maybe they evaluate using alternative service providers. Service organizations can determine how competitive they are. For internal service providers, installing fee-for-service billing entails costs to implement procedures to capture the needed cost information, develop bills, and make internal funds transfers; an alternative is to present bills for "informational purposes only," even if they are only estimates.

As part of outsourcing a function previously handled within an organization, the employees who perform the function are likely to be removed from the organization's payroll. In some outsourcing arrangements, they join, or even form, the vendor company that will provide the service.

Several factors influence decisions about whether to outsource a service. In favor of outsourcing, the vendor has a strong focus for its objectives: continuous quality service at a low cost. It specializes and concentrates its efforts. There are, however, potential negatives:

- Will the vendor be able to perform the services at sufficiently low cost to earn a reasonable profit without raising the costs experienced by the original organization?
- Will the people being transferred or laid off take with them essential skills and insights that the organization cannot replace?
- Will the people being transferred lose expected career opportunities?
- Over time, will the vendor lose too much feel for the goals and culture of the customer organization?
- Will the vendor remain competitive?
- Will the vendor be able to respond to the organization's new needs for capability and flexibility?
- If not, how difficult will it be to change vendors or rebuild capability within the organization?

How "virtual" can an organization's information resources function become? One cannot outsource all one's information resources concerns—this would mean that the organization would rely entirely on outsiders for its sources of information and for its information-based processes. Strictly speaking, one's employees could not develop even a spreadsheet on a personal computer.

At the other extreme, even providers of information technology and services do not attempt to be self-sufficient. They acquire at least some telecommunications equipment and services, computers, maintenance services, and generic software.

The decision to rely on outside vendors is not one of whether but of how much. Success lies in choosing an appropriate balance between internal and external work.

Future competitiveness demands attention to managing both internal and outsourced work well, not only for moment-by-moment continuity of service but also for overall long-term corporate capability and flexibility.

VISION AND INCENTIVE—ENSURING THE SUCCESS OF PROJECTS

How can an organization ensure the success of an information resources management project? Consider the seemingly simple example of maintaining telephone directories for an organization.

In a large company, one traditionally finds different printed directories for departments, plants, geographic regions, nations, and perhaps the entire worldwide employment. Additionally, individuals maintain personal directories.

How long does it take to list a new employee in a directory? It may be many months before the next edition is printed. If a person changes telephone numbers, how long will it be before everyone who needs to know knows? Of course, a great deal of work is expended to maintain, print, and distribute directories.

Much effort can be saved if there is a single, companywide computerized directory that everyone uses as part of an electronic mail system. Additionally, many opportunities for people to work together can be created and realized, especially if the directory contains people's work emphases, fields of expertise, facsimile numbers, and electronic mail addresses.

Recall the example of the company in which this kind of electronic directory is an integral part of a corporate culture that encourages employees to help each other answer questions and solve problems. An employee who needs to learn something describes that need in an E-mail message. The employee directs that the message be routed to employees registered as having specific areas of expertise. The system determines the recipients. Those recipients who can help are likely to do so because this company is in the consulting business and people who answer questions are more likely to be invited to work on current and future projects, thereby enhancing their careers.

Consider similarities and differences between the two strategies for telephone directories, one traditional and the other modern.

Both are parts of their respective companies' information resources management. At the core of each effort is the maintenance of an information resource, namely, a list of people in the organization and how to reach them. In each case, the list is intended to help people communicate with each other.

The modern approach is more aggressive in terms of information proficiency. There is a broader view of how effective an organization can be in using an information resource to accomplish work. And there is a broader vision of the role of a company telephone book. A directory can be used for locating expertise, not just specific people or organizations. There is a broader vision of people helping each other. Employees have a greater sense both of the rest of the organization and of their part in the organization. There is a broader vision of self-empowerment to find sources of solutions.

The modern example features more incentives to keep listings current and better mechanisms for doing so. Employees are more conscious of the role of the telephone book and their needs to be listed properly, can check their own listings, and have an easier, quicker method for making changes. A change is available to all people instantly.

Needs for printed directories can still exist. For example, one might want to give a customer a printed directory of people who support that customer. The modern solution can be designed to provide both specialized directories and, if needed, the traditional organizationwide telephone book more easily, accurately, and quickly than can done using traditional techniques.

Crucial to the modern solution are the incentives it encompasses—incentives for individual employees to maintain their listings and to communicate with other employees. Other factors include the availability of technology and people to implement the system. When the technology becomes available, the number of people-hours per year devoted to directory maintenance and publication should decrease after a transition to the new system. It is simply too cumbersome to collect and distribute directory information on paper or by diskette.

To ensure superior implementation of an information resources management project, you need to pay attention to information proficiency, not just information resources management. Take a forward-looking practical view of organizational needs and behavior. Ensure that there are incentives for the participants. Look at the possibilities opened up by technology. In so doing, you will win the allies needed to make the project succeed. And you will enhance the overall capability and flexibility of the organization as well as contribute to efficiency.

SYNERGY AND INNOVATION— INGREDIENTS FOR SUCCESSFUL PROJECTS

You doubtless know of projects that did not meet expectations—spreadsheet packages completed by vendors months behind schedule and still containing bugs or flawed administrative software that businesses have written for themselves. Projects can run smoothly though; they can meet objectives and do so on time. Here is a heartening example of information-proficient interorganizational synergy and of software development processes that produced excellent results.

A county crime lab undertook to automate its work tracking. Previously, the laboratory had kept paper records of its work. When new evidence was received, a case number was assigned. The case was recorded in a logbook. The evidence was sent to the appropriate part of the laboratory. After the analysis of the evidence was complete, the case was noted in the logbook as closed.

The new tracking system was targeted to run on a computer that the county was buying for this application as well as for a management system to help administer a jail that was being built. Computer terminals would be located on desks within the laboratory. With the county's programmers fully occupied developing the jail system, the laboratory put its software development project out to bid.

Obviating needs to debate hardware and programming languages simplified relations with potential contractors. But, by normal standards, the county seemed almost too casual in its approach to contractors—there was no written request for proposals for this project. Instead, prospective bidders interviewed laboratory management. Without a specification, bidders were free to propose their own innovations.

A contract was awarded based on a six-page letter bid that outlined functions the system would help the laboratory perform. As yet, neither the laboratory nor the contractor had laid out how information would be arranged when presented on terminals. There were no documented work flows.

The contractor and the laboratory management quickly settled on a new numbering methodology for cases, many of which consisted of several pieces of evidence received on different days. Enough common understanding seemed to exist to allow the contractor to proceed with a vigorous programming effort.

This was not a small application. Ultimately, the county would take possession of 100,000 lines of new software. Yet, the contractor spent only three to four people-months on this project, including all the time it took to make the bid, talk with the client about specifications, write and test key software, demonstrate essential system functions and gain the laboratory manager's agreement that the project was headed in the right direction, ensure that the software conformed to standards set by the jail management system, complete the software, install and start up the system, train the laboratory's staff, and collect payments as project milestones were completed.

This degree of programming productivity is difficult to achieve. At the time of this project, studies of large programming projects often reported averages of much less than 10 lines of code per person per hour. This project produced about 150 to 200 lines per person-hour. The difference did not lie in software tools that came with the computer; those tools consisted of a text editor facilitating the typing of program code, a compiler for translating that code into a form suitable for the computer's hardware, and utility software for managing program and data files.

The application included software that allowed crime lab employees to add, change, and delete items from nine lists: clients, employees, work activities, and so forth. It took an evening to develop and test one of these list-maintenance programs. Rather than serially coding eight more programs, the programmer tore apart the existing program, leaving a generic backbone of software with instructions for the compiler to copy into the program each segment specific to the first list. Based on this new program structure, producing and testing the other eight list management programs took only one more evening.

A decade later, this recognition of similarities between the various lists would be called *object-oriented programming*. For the crime lab system, the technique worked well for other groups of programs. Out of 100 software modules, only some of the 20 report-printing modules and a few others were programmed from scratch.

The laboratory's staff found that the system embodied logical enhancements and simplifications of familiar procedures. Training consisted of a few demonstrations, followed by Just Ask . . . learning from colleagues. The county programmers took over the software. The programming methodology, choice of names for modules and variables, and ability to recompile the entire system with one command proved adequate. The maintenance programmers never needed to consult with the contractor.

Here are some of the lessons of this project:

- Such information-proficient attributes as interpersonal and interorganization communication, competence, and trust can obviate needs for expensive and delaying paperwork such as memoranda of understanding, formal specifications, and technical documentation. Interorganizational synergy and empowerment work when the people are able and willing.
- Look before you leap. A little forethought often recognizes potentially repetitive work. A little work to develop innovative techniques often obviates much repetitive work.
- Keep software development teams small. One of the reasons programmer productivity is often less than 10 lines of useful code per hour is the administrative activity required for large teams. The team that produced the crime lab system consisted of 2 people, one of whom produced only the 20 report modules.

This project also illustrates the value of separating concerns about mission-specific software from those of generic software and hardware. Both the county and the contractor were well served because there was no reason to debate the choice of generic technology.

EMPOWERMENT AND BEHIND-THE-SCENES SUPPORT—AN EXAMPLE CONTINUED

Recall the international audit, tax, and technology consulting firm that leverages knowledge as a corporate resource. This firm provides an example of an innovative approach to building such a resource.

At one time, the company used competing generic software tools (Fig. 16–3) on its desktop computers. Backed by the company's chairman, the chief technologist orchestrated a change to standard tools for individuals. Then came preparation for the move to the groupware that facilitates companywide sharing of the firm's information resources.

The chief technologist commissioned a survey of a employees' experiences with technology. The best, it was found, featured implementing small projects for clients, whereas the worst involved national projects. A "reengineer from behind" strategy was chosen. No pilot project was done. The groupware was supplied simultaneously to each of the several thousand employees in the United States. Attention was paid to three issues:

- Technological *reliability* was viewed as a key to ensuring that each use of the tools is a success. The goal was, and continues to be, "zero defects." Short of that, any problems should not distract employees as they use the system.
- A successful, Just Ask . . . (Fig. 8–1) *learning strategy* was adopted. Encouraging employees to rely on their own intelligence and ability, the firm viewed formal training as a potential barrier to learning. A 20-page on-line "booklet" accompanied the groupware. Although some employees expressed concerns that they would not become optimally proficient, the company continued a policy of no formal training in the belief that the advantages of Just Ask . . . learning outweighed those employees' concerns. Consulting with colleagues was encouraged, and some employee-led lunchtime seminars were formed.
- The firm focused on *technology as an empowering tool*. Paralleling the training strategy, the company's view of empowerment allowed people to innovate at their own rate. There was no central plan specifying what applications people should tackle. There was no attempt to search for "best practices." Generally, people automated some traditional work before going on to create new techniques.

This informal strategy has built an international resource of knowledge. Every employee uses the resource and the tools that support it. One goal for the tools is to minimize the time people spend working with technology so that employees can spend more time working with clients.

The strategy has led to a change in the support provided for employees in their use of technology. "Help desks" have been supplanted by a distributed cadre of advisers, who are encouraged to focus on helping people learn how to do work better rather than on learning how to use the technology better. In the firm's U.S. offices, the ratio of employees to advisers is about 70 to 1.

LEADERSHIP AND SUCCESS—ANOTHER EXAMPLE CONTINUED

Recall the example of the high-technology corporation in which the chief information officer strives to be the "chief time officer," namely a key player in reducing the operating subsidiaries' process times. This corporation's attention to bottom-line results and to synergy between information resources practitioners and the business units drives the implementation of systems.

To initiate a new project, client and practitioner management agree on a project architecture. A joint client-practitioner steering committee is formed. Committee minutes are retained electronically for future reference. The project is divided into components so that teams are kept small. The teams are responsible for working out the details of the interpersonal communications between groups and technical linkages between modules. Normally, between two-thirds and 90 percent of the project participants are clients.

The corporation has a preference for modular projects that feature rapid adoption of new techniques. The chief information officer notes that phasing in a new system can take 3 times as long and cost 10 times as much as a quick changeover.

Modular design is important. The corporation has, at various times, started new business units, consolidated warehouses, and outsourced sales groups. The corporation requires systems that:

- Facilitate reorganizing, creating, and selling business units.
- Support doing business in many monetary units.
- Can be used in several human languages.

The systems also meet corporate security, legal, and operational needs. Modularity facilitates meeting operational necessities:

- Information security, including allowing only appropriate use by employees of other businesses, such as distributors of this corporation's products.
- Adherence to copyright restrictions—some of the software licenses acquired by the corporation do not permit use of the software on business partners' or employees' computers.
- The ability to disconnect from the corporate network a person or computer placing undue demands on the overall corporate system information resource.

The corporation has implemented a split between mission-specific information and technology and generic information and technology. Operational databases, including a worldwide inventory of parts and assembled products, provide up-to-date mission-specific data for employees who build and distribute products. Other copies of these databases are maintained, through daily updates, as generic information for use by other people throughout the corporation.

For the main manufacturing and distribution operations, the split means that the primary databases run unencumbered by other uses. Corporate effectiveness has been enhanced and information systems costs have been contained.

The split has also provided considerable convenience for the other information users. Employees have developed hundreds of analytic software applications. Analytic work, printing, and applications development, maintenance, and use are all decoupled from the operational needs served by the main databases.

Data and processing software are concentrated in two types of computers. Mainframe computers maintain the operational databases. Computers that serve local work groups store the data copies that are updated daily, along with other software and data used by people in their personal computers. Data is not stored in personal computers, thereby enhancing security, minimizing time spent administering and backing up systems, and facilitating computer exchanges in case of upgrade or failure.

Mainframe operations have been outsourced. The corporation maintains its own data communications network, believing that, as yet, there is no attractive outsourcing alternative.

Information resources costs are charged to the operating companies. Identifiable external computing and telephone costs are charged directly. Rates for other technology and services, such as desktop computers, are set by processes mimicking rate setting for a public utility. A committee sets the rates. The rate-setting process provides knowledge and feedback for both the information resources community and its clients.

The project management and cost allocation techniques reinforce this corporation's commitment to use the technology it sells as an effective tool to maintain its own competitiveness. Corporate goals, not technology, are the main drivers for its information resources endeavors.

17

Anticipating and Measuring the Benefits of Projects

*M*uch controversy has surrounded measuring the benefits of information resources management projects. Determining and communicating quantitative and qualitative benefits are key to choosing and marketing proposed projects, as well as to building credibility based on past successes. Enhanced information proficiency is a measurable benefit.

PRODUCTIVITY . . . ARE THE REPORTS REAL?*

Over a recent period of several years, there were a number of negative claims under the heading of "productivity gains—are the benefits from information technology real?" A popular conclusion seems to have been that productivity gains are small to nonexistent.

The problem for a reader of claims about productivity improvement, or the absence of it, is the lack of definition of what is being reported. One issue is that of "local" measurement versus "global" measurement within an organization.

Suppose that a corporation makes an improvement through automation that results in halving the staff devoted to a function while continuing to handle the same workload with the same quality. Dividing output by input, there is a 100 percent gain in productivity per person—locally. But what about for the entire company?

If the extra staff is laid off and no other functions are affected, there is a corporationwide gain in productivity per person—the same work is done with a smaller workforce. If, on the other hand, the extra staff is redeployed solely into improving the quality, but not the throughput, of other corporate operations, then there is an argument for no overall productivity gain. The company handles the same number of units of work with the same number of people. Thus, a local gain may or may not lead to a gain measured companywide.

This example points out another issue in focusing on quantitative measures of productivity. How does one recognize, in the productivity numerator, qualitative improvements in outputs? Where is the place for timeliness or customer satisfaction?

The composition of a unit of output can change. A car made today is not the same as one made 25 years ago. A new car has a special brake light, a sophisticated pollution-control system, and air bags.

---

*Adapted from Thomas J. Buckholtz, 1993. Material similar to portions of this section appeared in *Computerworld,* July 5, 1993, p. 70. Reused with permission of CW Publishing/Inc.

Preparation of an income tax return today is not the same as it was in the past. The rules have grown in complexity.

Today's unit of output can differ considerably from yesterday's. For processes that occur in offices, automation has facilitated accomplishing work. However, society continues to increase the requirements per transaction: more service or features to stay competitive, more complexity generated by new government programs, additional refinements in laws and regulations, new subtleties in interpretations of laws and regulations, and growing requirements for accountability and auditing.

In the final analysis, there are clear-cut productivity gains. In the 1990s, the U.S. Social Security Administration handles more accounts, with more timely public service, than it did in 1980. It does so based on procedural simplification and automation, with a significantly reduced staff (McDonough and Buckholtz, 1992).

A close look at many situations would lead us to conclude that gains have been achieved. Indeed, a more telling question than whether there have been gains is: How could today's work be accomplished at all if it were not for information technology?

A close second for serious consideration is whether society needs to roll back, or at least slow down the growth of, self-imposed complexity. Often, systems can be built to support the complexity, but should we have to expend the resources so that they can? Do we not have better goals to accomplish, with or without the systems? And how can people be informed members of society if they themselves cannot keep up?

CAN BENEFITS BE QUANTIFIED?

Productivity represents but one measure by which to judge an organization or activity. The more general question is: What other measures are there of anticipated or achieved success?

The question of the benefits of technology-based change has been controversial. Until the recent slimming down of corporations and improvement in corporate competitiveness and performance, there was noticeable sentiment that a significant investment in information systems, estimated at $1 trillion during a decade ending in early 1993, had not produced measurable improvement.

Any discussion about change and improvement leaves room for debate. Change and improvement are relative, not absolute, concepts; one must make comparisons.

*   *   *

A first conclusion about estimating benefits is that one must compare at least two scenarios.

Sometimes, one can institute change so as to have a laboratorylike comparison. Suppose that two groups perform the same function, say, insurance claims processing, with little difference in type of work, technique, and results. One group institutes a procedural change. If the types of work remain comparable between the two groups, comparing ongoing results leads to conclusions about the change and, presumably, to a decision as to which of the two techniques, old or new, is best for both groups.

Appropriate use of small-scale tests can serve as a proxy for this type of test, which compares two similar groups.

Often, there is no laboratory in which to compare alternatives. One can measure results only for the scenario that occurs. In making a change, one cannot measure precisely what would have happened without the change. If one does not make a change, it may be difficult to estimate what opportunities were missed. While only one of the scenarios can be observed, hindsight can be used to estimate the results of the other.

*   *   *

The second major conclusion about estimating benefits is that one must use some bases for comparing results.

One frequently used basis for comparison consists of estimating the present value of receipts and payments of money. For a future project, each transaction is estimated as to monetary amount and date. *Present value* refers to adjusting the amounts downward by a hypothetical interest rate, thereby reflecting the notion that a person would just as soon receive today, say, 95% percent of a particular future payment as wait until the anticipated receipt date to obtain the full value. The farther in the future, the lower the percentage. The overall present value for the project is the sum of the discounted receipts minus the sum of the discounted payments.

This method is useful, but its limitations should be recognized. For a future project the numbers are guesses. Even for a project consisting of an investment in a government bond, there are questions as to what discount rate the investor should use in computing the present value of each receipt. For most projects, the amounts and times of cash receipts and payments are estimates.

Beyond the numeric uncertainties lie questions of what to do with "financial intangibles." For example, an increase in information proficiency can be quantified (Fig. 6–1), but estimating its present value may be difficult. For information resources projects, there is usually something, such as a change in employee empowerment or morale, for which it is difficult to find a place in a present value equation. One should build a list ranking the most important financial intangibles, positive and negative, for use along with the calculated present value.

With this method, a choice between two alternatives is based on the difference between the two present values and on comparing the two lists of financial intangibles. For example, a decision might boil down, in essence, to choosing between an anticipated information-proficiency enhancement with unestimated financial impact and an estimated monetary advantage to the organization. Such a choice can be made based on principles.

*   *   *

In a world of why-not, there are likely to be many choices. Finding improvement projects is not difficult. No matter what criteria are used, it is necessary to choose between candidate projects and make the best use of resources.

For a specific change, you might anticipate enhancements in information proficiency; bottom-line earnings; constituents' perceptions; employees' health and safety; shareholder value, as reflected in stock prices; return on assets; service to your community; or overall cost-effectiveness.

To the extent that you can focus on major concepts and synthesize reasonable estimates regarding various alternatives, you can estimate quantitative and qualitative benefits of future alternatives or of the choices that have already been made.

*   *   *

Estimating benefits is important, even for ongoing and completed projects. You need to market the successes of your endeavors. To enhance your information proficiency, you need to review decisions so as to be able to apply lessons learned in making future decisions. You need to learn from past decisions, and that means using hindsight that is as close to "20/20" as possible to evaluate what happened and what might have happened.

You need to sharpen your skills at estimating benefits for hypothetical scenarios. After all, this is a key practice in evaluating alternative futures and making decisions. For decisions, at least two possible future scenarios must be imagined.

The real questions lie not in whether benefits can be quantified. They are instead: How well can you estimate future benefits, whether quantitative or qualitative? And how well can you make and market your decisions?

DELINEATING COSTS

"How much does our organization spend on information resources management?" People raise questions like this from time to time.

One answer considers obvious costs: equipment; services, including telephone and other telecommunications services; staff within information technology groups; and other staff members with titles such as computer programmer. This answer understates the costs for information technology and services, let alone information resources management.

There are additional costs for supporting information technology, such as the time of information technology clients who perform such informal work as:

- Helping colleagues become proficient with technology.
- Administering technology in their work groups—inventorying it, making backup copies of data, informing people and systems about changes in people allowed to use systems, and serving as a point of contact in case of an equipment failure.
- Helping select new generic technology.

There are costs for empowered activities related to information and procedures:

- Creating or modifying a computer-based procedure, such as the logic in a spreadsheet.
- Serving on teams that sponsor, create, or test innovation, such as a new work process based on information technology.

There are also all the other activities that change the organization's information resources:

- Entering data into a computer system.
- Reading a magazine or other source of information.
- Performing an analysis or making a decision.

Where to draw the line is up to you and your organization. Choosing "all of the above" may come close to including all costs the organization incurs—essentially all activities impact the organization's information resources.

Another choice is to include all costs related to generic information and technology and all costs to create and modify information systems-based procedures but to exclude the costs of clients' time to record and use data. This view holds that it does not matter who writes a computer program or what techniques are used—a financial analyst creating a new analytic tool using a spreadsheet package is doing work similar to that done by a professional programmer using a traditional programming language; all such costs are counted. For this view, you should include library and subscription costs just as you would fees for using outside services providing generic data.

Whatever method your organization chooses, as with measuring productivity and benefits, you need to apply definitions consistently (Fig. 10–3). People need to understand the basis and context for the comparisons they make. Deriving meaningful conclusions depends on comparing information that is consistent between groups and across time.

STICKING TO PRINCIPLES AND JUSTIFYING A PROJECT—AN EXAMPLE

This example, from a company that provides services based on information technology, illustrates that it can take more than a vision and a benefits estimate to launch a project. It also shows the transition of an endeavor from an informal project to a fully supported program.

This company's chief information officer manages several staff functions, including both internal information systems and the research leading to new customer services. Recognizing both forthcoming diversification of customer services and needs to modernize traditional services, the leader chartered a task force of a dozen people to recommend what significant changes should take place in corporate support processes and systems.

The task force decided to start with a clean slate. It envisioned the company taking charge of a fictitious similar company and designing, from scratch, the internal work processes for the new company. In two months, the task force produced a vision for new corporate work processes. It also produced a concept for how the actual company could make the transition from its current processes to the new ones.

The model for change was pursued. There was some support but little funding. No framework existed in which to pursue the changes vigorously. It was time to try a new approach to market the reengineering concept and reinvigorate the program. Several factors coalesced to give the effort a boost:

- The company prepared to spin off some of its operations, leaving a clearer sense of corporate direction. The company recognized needs to sustain its reputation for quality in its traditional service, as well as to pursue vigorously new services based on specific new technologies. Thus, the imperative for changing internal processes became more widely apparent.
- The notion of reengineering had become better known throughout the business community.
- The company hired a consultant, who:

  Verified the concepts and model generated by the task force and provided an improved analytic framework for moving the task force's recommendations from the realm of analysis to that of decisions.

  Provided resources needed to advance the project.

  Made the project more visible, partly because the company noticed that it was spending money for consulting services.

The company formalized the program by establishing funding, committing more personnel, and marketing the project both internally and externally. The focus for the project changed from "whether" to "what and how."

This example illustrates that it often takes more than estimates of benefits to launch a project. It was necessary to:

- Make people *aware* of the needs and potential for moving from the upper-left Coasting quadrant of the organizational climate chart (Fig. 7–2) to the upper-right Competing quadrant.
- Provide assurance and credibility for the concept of reengineering and for the *assessment* supporting the needs to institute change.
- Market the program to all senior management and then, with the help of all executives, to the entire company, thereby *activating* sufficient resources. With these three All A's steps (Fig. 7–1), the company *achieved* the start-up of this improvement program.

DOCUMENTING DECISIONS

As the last example, from the technology-based services company, illustrates, building an effective consensus for a project or program can require more than making a strong factual case. You must be able to present that case well. Unless you can make and implement a decision on your own and never have to justify your actions, you should consider the benefits of appropriate documentation.

All organizations share reasons for needing to be proficient at documenting decisions and actions. These reasons include:

- Documenting a decision provides material to help market and implement the decision.
- The work of developing and presenting a justification helps ensure that a satisfactory breadth of alternatives has been considered, that the alternatives have been researched adequately, that constituencies have been appropriately involved, and that a reasonable amount of support will accompany a decision.
- Knowing that actions will be documented encourages people to take the care necessary to avoid poor decisions and regrettable actions. Knowing that documentation will be kept discourages wasting time on options that will not stand the light of day.
- Documenting transactions, such as conversations during a contract negotiation, lessens threats of administrative appeals, avoids lawsuits, and helps win lawsuits when they do occur.
- Documenting decisions and decision-making processes provides a basis for improving information proficiency.

Governments have additional reasons for documenting decisions and actions. For example, policy and procedure encourage developing and keeping records so as to facilitate research into historic incidents and governmental processes.

Documentation does, however, generate risks. As society becomes more open and litigious, people are more likely to find past documents and interpret them in current contexts. Even supposedly transitory documents, like electronic mail messages, can be preserved in backup copies of computer systems' data. Any documentation has the potential to become controversial.

For a federal executive branch agency, a questionable or controversial action can come under scrutiny from any number of sources of 20/20 hindsight, such as allegedly wronged parties, the news media, public activists, political research groups, agency management, the agency's inspector general, the General Accounting Office, a congressional committee, and federal law-enforcement agencies.

Businesses are increasingly facing similar scrutiny. If a company does business with the federal government, any of the above sources of review can come into play directly. For any organization, there is potential for investigation by public activists, the news media, and other people.

All organizations face the challenge of finding a point of prudence—the right documentation, but not too much. Given the circumstances, you should expect a greater degree of documentation in governments than in most businesses. And you should expect that the amount of documentation within a business correlates with government regulation of that business.

REFERENCES

Buckholtz, Thomas J., 1993. Productive step forward. *Computerworld,* July 5, 1993, p. 70.

McDonough, Francis A., and Buckholtz, Thomas J., 1992. Providing better service to citizens with information technology. *Journal of Systems Management,* April 1992, pp. 32–40.

CHAPTER 18

Ensuring Information-Proficient Information Systems

Information proficiency applies to information systems as well as to people and organizations. A system's capability and flexibility depend on the extent to which designers build the system to be information-proficient. Some systems also learn from their users.

DATA DEFINITION—A KEY TO QUALITY

Consider the following example of an information system that used one piece of information for several purposes.

A retiree designates a conservator, who will handle all his financial and healthcare dealings. The conservator informs the retiree's former employer of the new mailing address for all items that would otherwise go to the retiree. The new address is recorded in the former employer's information system, which is designed to retain only one address per retiree. The system discovers that the address is outside the area served by the retiree's chosen health maintenance organization. The system automatically changes the retiree's coverage to a general policy that applies in the location of the conservator's address. The health maintenance organization continues to provide care but no longer receives premiums from the former employer's retirement plan. It takes a year for the conservator, former employer, health maintenance organization, and general insurance carrier to straighten out the situation.

Suppose that you are designing a system to support providing health insurance for a company's employees, retirees, and their families. From the above example, it is clear that you need to consider the issue of addresses. Each of the following could be a relevant, distinct address:

- Permanent residence.
- Location of convalescent home.
- General mailing address.
- Health conservator's mailing address.
- Accountant's mailing address.

Perhaps other addresses should be included. For example, for a family, there may be several addresses of permanent residences or convalescent homes.

This list of possible addresses can be called the "sufficient list" because it suffices in the following sense: If all such applicable data is current, then a mass mailing to all the addresses is sure to reach an appropriate address.

Designing this health insurance support system to minimize hassles for the employees and retirees, insurers, care providers, and the company may not be easy. You need to think of all the uses of the system and all the circumstances that might occur for the various constituents.

Perhaps data elements should be defined based substantially on their intended uses. In following that principle, you would consider having an address for mailings related to administrative matters such as offers of options for an employee or retiree to change insurance coverage, an address for dealing with the account on financial matters pertaining to claims, and so forth. Additionally, perhaps the company would like the system to record facsimile telephone numbers so that it can correspond by telephone when doing so would save money. This list of data elements is the "necessary list." These elements are necessary to perform the intended functions of the system and, presumably, to provide quality service to the system's constituents. The vocabulary for the necessary list differs from that for the sufficient list.

Perhaps, you, the system designer, will take a multitier approach, allowing recording of all the sufficient types of address information received but requiring only as much data as is needed to satisfy the necessary list (Fig. 18–1). This system will include rules, coded in software, to connect the primary inputs in the sufficient list to the useful concepts in the necessary list and to ensure that the necessary list is, and remains, completely satisfied.

There is a subtlety. The necessary list might contain an actual collection of addresses, or it might not. In the latter case, the necessary list consists of data "pointers" specifying, for example, which of the addresses from the sufficient list is to be used for administrative mailings.

If such a multitier approach is designed to allow for new types of items to be added to the sufficient list, changes in rules, and adequate follow-up to ensure consistency for extant cases after changes in rules, then you have a system portion that is not only capable but also flexi-

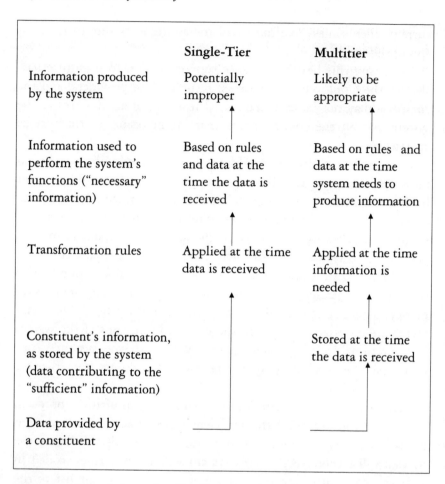

FIGURE 18–1   Information Handling, Based on Single-Tier and Multitier Data Definition.

ble. Postponing applying transformation rules provides added capability and flexibility compared to a single-tier approach in which newly received data is transformed by current rules and not retained as received (Fig. 18–1).

It takes more than this, however, to build a quality database. For example, issues about data elements that specify one address include the number of lines of address, numbers of characters, and consistency, such as between street address and zip code.

More broadly, there can be concerns about the history of the data. For example, if the company ever wanted to substantiate that it had made a reasonable attempt to contact a certain constituent about a certain issue, it might want to have in its active computer files a history of addresses. There are also issues of confidence in the data and of audits. For example, one might need to be able to retrieve a reference to the source of a recorded address.

Even more broadly, if all these complexities exist with regard to such a seemingly innocuous issue as addresses relevant to a company's retiree, then how difficult does data definition become in other systems?

While the issues surrounding data definition and data elements may not capture the imagination of many people, they provide one key to successful systems. To the extent that the design, use, and continued enhancement of a system occur so as never to misuse a data element, the system is pointed toward success.

Success with data definition fits within the quality paradigm. Adequate investment in planning and other start-up activities provides for capability and flexibility during the life of a collection of information.

PROCESS DEFINITION—ANOTHER KEY TO QUALITY

Process definition is another key to quality systems. Consider, for example, systems to aid in drafting contracts. A contract in the real estate marketplace might cover renting a home. A contract in the information technology marketplace might cover the purchase of some computing hardware, software licenses, and services.

Contracts include two types of components: specific conditions and general terms. The specific conditions provide specifications for products and services, prices, and delivery schedules. The general terms, also known as boilerplate, cover warranties, liabilities, provi-

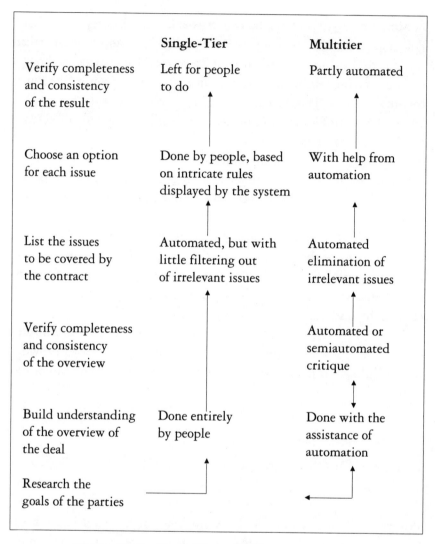

FIGURE 18–2   Single-Tier and Multitier Automation
for Generating Boilerplate.

sions mandated by law, and other general concepts appearing in many deals in the same marketplace.

Ideally, to write boilerplate, you first formulate an overview of the proposed agreement (Fig. 18–2, left column). What are the types of products and services, the pricing structures, and the other types of specific conditions? How do the parties intend to behave while the contract is active? When you believe that you have a reasonably complete understanding of the proposed transaction, you can list the issues that need to be covered in the boilerplate.

Next, you look for standard terms, used in previous contacts, that can describe the approach to each issue. For any issue, there are probably several distinct standard solutions. You try to find the solution closest to the intent of the deal or that of the party for which you work. If appropriate, you modify the chosen standard paragraph. You assemble a draft contract from such pieces and the specific conditions. You review your work for completeness and consistency. The parties to the proposed deal review the draft and negotiate differences.

A well-drafted document is an aid to negotiations. The document records areas of agreement. Differences are easy to spot and discuss. If there is a fundamental disagreement in overall expectations about the transaction, the parties need to discuss the overview of the deal. If not, they work on details.

Developing contractual boilerplate is an everyday occurrence. For simple transactions, such as renting a house, the nominal boilerplate can be a standard, printed form developed by a real estate association. The parties will probably use most of the paragraphs as printed; however, there may be some changes, for instance, regarding the renter's keeping pets on the premises. The specific conditions may fit into blank spaces provided on the form.

For more complicated transactions, including some in the computer and telecommunications marketplace, the processes of drafting and negotiating may consume months. Because the development of boilerplate may not be a top priority for people working on a deal and because of the way negotiations are conducted, the "reasonably complete understanding" of the structure of the deal may change from time to time.

For systems that automate the generation of boilerplate, the single-tier approach (Fig. 18–2) focuses on a pool of known paragraphs. In such a system, there is associated with each paragraph a precisely worded question that the system's user must answer. If the answer to the question is yes, the paragraph applies to a deal; if the answer is no, the paragraph is not used.

The strengths of this approach to automation are, among others, that it is easy to program the system's software, it seems to force the developer of the system to include a precise understanding of the applicability of each paragraph, and it appears to present a straightforward, one-step method for users to produce boilerplate. The weaknesses are found in matters such as whether all the boilerplate issues can be separated into independent paragraphs, whether a system so closely tied to its developer's choices of paragraphs and criteria will be appropriate, whether people can answer each question correctly, and what happens in case the parties need a customized paragraph. The questions through which the candidate paragraphs are selected or rejected will be both detailed as to the intent of the deal and precise in wording. People may misinterpret questions and there can be issues for which none of the paragraphs works.

The multitier approach develops in stages, paralleling the previously discussed human behavior for drafting contracts.

At the first stage, a person answers questions about the deal. The goal is not to produce paragraphs, but instead for the system to develop an understanding of the transaction and to verify the consistency of the concepts in the overview. If the concepts are not consistent, the system notifies the person. If the overview is consistent and the deal falls within the bounds that the system can handle, the person and system proceed to the next stage.

The system now goes through the relevant issues, assigning candidate paragraphs when it can rightly do so and asking the person to make choices when it cannot. The user's making choices will be simpler than in the first approach. Because there is an understanding of the overview of the deal, the choices will be limited and the questions can contain statements about context and be simpler. When the person is in doubt, the system can force the person to make a best choice in exchange for recording a reminder that modifications may be needed.

Just as with the multitier approach to data (Fig. 18–1), the multitier approach to process postpones decisions until appropriate times.

For this example, it is best to select paragraphs only after understanding the key points of the deal.

Attention to process definition is critical to getting work done, with or without automation tools. As with care in defining data, the choice and definition of underlying processes are crucial to the capability and flexibility of systems.

INFORMATION PROFICIENCY FOR INFORMATION SYSTEMS

Information proficiency is an important objective for information systems. How can the people who depend on a system be maximally information-proficient if the system itself is not?

The information in information systems includes both data and processes. As with *results* (Fig. 2–1), pieces of information are often neither elementary nor final. Many pieces of information have components. Many pieces of information are themselves components of other information.

Examples of elementary information are a traditional data field, such as a phone number or a name; a keystroke in a document; a pixel that is part of a picture; a component of sound; and a step in a process. Such elementary information can be used in combination with other similar units of information to form, respectively, a data record; a section of a memo, report, or letter; a picture; a segment of speech for a computer-generated movie; and a portion of a software program. Each of these items can be combined with similar items to form, respectively, a database, a complete report, a series of pictures constituting the video portion of a movie, the audio portion of a movie, and a complete software program. Of course, one can also mix different types of information. A movie includes pictures and sound. A newspaper page includes text and pictures. A spreadsheet includes data and processes.

What might a person want to know about such *items of informa-*

tion? Also, what knowledge might be relevant in an information system, either when the system is being developed or when it is in use?

- How does one refer to, and use, the item? For example, if a person is working on an insurance claim, how does one ask for information on that particular claim? Or, if one is writing a computer program to record credit-card transactions, how can the program invoke use of software that provides the date and time at which processing is taking place?
- How can one establish one's authority to use the item? This issue is especially important if the intended use includes changing the item or if the item contains information for which dissemination is restricted.
- What are the contexts in which this item exists? For example, the item may be a quoted sentence that a speaker presented as a hypothesis for discussion, not a sentence that the speaker thought to be fact.
- What information is supposed to be represented by an item? Recall the example of addresses related to health insurance policies. The one address stored for an employee might not apply for all the purposes for which it is being used.
- For what uses has this item been intended? For example, if the item is simulation software, what types and ranges of simulations can it handle?
- Where does the responsibility for avoiding untoward use lie— with the item's user or with a validation system built into the item? For example, in a simulator of planetary motion, does the simulator prevent the running of problems demanding physics more advanced than that which has been incorporated in the software?
- If used appropriately, how much confidence can one place in the use? To what extent is the confidence dependent on the specific use? When confidence is dependent on use, what information is produced by use of the item to indicate such confidence? For example, if the item produces statistical summaries of data, does it indicate numeric estimates of the confidence in the statistics?

Confidence depends on knowledge of accuracy, including a sense of what the information is supposed to represent; consistency, including a context into which to put the information; and other attributes (Fig. 10–3).

- What methods are available to test the quality of the item? For data, one might need references to sources. For software, one might want test procedures.
- What rules govern combining this item with others to form a new item?
- How was the item developed? By whom or what? From what sources? For example, if the item contains a decision, what factors led to that decision?
- What is the history of the content of the item? For example, for a person's address, what were previous addresses, and when and how were changes made?
- Does anyone own intellectual property rights to this item or some information contained in it? If so, what licensing provisions and procedures apply?
- What is the history of use of the item? For example, for a published paper describing a scientific discovery, what other papers have made reference to this paper? Or, for a unit of software, in what other software has it been used? This last question is especially important if the software unit is later found to have an error or if there is a proposal to change its range of applicability.
- If someone is interested in using this item, are there other items that might also be useful? For example, if a person wants information about one insurance claim, what other claims may be relevant? Cross-references among items can be very helpful.
- In what format is this item? For example, a person's name could be stored as a few dozen characters in a database, a verbal message in a voice mail system, or a pixel-based image of a portion of a page of text.
- What are the components of the item, and how can one answer questions, similar to those above, about each? For example, a date might include three component items: a month, a day in the month, and a year.

These are all questions of *metainformation*—also known as *metadata*—information about information. An item has content that might represent, for example, a number, a picture, some software, or the words, diagrams, and spatial layout for a book. An item also has external attributes that describe how to use it and internal attributes defining what it is made of. For one item, the answers to the above questions constitute metadata. Each answer can include one or more items of useful metadata.

In developing an item or a complete information system, to what extent should one take into account each concept that could be embodied in metadata? There is no standard answer. Perhaps, for a well-designed system, the best one can say is that the trade-offs were made conscientiously. Metadata needs to be available in situations in which its availability is worth the effort to have developed it.

One of the challenges of developing systems is providing useful metadata. For example, the need for written documentation about systems and their components was recognized decades ago. People need to be able to communicate to each other the purpose and design criteria of pieces of data and software. Today, metadata issues can also be addressed by object-oriented programming and other techniques. The need for metadata that can be used by other items within systems will present challenges for some time to come. Not only are there decisions to be made about which metadata to develop for any item, but also there are challenges to standardize the expression of metadata so that it can be used as widely as possible with as little effort as possible.

You may have noticed that metadata issues are similar to those considered by people and organizations making or implementing decisions. Successful treatment of metadata issues while developing systems parallels successful capturing of information-proficiency opportunities while conducting business. Success with metadata in systems involves trade-offs, as does success in devoting appropriate attention to any decision. Overkill can be as inappropriate as underattention. A metadata-oriented approach encourages thinking appropriate to developing flexible systems that can produce, for external constituents or other parts of the system, information that is useful and adequately qualified.

The successful system of the future will be information-proficient. It will be composed of, and provide, useful qualified data and processes. The metadata will be useful for people and other systems. These requirements will need to be met at a minimum of cost and in a timely manner.

ENSURING CONTINUING CAPABILITY AND FLEXIBILITY

Successful development of a lasting, evolving information system depends on ensuring capability and flexibility to meet challenges that the system will face over a long period of time.

Modularity and precise definition of data elements militate against risks from growing complexity and changing vocabulary. The example based on the health insurance administration system that stored only one address per policy illustrates this concept (Fig. 18–1). A system designer should anticipate proliferating needs for parallel information—several addresses in that example. Separating information into layers is also key. In that example, layering entails separating the sufficient list that collects addresses known for a particular insurance policy from the necessary list of addresses needed to communicate successfully with the system's constituents.

Modular definition of data elements also builds flexibility to combine elements in new ways. This is especially important in meeting people's demands for information synthesized from disparate sources. Such demands can require combining conceptually similar information, such as financial data for two merging companies, or distinctly different information, such as the text and pictures that constitute a newspaper.

A solid, well-understood, easy-to-use base of data provides the firm foundation on which to build current and future information system processes.

Similarly, care to define and modularize processes builds a capable, flexible resource. As with data elements, processing modules can be reused, replicated, and combined to meet future needs. As with data elements, layering and modularity provide benefits. Consider again the example of software to generate contract boilerplate. Developing the software in tiers so that the structure of the deal is "understood" before the software selects boilerplate paragraphs is a layered approach (Fig. 18–2). There will be many modules in each layer. These techniques facilitate keeping the software up-to-date with changes in contracting policies and laws. These techniques are essential if the software is to "learn" over time.

The long-term success of a system depends on maintaining useful, thorough catalogs of data elements and processing modules. These catalogs promote both the long-term utility of the entire information resource and the immediate economies of avoiding duplicate modules.

Layering and modularity (Fig. 16–4) support yet another long-term need. Eventually, pieces of technology are taken out of use. The organization must continue to do its work, with minimal interruption. Again, use of the layered, modular paradigm pays off.

Today, organizations routinely upgrade or replace computers without disturbing operations. Someday, however, today's computer and generic software product lines will cease to exist. Experience has proved that considerable trauma can occur as companies maintain obsolete generic technology and rescue the intelligence contained in software and data that depend on that technology.

Modularity and layering within the Peer Paradigm overcome traditional difficulties in making changes between types of technology. Newly developed applications software and data depend on software tools, not hardware. Therefore, it is possible to move between families of incompatible computers if there are compatible tools. This risk of having an "orphan" application has been shifting from the risk of a hardware line stagnating to the risk that a software tool will not be maintained in the marketplace. Even the latter risk can be minimized by using tools that exchange information with other tools.

Therefore, the main risk of facing a technically obsolete database or applications software system is poor practice on the part of the organization in maintaining its knowledge of, and control over, its own data, data definitions, software, and software control techniques. Building layered, modular, information-proficient systems minimizes this risk.

Capability and Flexibility Through Modularity and Standards

Recall the example of the software tools company that applies the principles of modularity, responsibility, and synergy throughout the layers of the Peer Paradigm for organizations, information, and accomplishments (Fig. 4–2). The company's advice to customers building *mission-specific* systems and its techniques for developing its own products, which are *generic tools* (Fig. 16–4), emphasize these three principles.

The corporation espouses the concept that designing a system for capability and flexibility rests on rigorous definition of interfaces between modules and vigorous enforcement of autonomy between modules. Within this framework, systems are built iteratively, with each module evolving from a minimally functioning placeholder to a fully capable peer participant. Subsequently, the interface definitions and intermodular autonomy provide long-term flexibility. An individual module can be easily enhanced when appropriate. New modules can be added when necessary.

The company emphasizes that this approach allows software developers to identify and tackle the highest-risk elements of a project early, thereby minimizing the risks rather than letting them grow while programmers produce the easier parts of a system.

Rigorous separation of the functions and communications within a module from the communications with other modules streamlines development, facilitates finding and fixing problems, facilitates making upgrades, and leads to reusing modules in subsequent systems. The company has observed a high degree of reuse, both when customers develop subsequent systems for similar applications and when the company extends its own product line.

A SYSTEM THAT LEARNS FROM THE PEOPLE WHO USE IT

An information-proficient system grows to meet changing needs. Consider the following example of a system that learns from the people who use it.

This system helps people analyze financial information. For instance, suppose a person asks the system to compare the income of banks. The system will ask the person to select appropriate concepts of "bank" and "income" from the definitions provided by people who previously used the system. If, for example, the individual does not want to use any of the previous definitions of income, the person creates a new one, which the system adds to its repertoire. Thus, this adaptive learning system builds dictionaries of data, such as the definitions of "bank," and procedures, such as methods of calculating income. The system and the people who use it are synergistically building an information-proficient resource.

The system can extract key financial information and auditors' statements scattered within reports filed by companies with the U.S. Securities and Exchange Commission. Uses of the information include spotting changes in a company's health or in its standing within its industry group.

The firm that developed the system is initiating a study to determine what can be learned and reapplied from building and using this adaptive system. It is time to achieve another step in corporate capability and flexibility based on another step forward in information proficiency.

P A R T *6*

Technology

19

Anticipating New Technology

*P*rogress in technology is based on "repetition."
Repetitive behaviors suggest opportunities for new
information technology products.

REPETITION—THE TRUE EXCITEMENT
IN INFORMATION TECHNOLOGY

"New," "improved," and "different" are important words in the language of sales. In the information technology marketplace, we hear about new models, improved technical attributes, and the concepts of faster, smaller, and lighter. "Less expensive" also sells well. But when all is said and done, the key to information technology is *repetition*. The basis for a major advance in information technology is the recognition of repetitive behavior. The advance is the successful automation of the behavior. Examples abound.

About two centuries ago, punched-card technology was invented to automate the production of repetitive patterns woven on French looms. More recently, punched-card calculators and early computers met needs for repetitive trajectory calculations for military projectiles. Uses of today's supercomputers emphasize repeated simulations within families of scientific and engineering problems, based on repeated use of algorithms that model specific laws of nature. People's understanding of the laws of nature is itself based on repetitive experimentation and validation.

Telecommunications technology answers and routes phone calls, sends and receives facsimile messages, and records verbal messages. All these communications advances arise from the recognition of, and application of automation to, repetitive behavior.

Advances in the designing of computer chips depend on recognizing unautomated repetitive practices in chip design work.

Personal computers took a major step forward based on the invention of the electronic spreadsheet. The family of personal computer technology owes its progress to recognition of both repetitiveness in accounting calculations and the usefulness of calculations based on numeric tables.

The successes of word processing and desktop publishing rest on the automation of steps that people perform to create and publish a document.

Generally, when society has mastered the fundamentals of some repetitive behavior, people take the opportunity to build tools to handle that activity. Often, the first tools are specific to the missions of a few organizations or the needs of one discipline. The main principles and parts of those tools often have far more uses than originally envisioned. General-purpose products emerge, multiplying the value of these principles by applying them to broad, repetitive needs.

The progress of information technology is measured by the transition of repetitive behavior from not automated to automated by mission-specific technology to automated by generic technology (Fig. 16–3).

OPPORTUNITIES FOR NEW PRODUCTS

Repetitive procedures in today's workplace suggest a number of opportunities for information technology products.

*   *   *

Consider the finding and filtering of information (Fig. 3–1). Making today's complex decisions demands both breadth and specificity of information. Typically, people first compile lists of relevant articles, books, documents, and other information. Second, they narrow their focus to review as much of the most relevant material as time permits.

Traditional support for this activity features indexing material by subject, author, and key words. Somewhat newer technology allows indexing all the nontrivial words in documents and responds easily to a request such as "find all instances of 'computer' within five words of 'telecommunications.'" A person can only hope to be formulating optimal queries; for example, a search for "computer" may overlook articles devoted to sophisticated pocket calculators, which are computers.

Forthcoming technology tools provide considerably more assistance in formulating search criteria, finding material, narrowing the field of material considered, and extracting useful information.

An information service, whether publicly available or run internally within an organization, will build a powerful index to knowledge. The service will use new linguistics-based tools to analyze the contents of documents and determine themes and contexts. For each document, the themes will be ranked by their relative strength. Also, because the tools understand relations between terms, a document that discusses computers, for example, will be linked to a more general concepts, such as information technology, even though the concepts are not explicitly mentioned in the document. Putting such information together results in document characterizations that allow new sophistication in matching searchers' intents.

The tools help people formulate appropriate searches, whether for a one-time need or for ongoing filtering of news. Ultimately, search criteria are reduced to strength profiles and other information matching both a searcher's intent and the cataloging technique for documents.

The searcher has two filters. The first is the number of documents to pursue, which can be determined by the searcher's available time and by the number and strengths of the matches. The second is the degree of detail to which the searcher intends to explore each document. The tools permit the person to ask for any degree of detail, from a few key ideas, through an abstract of, say, 5 percent of the length of the document, to the complete document. Flexibility abounds. If a 5 percent abstract proves interesting, the searcher can quickly ask for and receive a 10 percent version to find out the next most heavily emphasized concepts in the document and determine if further reading is appropriate.

To the extent that many documents are thus cataloged and searchers build profiles expressing their interests, people will have vital tools for extracting the most relevant information they need from the world's growing library of word-based materials. To the extent that salient aspects of recorded visual, audio, and numeric information are described in words, these materials become part of the searchable knowledge base.

*   *   *

The processes organizations use to generate reports, letters, and other documents present a prime opportunity for information technology products. While word processing and other traditional techniques play key roles in recording and formatting content, the potential has existed for a number of years to build tools that are even more helpful. Software is now coming into the marketplace to help people work as a group to develop a document.

Consider one opportunity. Picture yourself in charge of the development of a report. Staff reporting to you are coordinating the work. Some time ago you read a complete draft and sent the staff a number of suggestions. Other people did the same. Your staff worked diligently, reconciling the comments, performing any recommended research, and producing a picture-perfect final draft for your approval. You look at this draft. Now you will test some of the information proficiency (Fig. 5–2) of your organization by considering questions such as the following:

Question: What decision are you trying to make?
Answer: Whether to approve the report.

Question: What information would you like to have?
Answer: What happened regarding your last suggestions, what other suggestions were made, and what changes were made since the last draft you read thoroughly.

Question: What information do you have?
Answer: Perhaps, just a perfectly polished, supposedly final draft.

Question: What decision must you now make?
Answer: Whether to ask people to track down the answers to your questions (or, if someone sent you all the markups after the last draft, whether to review all this material), read the entire new draft, or just approve the report.

Question: What tool would you like your group to have in order to make all of you more effective in producing reports?
Answer: Software that would help a group of people manage the writing of a document.

Recognizing the needs, software developers have recently begun producing new products. Such software should allow any person working on the document to make comments and suggest changes electronically. It should keep complete drafts and a log of comments, proposed changes, and notes about how suggestions were acted on and why. It should answer the types of questions that forced you, in the example, to change the decision you wanted to make from whether to approve the report to whether to seek information about the recent history of suggestions and changes. Because several people need the answers to those and similar questions, such a software tool should save much rereading and other unneeded steps to complete documents.

*   *   *

There are more processes in the workplace than just filtering information and drafting documents, and there are other opportunities for new tools. While some procedures, such as processing credit-card payments, have been or are being virtually fully automated, there is still stylized work that can benefit from significant new automation.

There is opportunity for tools that make it easy for office workers to describe to a computer repetitive work flows and the criteria for making decisions. Such a tool should allow applications to be built incrementally. For work involving procedures not yet fully automated, the software should ask the person using it how to handle specific, as yet unautomated nuances. As the staff builds confidence and refines its procedures, the new understanding is added to the application. One example of a procedure in need of such tools is the generation of boilerplate for contracts (Fig. 18–2).

*   *   *

Another general opportunity is for the continued growth and expanded use of electronic commerce. Here, business transactions are conducted, or at least supported, via computing and telecommunications. Paper and unneeded personal contact are avoided in the processes of ordering and paying for goods and services. Electronic commerce has succeeded in some marketplaces, such as pharmaceutical distribution, securities trading, and just-in-time parts delivery for automobile manufacturing. As other marketplaces standardize transactions, the practice spreads. The information technology and services marketplace may be late in adopting these practices because standards on which deals are built have yet to be worked out.

Useful variants on electronic commerce exist. One organization custom-built a system for distributing pamphlets about its services. A customer calls the organization using the telephone portion of a facsimile machine. The call is answered by a computer. The ensuing dialogue allows the customer to choose appropriate publications by responding to questions using the touch-tone key pad on the facsimile machine. The questions are spoken by the computer. The computer then synthesizes and sends an image of the needed materials; the customer's facsimile machine prints the information. The entire transaction is handled during one telephone call. The information technology industry has begun to build and market similar systems.

Coupling the techniques of automating work procedures and of electronic commerce leads to a significant speeding of transactions and reduction of paper flow. As the two techniques become easier to deploy, there will be opportunities for products to integrate them.

*   *   *

Numerous opportunities exist for new tools that address repetitive work in many specialized fields of endeavor, as well as in widespread endeavors. The above examples illustrate how attention to people's activities suggests opportunities for new technology-based products.

DISCOVERING AN OPPORTUNITY

Society has discovered that being unable to walk or to see does not necessarily disqualify a person from performing effectively in the Information Age workplace. The mobility afforded by a wheelchair is adequate for many jobs. Technology allows blind people to read and write well. Hearing impairments are overcome, as are disabilities preventing proficient typing. Many people with disabilities achieve a full role in the workplace and the rest of society.

It is easy to appreciate the role information technology has played in fulfilling the needs of people with disabilities. For example, Braille printers are an early form of modern information technology for sight-impaired people. More recently, computers equipped with speech synthesizers speak the content of computer-scanned printed material.

Less well appreciated are the opportunities that attention to disability issues present to developers of information technology.

Traditionally, vendors understood their opportunities in terms of marketplaces for input and output devices that militate against specific disabilities. Established information technology vendors ignored much of this marketplace, leaving progress to individuals, many of whom knew people who needed special technology. Innovative techniques appeared, including:

- Speech generators.
- Software to enlarge text displayed on a computer screen.
- Accommodations for people who cannot simultaneously hold down one key on a keyboard and type another one.

Recently, there have been two steps forward in understanding disability-related opportunities that technology vendors have.

The first step took place as people realized that technology that was a necessity for some people could be a great convenience to many others. For example, as the current population ages, more people will want to look at enlarged text on computer screens. Concurrently with this realization, it became apparent that quality automated text scanning, computer recognition of speech, computer-synthesized speech, and other techniques were becoming feasible. Also, the U.S. federal government was both encouraging vendors to build accommodative technology and working toward passing the Americans with Disabilities Act. Traditional computer vendors began to take more interest in the potential in, and necessity for, producing accommodating technology.

The second step forward has been a subtler one. Technologists recognized that the best way to design accommodative products is to use a modular approach that distinctly separates input techniques and technology from a product's main processing technology and that similarly separates output techniques and technology from the heart of a product. These two separations greatly facilitate developing hardware and software products that can accommodate many input and output devices, and thereby many needs of people with disabilities. This modular separation also facilitates product design and development work. The breakthrough in thinking is, however, the realization that a modular product can be converted for use in a variety of human languages.

Thus, two steps forward in thinking have enlarged the visions of the marketplace for technology that is built to accommodate customers with disabilities. The first is a broader realization of the market for accommodative technology. The second is a competitive advantage in modular product design. Both of these steps fit the theme of searching out and finding opportunities based on repetition. In these cases, repetition is found first in needs for accommodative products and second in vendors' abilities to reuse a product in order to compete in several human language–delineated marketplaces.

Personal Computer—Mainframe, the Sequel?

Hollywood likes a sequel. There is an eager audience. The characters are already developed and ready for a new plot. Marketing is easy and profits are likely. "That's entertainment."

The information technology industry and entertainment industry are becoming more closely allied and have important similarities. In a comparison of the two industries, however, one difference is evident. Unlike Hollywood sequels, information technology sequels are based on familiar plots with new characters. Consider one of those plots.

The first generations of commercial computers consisted of machines called *mainframes*. Many companies built and marketed mainframes. Eventually, the marketplace focused on a leading company and its product line, companies that built clones of that product line, and a few other companies that sold their own families of computers.

Originally, mainframes ran one "job" at a time. Control of the hardware could be given to a single program without jeopardizing the running of other programs or the integrity of stored data. As needs grew to facilitate printing output and managing other peripheral activities, operating systems were developed. Demands grew. Operating systems were enhanced to handle several jobs at one time; several input and output devices at the same time; several people simultaneously using one job; increased complexity and diversity in input and output devices; communications with other computers; and the detection of, and recovery from, input, output, and other errors.

Although operating systems obviated some needs for repetitive programming, people found it necessary to learn how to adjust operating systems parameters to maximize overall efficiency. For some computer product lines, customers even needed to choose the most appropriate operating system.

As people continued to recognize types of work that computers could handle well, computer vendors and software companies produced applications development tools, for instance, for managing databases. Organizations that used computers now could acquire reasonably convenient software tools for describing the work that they wanted computers to perform.

A new profession arose. *Systems programmers* coped, computer by computer, with installing and testing revisions to operating systems; ensuring operational compatibility of applications software, applications development tools, and operating systems; tuning systems for optimal performance; devising strategies to minimize investments in technology; and dealing with errors and other special situations the operating systems and hardware could not handle. Systems programmers became a precious resource for an organization. Yet their direct connection to the goals of the organization came mainly through minimizing failures and the costs of software licenses and hardware.

Organizations found it increasingly difficult to change to newer supporting technology. They were constrained to use technology that ran the existing applications development tools and operating systems. Various marketplaces coalesced around groups of compatible or similar products. Vendors strove to maximize market share within such marketplaces.

Operating systems outgrew the memory capacities of older generations of hardware, thus encouraging equipment upgrades. Applications development tools also grew rapidly in size and internal complexity.

Programming staffs found it difficult to keep up with the growing complexity. Applications programmers were taxed by clients' demands for new features and new applications. Systems programmers began receiving requests to integrate previously separate systems. These demands spawned yet another new field, *systems integration.*

People recognized the need to handle new classes of calculations and new types of data; however, the combination of mainstream technology—the mainframe, its operating systems, the applications development tools, and the applications programs—and professional support lost flexibility and could not keep up. Operating systems became prohibitively expensive to maintain. Systems programmers, finding their work tedious and unappreciated, lost interest. Many applications programmers became more interested in developing new software than in maintaining and improving existing software. The applications programs were not sufficiently flexible to cope with the growing demands of users; indeed, some of the original coding could not be located and, therefore, could not be enhanced. While hardware prices did decrease, hardware vendors lost earnings as customers treated these products as commodities bought primarily on the basis of price.

Traditional technology and practices could not support future needs. A triumph was tarnishing.

This plot ends shortly, but not in complete despair.

Enter the hope for the future—the personal computer, along with related software, hardware, communications networks, and the enthusiasm of the general public. Enter the hope for a new generation of beneficial applications. Enter the hope for methods and technology featuring ease of use and reduced costs. Enter the hope that society's next generation will avoid repeating the problems of the past.

An all too familiar story? Yes, because it is being repeated.

The personal computer is becoming "Mainframe, the Sequel." The personal computer is the new lead character, but the plot is the same.

Indeed, perhaps only one supporting role has changed. The systems programmer is replaced by a combination of technically enthused and literate computer users, *local area network and database administrators,* and systems integrators.

Is the only remaining mystery the ending? Will there be yet another generation of starring technology? If so, what will fill the following blank? "_____—Personal Computer, The Sequel—Mainframe, The Sequel II." And to what extent will the plot differ the third time?

TECHNOLOGY TRENDS AND PRODUCT OPPORTUNITIES

Advances and changes in technology create opportunities for new products. Computing and telecommunications speeds and capacities continue to increase, as does the amount of information that can be stored in a given volume of space or with a given weight of equipment. Generally, the size, weight, and prices of hardware continue to decline. Simultaneously, there are considerable advances in the abilities of systems to understand and produce speech and other sounds and to capture, store, and produce images.

Consumers are beginning to recognize the merger of telecommunications and computing, along with the combining of movies, television, and other forms of entertainment with computerized data and techniques. There is growing overlap in information content, as well as delivery techniques (Figs. 10–1 and 10–2).

Opportunities for new products and services abound. One can conceive of multiparty communications services that provide general news, interactive entertainment, social interaction, volumes of fact and fiction, financial news, financial services, and various types of processing services. Technology may combine the products we know today as telephones, television sets, and computers. Communications may take place via television cable, telephone lines, airborne or fiber-carried light waves, or various combinations.

The potential for new products is made even more inviting by the possibility that current products will not adapt easily to meet new needs. We can envision a new generation of television. It is possible that the technologies associated with current personal computers will prove too inflexible. A new generation of computer communicators may take hold, not only capturing the opportunities of the future with easy-to-use technology but also avoiding some of the accumulated complexity and related software maintenance costs of the past.

Perhaps the greatest challenge society faces within the vast potential for new technologically driven products is to make operational sense out the opportunity. For example, we need to be able conceptually to separate information from techniques for transmitting and manipulating information (Fig. 10–1). Current vocabulary does not always help avoid confusing the two. For instance, terms such as *movies* or *films* denote both information content and delivery techniques. A piece of software can represent data in one context and technique in another. The layered Peer Paradigm (Figs. 10–2 and 16–3) for information and technology presents a foundation for overcoming such confusion.

Standards for information expression, storage, and transmission need to keep pace. With standards, the information consumer may receive more easier-to-use services earlier. There will be competing products and services, but standards can help products and services work together. Without adequate standards, it will take yet more products to provide bridging interfaces between the growing repertoire of techniques and technologies (Table 19–1). Without adequate standards, customers' costs increase as buyers pay the price to link disparate technology.

It remains to be seen whether the institutions that historically developed such standards will be able to keep up with the needs of the future. Perhaps society will move, as it seems to be doing, toward market-determined standards in the information technology marketplace. If so, it remains to be seen to what extent vendors will ensure availability of external specifications for products.

More generally, we need to adopt a useful, easily understood model for technology and its deployment (Figs. 10–2 and 16–4, respec-

TABLE 19–1   THE VALUE OF STANDARDS AND THE COST OF INTERFACES

Number of Products	Complete set of standards for communicating between products			No standards: Each product defines its own interfaces		
	Interfaces			Interfaces		
	In the products		In bridge products	In the products		In bridge products*
	I	O		I	O	
1	1	1	0	1	1	0
2	2	2	0	2	2	2
3	3	3	0	3	3	6
4	4	4	0	4	4	12
10	10	10	0	10	10	90
100	100	100	0	100	100	9,900
1000	1000	1000	0	1000	1000	999,000

*Assumes that all pairwise interface bridges are built.

Legend:

I = Input

O = Output

tively). Envision a societywide implementation of this model. To the extent that modules in the paradigm are defined with standard linkages to other modules, products and services fit together with synergy. Compatibility of interfaces within a given peer layer is important, as is compatibility of linkages between layers. To the extent that both are achieved, technologists develop drop-in modules that plug into their places in an overall technology framework. This vision will be facilitated to the extent that the modules can be described without technical jargon and that most users need not be concerned with the details and even the choices of generic components. If society succeeds at this task, our dreams of being able to move vast amounts of information quickly and inexpensively will be realized. We will be able to take advantage of such telecommunications services without having to worry much about choosing among competing types of services. Vendors will provide competitively priced overall service without forcing customers to become enmeshed in technical choices or in the challenges of integrating various technologies that provide the bases of the services. We will be able to communicate in any medium with other people and machines via store-and-forward message services.

Similar potential exists for data and processing services. There can be a robust assortment. The customer wants to choose among sources of information and processing services. Remote services will provide data, such as news, knowledge, entertainment, and financial market data, on demand. Simulations and other processing capabilities will be available.

In fact, there will be so much information and so many choices that technology will be needed and available to help people filter out most of the choices, use what they need, and integrate information from the chosen sources.

In homes, workplaces, and people's pockets will be found devices that integrate computing and communications. Handling text, images, and sounds, these devices will be applied to doing personal work and storing personally interesting information. There will be continual growth in application of these devices.

To the extent that the Peer Paradigm is executed so that the various modules can grow independently in capability, people will have access to extensive, useful, low-cost information when and where they need it.

Vigorous progress in pursuing a robust, easily integrated melange of technologies that provides the capabilities permitted in the Peer Paradigm will go a long way toward improving the information proficiency of people and organizations. It will provide numerous opportunities for new products. It will hasten the development of new types of generic products, including ones that address work previously thought to be mission-specific.

There will always remain areas of behavior that are reserved for people. These areas will continue to present challenges for vendors to develop new products and, with or without those products, for people and organizations to improve their proficiency in making and implementing decisions.

CHAPTER *20*

Acquiring Technology and Services

Deploying an optimal information resource depends on skillfully acquiring technology and services. For both buyers and sellers, success in the information technology marketplace is a two-way street. Buyers and sellers have opportunities to improve their own practices and to help each other toward mutual success.

QUALITY BUYING—MANAGING
RELATIONS WITH VENDORS

There is a good deal of similarity between being a buyer in the information technology marketplace and being a buyer in any other marketplace. There are also differences. Consider the following advice on succeeding as a buyer in this evolving marketplace.

*   *   *

Know what you are looking for. In evaluating technology and services, you should consider several aspects:

- The usefulness of the product.
- The internal quality of the product.
- Relations with the supplier.
- Maintenance and eventual replacement of the product.

The best test of usefulness is to have intended users do their work using the technology or service. You will discover both how useful the product is and how readily people learn to use it. For off-the-shelf products, a partial substitute for experimenting in your own organization is to review how well other organizations do similar work using the product.

For custom products, you can learn from other organizations that have put into use similar products from the same supplier. Especially when there is a high degree of new technology like custom software, you need to evaluate projects that have been completed for other customers. You should learn how the customers managed these projects and relations with the vendor, as well as how well the vendor performed.

For any product or service, you should know where both it and its intended impact fall in your organization's current and likely future implementation of the Peer Paradigm (Fig. 16–4). The long-term utility of the product depends on how broadly it supports, and coordinates with, many other modules. Long-term usefulness also depends on the product's current and future competitive posture (Fig. 20–1).

The internal quality of the product depends on a lack of bugs and a design that facilitates enhancements. For off-the-shelf products, you want technology that will grow with your needs, and you want your organization to grow through the use of increasingly capable tools. Avoid products for which there will be no improvements.

You want to avoid obtaining a custom product that will become an "orphan." Be sure that you will need minimal effort to make the product fit with your future needs for mission-specific techniques and your future deployment of generic technology. Customizing a software package or database presents a special challenge. You may need to ensure that the material specific to your organization constitutes separate modules that can be easily maintained and integrated into future versions of the generic product. If appropriate, you should require the supplier to incorporate the custom work in the next off-the-shelf version of the product.

There are many factors to consider in evaluating suppliers. Even when a supplier's past performance has been exemplary, you may find telling symptoms of impending problems. You should consider:

Product: Coasting	**Product:** Competing

Customer objective:
  Contingency escape plan
	Customer objective:
	  Growth in parallel
	  with the product

Product: Recollecting	**Product:** Striving

Customer objective:
  Escaping quicksand
	Customer objective:
	  Leading-edge competitive
	  advantage

Figure 20–1   The Customer's Objective, Given the Competitive Posture of a Product.

- Responsiveness and image:
    Does the vendor emphasize helping customers achieve their own bottom-line results? (A "positive")
    Does the supplier convey an "if we make it, they will buy it" image? (A "negative")
    How responsive to you has the supplier been?
    Is the vendor so responsive that you wonder how it can afford to maintain its staff?
    Is the vendor's responsiveness uniform throughout its organization?
- Corporate competitive posture:
    Which competitive posture (Fig. 7–2) currently describes the vendor?
    Which postures will apply in the future?
- Stability of finances and operations:
    How significant are any downturns or increases in earnings or revenue?
    What are the vendor's financial objectives? For example, does the company emphasize short-term revenue or long-term earnings?
    Has the supplier changed business strategies recently? If so, were the changes based on customers' needs or the supplier's need to shore up finances?
    Have there been changes in lines of business? What impact will the changes have on the company's ability to meet your needs?
    Is there likely to be personnel turnover that will affect you as a customer?
    Are there any lawsuits or governmental investigations that are likely to drain key resources?
- Unity between sales, engineering, and financial staffs and goals:
    Do these functions seem to work together? If not, what impact will the vendor's disunity have on you?
    Does the vendor produce incompatible products that compete with each other?

Is the sales staff working with you able to explain the whole product line?

- Product strategy, especially with respect to linkages to the supplier's other products and to other vendors' products:

    Is this supplier's business strategy with respect to open interfaces compatible with your organization's strategy and needs?

    Do the product lines remain current in the marketplace?

Based on experience, yours and that of people you know, you can probably add to this list of topics and questions.

You should be observant. For example, a supplier's deemphasizing its large-computer leasing program may be a tactic to provide short-term improvement in financial statements by booking more purchases. It may also be a symptom of a longer-term problem that has just been compounded by giving away a lucrative leasing program.

* * *

When you formulate final objectives for a business arrangement, use what you have learned. If you negotiate a contract, refine what you know by learning from the negotiations. Use all that you know in order to enhance your position. If the proposed agreement is not adequate, consider looking for other suppliers.

If your agreement covers consulting or the development of unique technology, special care is needed. Observe the supplier's attitude toward such key project aspects as:

- Your organization's role in the project.
- Setting milestones by which you can measure progress.
- How likely it is that, if the vendor believes you are headed in a poor direction, the vendor will tell you, even if it means risking a decrease in business?
- Your organization's role in designing and testing technology products.
- What products or rights you will acquire.
- Your ability to stop or redirect the project.

Of course, you need to be confident that your own organization can carry out its responsibilities. Your organization:

- Must have the stamina to see the project through to completion.
- Must remain in charge of the overall effort.
- Should not meddle with the supplier's internal operations.
- Must not interfere in the vendor's relationships with its suppliers and subcontractors.

*   *   *

After you come to an agreement with a supplier, maintain vigilance to ensure a successful relationship. Consider the following example.

A customer hires a company to provide microfiche filming and filing technologies, a state-of-the-art computer and software system, and a unique add-on hardware system. The supplier delivers the computers and the first software components on schedule. The microfiche technologies and procedures go smoothly into place. The customer finds that these deliverables both satisfy contractual obligations and are quite useful. Subsequent software modules also arrive on time and work flawlessly.

The customer ceases making inspections of work in progress. Meanwhile, the supplier's team producing the add-on hardware is falling behind schedule. Although the delays are not the fault of the customer, continued customer attention to this part of the project might have spurred the supplier to stay closer to schedule and certainly would have alerted the customer's operational management to plan for a delay.

For projects that emphasize consulting or development of custom technology, there is no substitute for a customer's staying abreast of the vendor's progress and maintaining the project's goals. Many such projects have overrun their budgets, failed to maintain their schedules, failed to produce significantly useful results, been scaled back, or been canceled.

Sometimes, a lack of customer competence or steadfastness contributes to the problem. In many cases more appropriate customer involvement can either save the project or lead to canceling it earlier. Customers control the outcome.

ORDERING VERSUS PROCURING—
A USEFUL DISTINCTION

"Acquiring technology and services takes too much effort." This statement is ubiquitous in business and government. What can be done to reduce this overhead?

"Procurement" is a big word in Washington, D.C. The U.S. federal government spends at least $20 billion dollars each year on computing and telecommunications, to say nothing of larger expenditures on other goods and services. Attention focuses not only on the dollars spent but also on processes. "There ought to be a better way."

Changes in federal procurement policy take time and often focus on refinements, not overhauls, of existing laws, regulations, and procedures. Yet there have been practical breakthroughs to streamline federal acquisitions. A key observation is the difference between a procurement and an order. The important development has been to exploit that difference.

Procurements take time. A multi-hundred-million-dollar purchase project often takes a few years from the start of the project to the award of a contract. Then, the government orders goods and services.

The federal government has begun to use a number of techniques to facilitate acquisitions:

- Pooling procurements across organizations. Aggregation avoids duplicative procurements and often results in lower-priced bids. While such a project takes more work than a smaller procurement, each organization contributes less effort than if it had done its own procurement. When the contract is awarded, all organizations place orders.
- Providing for advances in technology. A procurement can permit the acquisition of future technology. Minimal extra effort to specify so-called "technology refreshment" pays off handsomely, but buyers should take care not to order new products that are untested or overpriced.
- Acquiring organizationwide licenses for software.
- Prequalifying vendors and running quick competitions. When buying services, the competitions are for task orders.

> With contracts already in place, both buyer and bidder focus on specifications, schedules, and prices.
>
> For commodity technology, an electronic marketplace is appropriate, either to allow a customer to compare prices before placing an order or to allow vendors to bid quickly for a certain piece of business.

These techniques enhance federal procurements and they should work well for businesses.

*   *   *

Regarding technology refreshment, a customer and vendor can agree today on prices for products not yet announced. Doing so facilitates ordering future products and provides a future win for both parties. The customer orders the new products without obtaining a new contract. The vendor enjoys low-cost sales and the evident advantages it has over a competitor who would have to negotiate a deal.

The simplest approach features a "similar discount" technique in which the supplier guarantees the customer the lower of two types of prices. One is, of course, whatever prices will be available to other customers. The other is based on the ratio(s) implicit between the list price(s) at the time of contract signing for the original product(s) and the price schedule agreed on for the original product(s). At any future time, the customer applies the same ratio(s) to the list prices of products in order to obtain a pricing structure.

ORGANIZATIONWIDE SOFTWARE LICENSES—A WIN-WIN SOLUTION

When you buy a car, you do not review the sales contract to see what limits it puts on your use of the vehicle. If you do read the contract, it is probably to review the list of optional accessories to be bought, verify the delivery date and warranty provisions, and check the price and financing. When you buy a computer, the situation can be similar.

So why does software present such a problem? Why do you have to worry about the number of machines, or their processing power, for which the license applies? Why may you have to specify even the serial numbers of the machines? Or why do some software licenses specify a maximum number of concurrent users and why does the licensor have either to code such a limit into each copy of the software or to provide a service to authorize increased usage?

All the traditional software pricing schemes have bases in realities that apply sometimes but not always.

Pricing based on numbers of machines and the speed of machines dates from the era of the large computer that could run only one application at a time. Today, the use of mainframe applications software is dependent mainly on the needs of the using organization, not on the number of computers or their speed. On the desktop, software prices usually do not depend on the speed of the computer; that would be difficult and prohibitively expensive to implement. But personal computer software prices often do depend on the number of machines licensed individually or the maximum number of users allowed simultaneous access to a copy from a "server" machine that stores software for a group of computers.

Such pricing and the associated administrative burdens present a needless drag on the competitiveness of customers and their software vendors. Vendors incur the costs of implementing pricing and access-limiting schemes; producing, storing, and shipping physical copies of software; and registering, collecting fees for, tracking, and supporting individual licenses. A customer pays prices that reflect all these vendor activities. The customer also has similar burdens: ordering, receiving, paying, possibly reshipping, inventorying, and so forth. The administrative burdens for both parties are magnified by product upgrades and corrections. Yet, many of these steps and physical copies are unnecessary in an era in which software and manuals can be distributed electronically and in which many people use third-party books in place of vendors' manuals.

One can eliminate these burdens. Consider the following concept for an "organizational license" covering the customer's entire operational needs.

In the simplest such arrangement the licensee pays once for a perpetual license for copying and use, limited only to use for the benefit of the licensee. Use by consultants and employees on their own machines, for the business of the licensee, is allowed; however, rights to relicense the software to other parties are not included. A warranty is included. Each upgrade or version for future machines is provided if an annual fee, specified in the original contract, is paid up when the new release becomes available in the marketplace. When the license commences or a new software version is released, the vendor supplies one copy, or a few copies, of the software and documentation.

To cover a product line, and thereby eliminate potential disputes over "new products" versus "upgrades," such a license agreement includes "any product that partly or wholly obsoletes in the marketplace" a product already covered under the agreement. The agreement includes the software for all types of computer operating systems and computers, current or future, for which the vendor produces the product. The contract can cover "related products," that is, satellite products whose use or main utility depends on an already-licensed product. The agreement can also cover unrelated products through the "similar discount" technique.

Other items and services—additional physical copies of the software or documentation, training, consulting services, and rights to grant sublicenses—are priced separately. Separate pricing provides for rational pricing for mutually understood units of service.

This type of license provides each customer with a convenient basis for standardizing on particular product lines, thereby building a uniform base of software on which to share innovative techniques developed in the organization. Along with reducing or eliminating costs to order new copies, experience has shown that such licenses can feature attractive fees.

One corporation's experience with a dozen such licenses showed that savings of 90 percent from list price were always achieved, whether the software was widely used in the company or not. The savings figures were based on estimates of the number of computers in the corporation into which the software was put. Savings on software upgrades were not estimated but, if expressed similarly as a percentage saving per copy, would have been well above 90 percent. Also, it was observed that software developers willing to consider this innovative business practice tended to keep their products technologically competitive.

Vendors that follow this pricing methodology face at most three challenging pricing issues: the one-time price for an organizational license, the annual fee covering upgrades and, possibly, fees to be paid by a licensee that wants to sublicense the product (e.g., if the licensee desires to market software it has developed that requires the licensed software). All other fees, for providing extra physical copies of the software, for example, can be based on reasonable markups on actual or anticipated costs of service.

For some vendors, the organizational license has become an attractive, low-cost way of doing business. These vendors have solved the two key pricing issues: initial fees and annual fees. If the software works well and the extra services are priced separately, there is essentially no cost to support the basic use license for a given customer. Revenues from licenses can be used to pay for product development, to reward sales personnel, or to pay dividends to shareholders.

VALUE AND COST

The more directly an information technology project can be associated with the goals of an organization (Figs. 12–4 and 16–3), the more likely it is that the activity will be viewed in terms of value. The more an activity is associated with building an infrastructure of generic technology, the more likely it is to be viewed in terms of cost.

A focus on cost tends to be fraught with other perceptions. Starting with the mainframe era and continuing to the present day, people have tended to emphasize the price of computers. Yet, decades ago, the costs of buying or leasing large computers became typically a small fraction of the cost of the entire automation effort that the machines supported. Other items, each often of comparable or greater cost, include systems software and applications packages, developing mission-specific software, maintaining that software, and the necessary peripheral technology including data storage units and communications systems.

For small computers, there are at least two thoughts that customers can use to put the cost of the computing hardware into perspective. The first can be expressed by an analogy with a stereo system: eventually one will have paid more for tapes and compact disks than one paid for the stereo. Likewise, the cost of software will eventually exceed the cost of the computer hardware; this will happen especially quickly if the computer is used extensively for developing spreadsheets, database applications, or other custom procedures. The second notion is that the cost of connecting the computer into a network and maintaining that connection is significant.

Excluding the most sophisticated supercomputers, in today's marketplace treating computers as commodities is the norm. For years, consumers have tended to overemphasize the price of hardware in their planning. The good news for them is that hardware prices are becoming even lower. The main challenge is to focus on the project components other than computing and storage hardware, emphasizing work that adds overall information proficiency and competitive advantage and learning how to control the costs of entire projects.

Recall that the continuing growth of capability and utility of generic technology provides one indication of progress in the field of information technology. Yesterday's mission-specific technology becomes tomorrow's generic technology. Marketplace competition is likely to continue to force decreasing prices for the ever-growing repertoire of generic technologies and services.

QUALITY SELLING

In what activities should one pay attention to quality? The answer may seem obvious: All activities. Organizations, however, do not necessarily give equal attention to each aspect of their work.

Today, vendor attention focuses on quality in products and services. There has also been progress in the quality of postsale relationships, whether based on service or stronger partnerships between buyers and sellers.

It is time for buyers and vendors to focus firmly on quality in relationships between would-be customers and sellers. A shorthand term for this could be "quality selling," although broader concepts, such as marketing, are included. Customers have two opportunities to improve the quality of their relationships with vendors. One is to observe vendor behavior and factor those observations into purchasing decisions and negotiating strategies. The other is to encourage improved vendor practices.

* * *

Responding primarily to customers' *wants* tends to position a vendor as a provider of cost-interpreted services or products. Responding to customers' *needs* positions a vendor as a source of insight and value. If a customer says "I want . . . ," a sales force can simply give the customer what he asked for or it can also try to understand the customer's true need. The customer may not realize all the ways the vendor can help the customer toward improved competitiveness.

The consideration of wants and needs has parallels. Does the sales effort emphasize the vendor's products and technology or the customers' goals and results? Does it focus on a customer's information technology professionals or their clients?

The Peer Paradigm (Figs. 16–3 and 16–4) sheds light on the question, "Who is the client?" If the customer organization is a business, the client for *goals and results* is a diverse group that includes the business's customers, shareholders, internal groups and employees, and probably other constituents. The client for *generic technology* may be a group that coordinates the business's infrastructure of behind-the-scenes information technology. That customers and vendors understand who the client is can lead to focused, successful presales relations. On the other hand, when a vendor markets generic technology to a customer's senior management, the outcome is problematical. Executives are interested in business results. A poorly aimed sales pitch for a piece of technology infrastructure can delay a customer's technology-intensive projects.

*   *   *

Along with the question of who the client is comes the matter of a long-term view of business relations. Does the vendor seek single sales, obtaining individual pieces of business based on a growing reputation but little or no lock on a customer's work? Or does the vendor seek to become so integral to a customer's operations that the customer cannot dislodge the vendor?

There can be considerable room for misunderstanding in presale presentations and negotiations regarding creative services. Consider, as an example, a vendor selling services to facilitate reengineering information-based business processes. The service often involves developing prototypes of new work procedures and screen displays to support the procedures. This enables the customer's people to get a feel for using a computer to do the reengineered work. The vendor also offers follow-on services to develop complete applications.

A typical customer has a traditional, complex system of computer software for managing business operations. The customer wants to develop concepts for reengineering that work and wants to be able to try out the mock-ups of how transactions will be handled after reengineering. Later, the customer may want this vendor to develop the entire application.

A question of proprietary rights needs to be settled before there is a business relation between the vendor and the customer. At one extreme, the customer owns the prototype screen designs and essential software that supports them—the vendor seeks reputation. At the other extreme, the vendor owns the intellectual property and places restrictions on the customer's use of it—the vendor wants a lock on future business. Clarification is essential prior to detailed negotiation or any work.

Similar fundamental issues may arise regarding any business relationship in which new software or data is to be developed.

*   *   *

Vendors must decide to what extent to discuss future enhancements to their product lines. Future products can include both direct descendants of current products and other products that will coordinate with the main family of products.

The timing of preannouncements of descendent products has proved crucial. If the announcement is made too early, sales of the available product decline; potential customers decide to wait for the new product. If the announcement is made too late, sales of the new product line suffer; potential customers look elsewhere for state-of-the-art products.

*   *   *

More subtle is the question of related products. For example, a salesperson promoting a new personal computer software package is giving a presentation to a buyer representing an entire company. The vendor is contemplating developing a series of other products that will coordinate with the current one. To what extent does the salesperson discuss the other products? In one such instance, a prospective buyer became worried over the potential cost of future products related to the one under consideration. The buyer's organization acquired a competing product. As it turns out, the would-be seller did not produce the future products.

SALES COMPENSATION—IS IT TIME FOR A CHANGE?

You may have heard the phrase, "Sell it at a loss and make it up on volume." Can we assume that no one wins when this happens?

The vendor loses; prolonged use of this technique leads to bankruptcy. Any customer interested in vendor-supplied service or in a continuing supply of the product loses as well.

The vendor's sales force, however, wins, at least in the short run. It receives commissions based on gross sales, which are artificially inflated by prices that were set below costs.

A vendor planning to stay in business would not allow this practice to continue. While selling at a loss provides an extreme example, most vendors are missing a significant opportunity when they set sales compensation plans.

What are the objectives of the vendor's stockholders? Excepting perhaps the case of a start-up firm, the owners want the promise of a steadily growing stream of good earnings from their investment. Presumably, this will require offering continually competitive products at reasonable prices.

What about the customers? Their interests are the same: sound products, an up-to-date product line, good service, and vendor stability, as well as good earnings and good earnings prospects.

Maximizing short-term vendor revenue is hardly the customer's goal; it turns out that it is not the goal of the vendor's stockholders either.

Both parties to a business deal have the same interests. Yet sales forces are typically rewarded for revenue, not earnings, and compensated on a short-term basis. Today a member of a sales force typically receives a base salary and a commission based on business sold. The basis for the commission often is quarterly revenue generated. Perhaps it has traditionally seemed too difficult to base compensation on anything more complex than these two components.

The competitive vendor of the future should reward its sales force based on the mutual interests of stockholders and customers. A sales force, after all, is an integral part of the customer-vendor relationship. The overall profitability of the vendor and the profitability of the sales made by an individual could provide improved bases for commissions. For each of these two bases, one can consider short-term results, such as for the recent year or quarter, and longer-term results as well.

For a short-term companywide plan, the company can consider rewarding the sales force based on a percentage of the after-tax earnings for the prior quarter-year. For compensation calculated on a longer-term companywide basis, or for any compensation based on profitability of individual product lines, the company will need to rely on techniques such as use of business plans and profitability projections, delayed compensation, and compensation in equity, not cash.

A company that makes the effort to behave this way will send positive signals to its potential customers, investors, and sales staff. When business is conducted, the sales staff will be working toward the objectives of the company's investors and customers.

VENDORS' ADJUSTING TO THE PEER PARADIGM FOR PROJECTS

Adjusting to the Peer Paradigm for projects (Fig. 16–4) represents a major step for vendors. The paradigm features modular deployment; it also features horizontal integration within each of several broad client areas: areas of mission; groups of people; information used to make decisions; and mission-specific data, processes, and technology; as well as each of three layers of generic data, processes, and technology.

A vendor supplying a module, in the sense of the paradigm, has the challenge of providing technologies or services that integrate both horizontally with peer products and vertically with processes and products in adjoining layers of the paradigm. These considerations will work in favor of vendors that supply technology and services with *open interfaces,* which work with other products and services.

In designing a product, a vendor traditionally has had the choice of building *proprietary interfaces,* thereby aiming for a large portion of a marketplace that is likely to be "small," or of featuring open interfaces and anticipating a smaller fraction of a marketplace that is likely to be "large." Customers' needs and the new paradigm favor the latter course. To the extent that a smaller portion of a larger marketplace is larger than a larger portion of a smaller marketplace, a vendor should have more business from building products with open interfaces.

A product with open interfaces to other products need not be without proprietary features or proprietary internal technology. In the past, vendors have used proprietary features to obtain new customers based on capabilities not found in competitors' products and to retain business based on the amount of difficulty existing customers would have in changing to a competing product line that does not have identical features. While this strategy will remain valid, some customers will discourage use of proprietary features or even shy away from products that have them. Customer management may not want to take the risks associated with depending on one product line.

IS THE SIZE OF THE MARKETPLACE FIXED?

One of the oft-used measures of the success of business is its market share—the fraction of some market that consists of purchases of that business's products. An example is the fraction of the personal computers sold during a particular year made by a certain company.

Market share can represent a valid measurement and a meaningful concept; however, undue attention to it can limit a supplier's thinking. A vendor can begin to believe that it is competing only with competitors in that one market and that the market has a certain size. However, a vendor should not ignore the possibility that it—along with competitors in that market and even entities outside that market—can take steps to enlarge the market.

The benefits to a vendor of a larger market seem obvious. Even with a decreased market share, there can be increased sales and, presumably, increased profits.

Consider a vendor that is close to finishing development of a new type of product. This product will have little direct, immediate competition. Consciously or not, the vendor will make decisions affecting the size of the early marketplace. That market will be bigger to the extent that the product is publicized well, easy to obtain, and works with other products people already use. The market size also depends on the extent to which other products are developed to work with this one. Inherent in each of these factors is the perceived utility of the product.

Already the vendor faces decisions. The market for this product will depend on how well the product works with other vendors' current and future products. Some of those products may represent competition to the vendor.

Some of these decisions involve product design, for example, the extent to which the product will embrace technical standards and provide linkages to other products. This issue of open versus proprietary interfaces continues to be worked, product by product, although the trend today is toward open interfaces.

Perhaps not so obvious is the answer to this question: To what extent should a vendor facilitate development by rival suppliers of direct competition for new product? A vendor's first reaction is likely to be negative, but history and theory suggest that this reaction may not always be the best. Cloned products and other close competitors add legitimacy to a product in the eyes of prospective buyers. If more than one vendor is selling in a marketplace, buyers realize that several parties have already bet that there will be a healthy marketplace. Buyers are more confident that they are not engaging too early in a market, are more comfortable with the potential for success through such products, and can be more confident that they will not pay too much. Buyers like the comfort of knowing that there are second sources.

For example, the availability of specifications for personal computers led software developers to be interested in those machines. People buy such computers because of the software that runs on them. The snowball effect of software availability and cloned hardware added to the market for all these products. Dramatic advances in the market for various types of personal computer software and add-on peripheral hardware took place when there were competing products. A good strategy for a vendor can be to encourage cloned competitors and to stay ahead of the competition in terms of product features and quality.

There is also a broader picture, beyond decisions that influence the size or speed of development of a single market or some closely related markets. How fixed is the size of the overall market for information technology?

Potential buyers of information technology make trade-offs. What is the best investment of resources, including money and time? Regarding money, the decision is made among information technology, other spending, savings, and, for a business, dividends. Even for entities with rigid budgeting, decisions need to be made in one period whether to spend all the information technology budget, whether to shift monies into or away from that budget, and how much to budget for information technology for subsequent periods.

The size of the market for information technology is not fixed. Customers' perceptions about the relative values of various possible investments are crucial. Many of those perceptions are shaped by members of the information technology community, including people working for vendors, customers, academic institutions, or the press.

The keys to the size of the overall market include more than the production of worthwhile, synergistic products. Customers and vendors must continue to demonstrate the worth of technology-intensive investments. Their dialogue must focus on realistic, mutually understood plans for beneficial deployment. To the extent that discussion between the information technology community and its constituents focuses on results and does not confuse customers with jargon, the marketplace can and will expand.

QUALITY DEAL-MAKING—SIMPLIFYING NEGOTIATIONS OVER BOILERPLATE*

They agree on the specifications. They agree on the schedule. They agree on the price. Do they have a deal? Not immediately. Probably not for weeks. Perhaps not for months. Maybe never. The delay occurs over pages of fine print boilerplate.

---

*Adapted from Thomas J. Buckholtz, 1993. Material similar to portions of this section appeared in *Computerworld,* March 15, 1993, p. 33. Reused with permission of CW Publishing/Inc.

While prevalent in the corporate-to-corporate information technology marketplace, such negotiation and delay are avoided in other marketplaces. Haggling over boilerplate for each shipping container would sink international commerce; but this does not happen because the international maritime marketplace came to understandings centuries ago. The American Institute of Architects publishes standard boilerplate for its field. State real estate associations publish widely used boilerplate for the purchase and rental of homes.

What happens in the information technology marketplace when two would-be partners, BuyCo and SellCo, have agreed on specifications, schedules, and prices?

First, they decide whose boilerplate is to be used. Usually, SellCo wins this first skirmish in the so-called battle of the forms. Then, they decide who will word-process amendments.

Then, they negotiate. BuyCo cannot hope to abide by a requirement to return or destroy all copies of SellCo's software when use ceases. The two parties do not agree on rights to custom software developed under the contract. They disagree on SellCo's liabilities for various possible types of damages. BuyCo wants price caps in case of subsequent purchases. BuyCo demands, and has always previously gotten, stronger coverage in case of a third-party claim over alleged proprietary rights violations by a vendor. There are dozens of such issues.

BuyCo's project management discusses each issue with SellCo's sales force. They compromise, subject to review. Lawyers, procurement staff members, and management perform their reviews. If they suggest new wording, more discussion ensues.

Often, all goes well, paragraph by paragraph. Sometimes, however, negotiations take strange twists. For example, on a scale of 1 to 10, BuyCo's position starts at 3, SellCo's position starts at 7, the negotiators settle at 5, and SellCo's next draft of the boilerplate comes out at 8—"worse," from the buyer's perspective, than SellCo's earlier approved position.

Negotiations over one provision are usually independent of negotiations over others. Seldom, if ever, is there a suggested price change because of a boilerplate issue.

During the discussions, the clock continues to run. BuyCo cannot derive competitive advantage from products and services it has not received. SellCo is not receiving revenue on this would-be deal.

Usually, the parties complete a deal. Even this can be a somewhat curious victory. After one several-month negotiation, a SellCo could not deliver its products on time. A distributor of SellCo's equipment then signed the same contract and met the schedule. The customer paid the anticipated prices, but SellCo and its distributor shared the profit.

A noticeable fraction of the time, negotiations are abandoned after two to six months. For example, one BuyCo recognized a quagmire in negotiating with a SellCo, took one week to evaluate a competing product, and signed a deal based on its boilerplate three weeks later with the second vendor. BuyCo's demands proved to be within the bounds allowed by the marketplace. SellCo lost what would have been its second-largest sale.

Each year, thousands of talented managers, technical staff members, procurement staff members, and lawyers devote significant fractions of their work to negotiating computing and telecommunications boilerplate.

Is this productive? Is it necessary? Sometimes it significantly improves a business arrangement or prevents a deal that would have been built on false expectations. More often, the parties would be happy with marketplace-standard wording and the comfort that most business was done based on it. The comfort might be more important than the nuances of the boilerplate paragraphs. If not, at least the two parties would know well the starting point for their negotiations and would discuss fewer issues. Unfortunately, there is no marketplace-standard wording. Indeed, there is insufficient agreement on the standards for business transactions.

Society can free millions of people-hours tied up annually by boilerplate negotiations. The BuyCo's would rather spend money on more products and services instead of negotiations. The SellCo's want to make those extra sales and to lower the costs of sales. Both groups want to do business more quickly, and both have better uses for the time of talented employees.

Several major vendors' chief executive officers need to recognize the priority for a project to standardize boilerplate. If those people commit modest but sufficient resources, enough buyers and other vendors will join the effort. Standardizing boilerplate for the information technology marketplace will enhance competitiveness and productivity for both buyers and sellers. It would be a quality improvement—quality in the process of arriving at a business relationship.

Additionally, such standardization is needed to make electronic commerce—the conducting of business electronically, which information technology supports in financial and other markets—a reality for information technology and service transactions. The information technology marketplace need not be the last to take advantage of this technique.

INTELLECTUAL PROPERTY—SOME CONTINUING CHALLENGES

The topic of intellectual property presents continuing challenges in the information technology marketplace.

*   *   *

The future portends the merger of many forms of information (Figs. 10–1 and 10–2) and, hence, the potential overlapping use of all forms of claims of proprietary rights. Future information-based products will embody not only proprietary hardware, data, and software, but also picture images and sounds. What happens when the images include segments of movies and television programs, protected by their own copyrights, or a high-quality image of a famous painting that is part of private collection? What happens when the sounds include professional recordings for which the musicians expect royalties?

One challenge involves finding workable procedures for protecting rights to creative works, licensing derivative rights, and collecting compensation.

Specific types of rights have served specific areas of endeavor, for example, patents for inventions and copyrights for books, music, and movies. Stress is already evident in the information technology marketplace. Some software is protected by copyright, other software by patent. Hardware might be protected by patents but, when a computer chip contains read-only memory, the contents of that memory may be copyrighted. A product may be named with a newly invented word to allow protecting its name.

*   *   *

When there is a sound basis of protection regarding proprietary rights, the challenge shifts to how to license the rights. This challenge can be magnified if licensees want to incorporate parts of the material into other items.

The question of royalties is but one part of the issue of pricing products based mainly on intellectual property. Software can be priced much like a book and sometimes is. Yet much mass-marketed software is priced at several times a typical mass-market price. Is the price of such software based on value? It seems difficult to establish what that value is, other than what the market will bear.

Pricing challenges may increase as the types of information sold as a unit increase. Should an encyclopedia on a CD-ROM be priced as an encyclopedia or as a CD-ROM? Should access to such data from an on-line service be priced by the minute, by the amount of material read, or as if the customer is "renting" an encyclopedia and paying separately for information delivery costs?

Separating the price of a use license from the prices associated with supporting usage provides a key to addressing such questions.

*   *   *

Another challenge involves mixing off-the-shelf material with material developed for a specific customer. Many customers have asked software vendors to make customized versions of standard products. In such a case, who owns the changed or new parts of the software? Is a nonowner allowed to use the new material? The answers lie in the agreement between the parties. Will the vendor produce a new customer-specific version when a subsequent general version is produced? Again, it depends on the agreement between the two parties; in some cases, an innovative solution that could serve the interests of both parties would be to require the vendor to include the special features in future general versions. The modularizing of software development, the development of increasingly flexible software, and the growing willingness on the part of customers to rely on generic software may be reducing some needs to address these issues; however, one can speculate about what might happen as the intellectual property marketplace addresses similar issues in the broader context of multimedia information.

* * *

Another question yet to be settled in the marketplace involves software royalties in case the capacity of the underlying computer is changed. Virtually absent with respect to single-user personal computers, this topic has proved contentious regarding some mainframe and minicomputer software licenses. Similarly, the personal computer software marketplace seems to have solved the question of transferring licenses when a computer is sold or otherwise transferred to another party, but the issue of transferring software presents challenges regarding transfers of larger computers.

* * *

Another problem involves cessation of use of leased intellectual property. Requiring a licensee to "return or destroy" each copy of some software in order to stop paying a licensor is inappropriate. Good practice demands that the licensee make backup copies. It is difficult to expunge those from archival material. Cessation of use might be a better criterion for terminating what is, after-all, a "use license."

* * *

Challenges regarding intellectual property are likely to be found in the information technology marketplace for some time to come.

Reference

Buckholtz, Thomas J., 1993. Too many deals are lost over the fine print. *Computerworld*, March 15, 1993, p. 33.

Conclusion

21

Putting It All Together

*I*nformation proficiency is the bright light in our future.

INFORMATION PROFICIENCY—
OUR FUTURE

Tomorrow . . .

Information proficiency is still the key to success. It provides the competitive advantage sought by everyone.

From individuals and small organizations to large countries, the value of defining and achieving goals by making and implementing decisions effectively is of paramount importance. The emphasis on information proficiency magnifies the momentum of traditional quality-enhancement programs. Information proficiency also forms the basis for extending and surpassing the achievements of traditional automation, process reengineering, and knowledge-base building.

Information proficiency equates to competitive advantage. The most successful individuals and organizations embrace and customize information proficiency for their own needs and constantly achieve innovations in their information resources and decision processes. As a consequence, the quality and speed of decisions increase.

Information-proficiency coaches and catalysts are prized employees. Their inspiration and ideas are highly valued for the competitive advantage they generate. People's contributions to improved information proficiency are measured, recognized, and rewarded.

With improved information and techniques, more and more types of decisions are becoming routine and automated while individuals and groups focus on making complex decisions. Both people and systems benefit from abundant, qualified information. An individual or system derives from qualified information the confidence with which a decision can be made. If the confidence level is too low, the tools are at hand to specify and pursue additional information.

*   *   *

The benefits of *information proficiency* are powerful and far-reaching.

*   *   *

People find it easy to do business with all types of organizations. One-stop shopping, whether via telephone, computer, or two-way video, abounds. Customers choose products and services based on instantaneously presented comparisons provided by information intermediaries. These intermediaries synthesize product and price information from a multitude of suppliers and present comparisons tailored to each customer's needs. Orders are placed electronically; payments are handled automatically.

The ease of shopping extends to information itself. Information intermediaries provide ready access to literature, entertainment, educational materials, news, and data. Similarly, modern techniques facilitate locating facts on governmental activities, public proceedings, and one's own accounts with various government programs and services.

Convenience abounds. A change of address, posted once, reaches all constituents. People direct information to their location, be it home, business, car, or hotel room. The individual may choose to read the information, listen to it, print it, or simply store it for future use.

Organizations reap tremendous, continual rewards from information proficiency. For example, military use of information proficiency provides varied data—geographic, socioeconomic, intelligence, readiness, and environmental—conveniently merged and presented for making timely decisions.

Organizations build information resources that continuously capture, synthesize, and leverage collected experience. These knowledge bases empower employees and build keen competitive advantage.

Policy decisions, based on growing needs both to think globally and pay attention to details, are increasingly complex. Through information proficiency, people come to appropriate decisions efficiently while drawing from the largest body of information and most complete range of techniques ever assembled. Information-proficient information systems facilitate gathering, evaluating, and selecting options, as well as communication between decision makers and other interested people.

Information-proficient coordination among various organizations provides appropriate integration of programs involving more than one type of group—private-sector businesses, charities, and federal, state, and local governmental agencies. Examples include coordinated endeavors for law enforcement, administration of governmental benefits programs, and business conducted by virtual corporations.

Learning is highly effective. By measuring group and personal information proficiency, organizations and individuals formulate targeted education plans. Training programs emphasize on-the-job learning over formal instruction. Information technology facilitates team learning for groups in various locations—locally, nationally, or worldwide—and reduces needs for on-site instructors. Training providers use the quantification of their customers' information proficiency to sharpen their training services.

The information resources management community serves as a catalyst for improving organizations' products, services, and information proficiency. This community is dividing into two groups. The information-proficiency component focuses on organizations' missions and plans, organizational improvement, information, and mission-specific procedures and data. The technology infrastructure component builds an integrated infrastructure of generic information and technology.

Overall consolidation of the generic information and technology infrastructure provides a flexible, reliable resource of information and the means to use it. Groups that specialize in high-quality, low-cost service provide core administrative and operations-support systems, either as software or as services. Customer organizations develop mission-specific applications around the core systems.

Industrywide consolidation has produced vibrant products and services, combining "high-definition television," two-way communication, commandment by voice, telephony, sophisticated computing, and access to entertainment, news, images, and data. Technology developers and vendors provide products that work compatibly. Hardware components are deployed as interchangeable commodities. Software products and information services are routinely licensed for use by an entire organization.

Information proficiency is and will continue to be the focus and catalyst for advancement.

AFTERWORD

You have a framework and many useful techniques for thriving in the Information Age.

Your Key to the Information Age

Your key to the Information Age consists of many concepts and suggestions you obtained from reading this book, including:

- Information proficiency—the concept, its importance, and a program to measure and enhance your own information proficiency, as well as that of your colleagues and organizations.
- A framework for understanding, discussing, and thriving in the Information Age.
- The Peer Paradigm for organizational behavior, and ways you can use it.
- The All A's program for improving information proficiency and other aspects of an individual or organization.
- The Just Ask... approach to effective learning.
- A methodology for choosing appropriate general-purpose education and a framework for suppliers of training to improve their products and marketing effectiveness.
- A practical program through which information technologists and their clients build synergy and produce needed results for their organizations.

- Appreciation of the ongoing change in paradigm for building information systems.
- A practical approach to dividing work between information technologists and their clients.
- An appreciation for information as a resource, along with tips for dealing with information, building information resources, and enhancing the role of information systems.
- A method for categorizing information and information technologies.
- Recognition that *repetition* is the key word in developing new information technologies.
- Practical insight into, and hands-on advice for, buyers and sellers dealing in the information technology marketplace.

—And, I trust,—

- Numerous ideas and plans you have developed for yourself as you read this book.

Using Your Key

You now have a framework for understanding and thriving in the Information Age. It starts with your goals, the results you hope to achieve. It includes the people and organizations with which you deal. It includes information and technology.

You now have your key to the Information Age—concepts, programs, and techniques to help you.

- Keep track of broad, contextual dreams, issues, and thoughts. "Think globally" and base decisions on principles.
- Pay attention to the information proficiency of your organizations, your colleagues, and yourself. Measure it. Improve it. Make informed, well-considered decisions. Implement your decisions effectively.
- Be aware of the value of information resources. Nurture those re-

sources. Ask questions about the information you use. Encourage other people to do the same.

- Capture the potential for general managers and information resources managers to build a better, more synergistic organizational agenda. Extend this opportunity to all employees and other participants in your organizations.
- Deploy capable, flexible information systems to meet your changing needs. Exploit technology, but do not allow yourself to be distracted through overattention to it.

These are Information Age opportunities for you and for society. We will need our best information proficiency to capture them fully. Apply your key to the Information Age!

Best wishes to you in these exciting, challenging times.

FURTHER READING

The following are publications from which you can gain further perspective. The books and articles are listed in the order in which related topics appear in this book.

Introduction

- Impact of the Information Age

Shultz, George P. 1993. *Turmoil and Triumph—My Years as Secretary of State*. New York: Charles Scribner's Sons.

Goals and Results

- Principles and paradigms

Barker, Joel Arthur 1993. *Paradigms—The Business of Discovering the Future*. New York: Harper Business.

Covey, Stephen R. 1991. *Principle-Centered Leadership*. New York: Simon & Schuster.

- Public sector goals and results

Osborne, David, and Gaebler, Ted 1993. *Reinventing Government—How the Entrepreneurial Spirit Is Transforming the Public Sector*. New York: Penguin Books (USA) Inc.

People and Information Proficiency

- Impact of Information Age changes on work

Alder, Paul S. 1992. *Technology and the Future of Work*. New York: Oxford University Press.

Little, John D.C. 1994. Information Technology in Marketing. In *Information Technology and the Corporation of the 1990s*, ed. Thomas J. Allen and Michael S. Scott Morton, pp. 454–474. New York: Oxford University Press.

Osterman, Paul 1991. The Impact of IT on Jobs and Skills. In *The Corporation of the 1990s*, ed. Thomas J. Allen and Michael S. Scott Morton, pp. 220–243. New York: Oxford University Press.

- Leadership

Gardner, John W. 1992. *On Leadership*. New York: Macmillan.

- Information Age changes between and within organizations

Davenport, Thomas H. 1993. *Process Innovation–Reengineering Work through Information Technology*. Boston: Harvard Business School Press.

Hammer, Michael, and Champy, James 1994. *Reengineering the Corporation*. New York: Harper Business.

Rotemberg, Julio J., and Saloner, Garth 1991. Interfirm Competition and Collaboration. In *The Corporation of the 1990s*, ed. Thomas J. Allen and Michael S. Scott Morton, pp. 115–121. New York: Oxford University Press.

Rothschild, Michael 1990. *Bionomics—Economy as Ecosystem*. New York: Henry Holt and Company.

- Success through Peer Paradigm behavior

Bromley, D. Allan 1994. *The President's Scientists—Reminiscences of a White House Science Advisor*. New Haven, Connecticut: Yale University Press.

Galbraith, Jay R. 1993. *Competing with Flexible Lateral Organizations*, 2nd ed. Reading, Massachusetts: Addison-Wesley Publishing Company.

Harrington-Mackin, Deborah 1994. *The Team Building Tool Kit— Tips, Tactics, and Rules for Effective Workplace Teams*. New York: American Management Association.

Moody, Patricia E. 1993. *Breakthrough Partnering—Creating a Collective Enterprise Advantage*. Essex Junction, Vermont: Oliver Wright Publishers Inc.

Von Hippel, Eric 1994. Innovative Cultures and Organizations. In *Information Technology and the Corporation of the 1990s*, ed. Thomas J. Allen and Michael S. Scott Morton, pp. 125–148. New York: Oxford University Press.

■ Virtual organizations

Davidow, William H., and Malone, Michael S. 1992. *The Virtual Corporation*. New York: HarperCollins.

■ Decision making

Clemen, Robert T. 1990. *Making Hard Decisions—An Introduction to Decision Analysis*. Belmont, California: Wadsworth Publishing Company.

March, James G. 1990. *Decisions and Organizations*. Oxford, England: Basil Blackwell.

March, James G. 1994. *A Primer on Decision-Making—How Decisions Happen*. New York: Macmillan.

■ Quality

Bank, John 1992. *The Essence of Total Quality Management*. Hemmel Hempstead, England: Prentice-Hall (UK) Ltd.

■ Measuring organizational quality improvements

Kinlaw, Dennis C. 1992. *Continuous Improvement and Measurement for Total Quality*. San Diego: Pfeiffer & Company.

Newman, Constance Berry 1992. *Presidential Award for Quality—1993 Application*. Washington, D.C.: United States Office of Personnel Management.

- Organizational improvement

Mohrman, Susan Albers, and Cummings, Thomas G. 1989. *Self-Designing Organizations*. Reading, Massachusetts: Addison-Wesley Publishing Company.

Senge, Peter M. 1990. *The Fifth Discipline—The Art and Practice of the Learning Organization*. New York: Doubleday.

- Organizational learning and All A's improvement programs

Beer, Michael, Eisenstat, Russell A., and Spector, Bert A. 1993. Why Change Programs Don't Produce Change. In *The Learning Imperative—Managing People for Continuous Innovation*, ed. Robert Howard, pp. 217–231. Boston: Harvard Business School Press.

Rogers, Everett M. 1983. *Diffusion of Innovations*, 3rd ed. New York: Macmillan.

- Catalyzing change from within an organization

Cohen, Allan R., and Bradford, David L. 1991. *Influence without Authority*. New York: John Wiley & Sons, Inc.

Information and Information Resources Management

- Simulations

Gredler, Margaret 1992. *Designing and Evaluating Games and Simulations*. Houston: Gulf Publishing.

Knepell, Peter L., and Arangno, Deborah C. 1993. *Simulation Valida-*

tion—A Confidence Assessment Methodology. Los Alamitos, California: Computer Society Press.

- Working with Information

Horton, Forest W., and Lewis, Dennis 1991. *Great Information Disasters*. London: Aslib, the Association for Information Management.

MacNeal, Edward 1994. *Mathsemantics—Making Numbers Talk Sense*. New York: Viking Penguin.

- Sources of information

Krol, Ed 1993. *The Whole Internet—User's Guide & Catalog*. Sebastopol, California: O'Reilly & Associates.

Starer, Daniel 1994. *Who Knows What*. New York: Henry Holt and Company.

- Information security

Computer Science and Technology Board 1991. *Computers at Risk—Safe Computing in the Information Age*. Washington, D.C.: National Academy Press.

- Competitive advantage and value-adding information resources management

Badaracco, Joseph L., Jr. 1991. *The Knowledge Link—How Firms Compete Through Strategic Alliances*. Boston: Harvard Business Review Press.

Keyes, Jessica 1993. *Infotrends—The Competitive Use of Information*. New York: McGraw-Hill.

McKinnon, Sharon M., and Bruns, William J., Jr. 1992. *The Information Mosaic*. Boston: Harvard Business School Press.

Patterson, Marvin L. 1993. *Accelerating Innovation*. New York: Van Nostrand Reinhold.

Porter, Michael E. 1985. *Competitive Advantage—Creating and Sustaining Superior Performance.* New York, Macmillan.

Strassmann, Paul A. 1990. *The Business Value of Computers—An Executive's Guide.* New Canaan, Connecticut: The Information Economics Press.

Westney, D. Eleanor, and Ghoshal, Sumantra 1994. Building a Competitor Intelligence Organization: Adding Value in an Information Function. In *Information Technology and the Corporation of the 1990s,* ed. Thomas J. Allen and Michael S. Scott Morton, pp. 430–453. New York: Oxford University Press.

- Educating executives about information technology

Hoffman, Gerald M. 1994. *The Technology Payoff—How to Profit with Empowered Workers in the Information Age.* Homewood, Illinois: Richard D. Irwin Inc.

Information Systems

- Information systems management

Cash, James I., McFarlan, F. Warren, and McKenney, James L. 1992. *Corporate Information Systems Management—The Issues Facing Senior Executives,* 3rd ed. Homewood, Illinois: Richard D. Irwin Inc.

Tapscott, Don, and Casten, Art 1993. *Paradigm Shift.* New York: McGraw-Hill.

Walton, Richard E. 1989. *Up and Running—Integrating Information Technology and the Organization.* Boston: Harvard Business School Press.

- The role of credibility in justifying and marketing a project

Kouzes, James M., and Posner, Barry Z. 1993. *Credibility—How*

Leaders Gain and Lose It, Why People Demand It. San Francisco: Jossey-Bass.

- Information systems design and implementation

Jones, Caspars 1994. *Assessment and Control of Software Risks.* Englewood Cliffs, New Jersey: Prentice-Hall.

Martin, James 1989, 1990, 1990. *Information Engineering, Books I, II, and III.* Englewood Cliffs, New Jersey: Prentice-Hall.

- Object-oriented techniques

Booch, Grady 1994. *Object-Oriented Analysis and Design, with Applications.* Redwood City, California: Benjamin Cummings.

Information Technology

- Technology and industry trends

Bromley, D. Allan 1992. *Grand Challenges 1993: High Performance Computing and Communications.* Washington, D.C.: United States Office of Science and Technology Policy.

Computer Science and Technology Board 1990. *Keeping the U.S. Computer Industry Competitive.* Washington, D.C.: National Academy Press.

Computer Science and Technology Board 1994. *Realizing the Future.* Washington, D.C.: National Academy Press.

National Institute of Standards and Technology 1994. *Putting the Information Infrastructure to Work: A Report of the Information Infrastructure Task Force Committee on Applications and Technology.* Washington, D.C.: U.S. Printing Office.

Price Waterhouse World Firm Technology Center 1993. *Technology Forecast, Version 4.0.* Menlo Park, California: Price Waterhouse.

- The roles of standards in the marketplace for technology

Besen, Stanley, M., and Saloner, Garth 1994. Compatibility Standards and the Market for Telecommunications Services. In *Information Technology and the Corporation of the 1990s*, ed. Thomas J. Allen and Michael S. Scott Morton, pp. 149–183. New York: Oxford University Press.

Vernon, Mary K., Lazowska, Edward D., and Personick, Stewart D. 1994. *R&D for the NII: Technical Challenges*. Washington, D.C.: EDUCOM.

INDEX

project architecture, 240–242
proprietary interfaces, 305
proprietary rights, 312
prototype systems, 121–122

Q
quality
  buying, 290–295
  data definition, 256–259
  deal-making, 307–308
  further reading, 327–328
  of information, 40, 187
  information proficiency and, 65–70
  information resources, 148–149
  information systems, 256–262
  of information systems, 229–233
  involving customers in product design, 44
  movement toward, 120
  process definition, 259–262
  selling, 300–303
quality control, 68
quantitative measures, productivity, 244–253
questionnaire, measuring information
    proficiency, 73

R
rating method, value of information resources
    community, 170–177
real estate market, 41–42
reengineering business, 167–168
regulation, staff function and, 170–177
repetition, 274–287
responsiveness, 292
restorative systems, 230
results
  examples of, 10–11
  further reading, 325
  goals and, 190–191, 198
  organizational, 176
  producing, 29–30
  synergy between customer's mission and com-
    pany's mission, 50
  types of, 11
results standards, 175, 176
retained information, 20
royalties, 312, 313

S
sales
  compensation, 303–305

employment in, 36
  office space, 41
secretarial work, 35
security, of information, 145, 148–149
selling, 300–303
service
  continuous, 229–233
  staff function and, 170–177
shopping from home, 42
shoreline preservationists, 28
similar discount technique, 296
simulation
  benefits, 125
  example, 122–126
  of global economics, 126
  limits, 124–125
  purpose of, 122
  software, 124
  utility of results, 123
  video games, 129–131
simulator, future of, 130–131
single-tier approach
  generating boilerplate, 260, 261–262
  information handling, 258
society
  decisions and, 61–65
  Information Age and, 33, 56–67, 279–281
  modular, 13–14
  perceived differences, 64
  quality movement, 66
  self-imposed complexity, 245
software licenses, 296–299
solar system, simulation of, 123–125
sources, knowledge of, 147
staff function
  information resources management, role in,
    168–170
  leadership roles, 170–177
standards
  information resources, 174–175, 285
  modularity and, 269–270
  technology, 175
  value of, 286
statistical data, 131–132, 147
sticking to principles, 24–27
stovepipe paradigm, 218–220
strategies
  assigning information resources
    responsibilities, 197–200
  information resources, 141–142